UBUNTU
AND THE
RECONSTITUTION
OF COMMUNITY

WORLD PHILOSOPHIES

Bret W. Davis, D. A. Masolo, and Alejandro Vallega, *editors*

UBUNTU AND THE RECONSTITUTION OF COMMUNITY

Edited by James Ogude

INDIANA UNIVERSITY PRESS

This book is a publication of

Indiana University Press
Office of Scholarly Publishing
Herman B Wells Library 350
1320 East 10th Street
Bloomington, Indiana 47405 USA

iupress.indiana.edu

Library of Congress Cataloging-in-Publication Data

Names: Ogude, James, editor.
Title: Ubuntu and the reconstitution of community / edited by James Ogude.
Description: Bloomington, Indiana : Indiana University Press, [2019] |
Series: World philosophies | Includes bibliographical
references and index.
Identifiers: LCCN 2019010093 (print) | LCCN 2019013581 (ebook) | ISBN
9780253042125 (ebook) | ISBN 9780253042101 (cloth : alk. paper) | ISBN
9780253042118 (pbk. : alk. paper)
Subjects: LCSH: Ubuntu (Philosophy) | Philosophy, African. |
Humanism—Africa. | Social groups—Philosophy.
Classification: LCC B5315.U28 (ebook) | LCC B5315.U28 U27 2019 (print) |
DDC 199/.68—dc23
LC record available at https://lccn.loc.gov/2019010093

1 2 3 4 5   23 22 21 20 19

CONTENTS

ACKNOWLEDGMENTS

THIS PUBLICATION WOULD NOT HAVE BEEN POSSIBLE WITHOUT the support and generous funding that we received from the Templeton World Charity Foundation to undertake a research project aimed at deepening our understanding of the southern African concept of Ubuntu. The funding was given in honor of Archbishop Emeritus Desmond Tutu in 2013 for a University of Pretoria project I am heading called "The Meaning and Value of Ubuntu in Human and Social Development in Africa." The aim, according to the foundation, was "to increase the knowledge and awareness of Ubuntu, and in the process contribute to the transformation of African communities and societies." This book, I hope, constitutes one such important attempt at extending our grasp and understanding of the relational idea of personhood, our connectedness as human beings, and the totality of our environment—Ubuntu. Thanks too to the vice chancellor and principal of the University of Pretoria, Cheryl de le Ray, who had insisted that I become the principal investigator of the Ubuntu project, barely four months into my job at the university. I hope the publication of this book will be a vindication of your confidence in me.

The majority of the chapters published in this book originated from a colloquium held at the University of Pretoria on June 4–6, 2014, on theorizing the concept of Ubuntu in relation to notions of personhood, self and community, interstate relations, and spiritual values in Africa. I am deeply indebted to D. A. Masolo, one of Africa's foremost philosophers and an authority on discourses about self and community in Africa, who gave the keynote address and set an important tone to the colloquium and many others that followed in subsequent years, as we wrestled with what Desmond Tutu meant when he insisted that Ubuntu teaches us, among other things, that ethical responsibility comes with a shared identity. Thanks too to the late Augustine Shutte (may God rest his soul in peace), whose pioneering work on Ubuntu inspired my initial thoughts on this project. Until his death, Shutte remained an avid supporter of this Nguni concept, insisting that there was much that this philosophical thought could contribute to the world and European mainstream philosophies in general. My gratitude also goes to the contributors to this volume, many of whom remain

"Ubuntu Fellows" at the Centre for the Advancement of Scholarship at the University of Pretoria, where the Ubuntu project is housed. Their participation at the colloquium added immense insights to the debates on the concept. Thanks also to the other cluster leaders on the project, professors Julian Muller, Christof Heyns, and Maxi Schoeman, for having shown faith in my leadership and for your insights as we battled to put together the proposal for funding.

Some of the chapters in this book have been published before, and we wish to thank the editors for having granted us permission to reproduce those chapters in this volume. Aspects of chapter 5 by Dirk Louw have been published in the following outlets: C. W. Du Toit, ed., *Power Sharing and African Democracy* (Pretoria: Research Institute for Theology and Religion, 2010); *Tijdschrift voor Filosofie* 77, no. 1; and Dennis Sullivan and Larry Tifft, eds., *Handbook of Restorative Justice: A Global Perspective* (London: Routledge, 2006). Chapter 10 by James Ogude and Uni Dyer was first published in a German journal, *Polylog* 34 (2015), and the paper has been reproduced here in English with some minor modifications.

Finally, thanks to my research assistant, Uni Dyer, whose invaluable work in undertaking a deep literature review for my work on Ubuntu, organizational skills during the range of colloquia we convened, undying commitment to indigenous knowledge systems, and rare insights into the broader implication of the project made her more than an assistant researcher. She also helped put the chapters together and communicate with the contributors. When Uni left for her PhD studies at the University of Wisconsin, she handed her duties over to the center's project assistant, Kirsty Agnew, who was equal to the task and continued to support our ongoing activities with dedication. Last, but not least, thanks to the center's administrative assistant, Cecelia Samson, who was responsible for the travel and accommodation arrangement for our delegates when they attended each and every colloquium.

UBUNTU
AND THE
RECONSTITUTION
OF COMMUNITY

INTRODUCTION

James Ogude

IN 1994, WHEN ARCHBISHOP EMERITUS DESMOND TUTU EVOKED the concept of Ubuntu in the course of mediating the South African Truth and Reconciliation Commission (TRC), a process whose primary objective was to initiate the nation's healing by coming to terms with painful narratives and memories of a past that continued to manifest itself through racial schism and socioeconomic inequality, little did he know that he was introducing a new grammar framing South Africa's postapartheid politics and its many possible futures. Soon the concept of Ubuntu, at least in his view, promised to capture and provide the theological and philosophical lexicon for a society groping for precisely the kind of language that was both humane and capable of rallying together once-antagonistic national groups and constituencies for a fresh social and political beginning that recognized the past as a distant and repudiated moment while committing to define and build a new future. On his part, Tutu was also searching for a possible synergy between Christian and African value systems by injecting the idea of Ubuntu, understood by him as a special gift from African modes of thought, or *gnosis*, as Mudimbe (1988) would have it, whose core meaning bore a special relevance within contemporary South Africa. Tutu was groping for a language that would point to the basis of the common humanity and shared identity of all humans while acknowledging contingent differences that allow people to live their humanity with the richness of cultural diversity. The idea of Ubuntu, premised on the belief that the full development of personhood occurs only in circumstances of already-established human conditions of mutual dependency, provided Tutu with a second handle on South Africa's tortured political past.

Central to Ubuntu is the idea that an individual's humanity is fostered in a network of existing human relationships, as captured aptly in the Zulu proverb that he helped make popular, though it is by no means conceptually absolute or univocal: *Umuntu ngumuntu ngabantu*, which roughly translates as "I am because you are; we are because you are." Put differently, the idea of Ubuntu forces us to ask what makes human experience possible. As D. A. Masolo writes, "If there were to be differences in views regarding the principles on which our beliefs about the world are based, they most probably would be traceable to beliefs about what the constitutive nature of the person is, which we often trace back to a pool of axiomatic beliefs within the respective systems of our cultural heritages" (2010, 12). In his search for new and fresh ways of reconstituting a divided South African society, Tutu fell back on ideas embedded in the beliefs of his people in order to find the right concept with which to frame relational forms of personhood. Yet he also guided the use of such neologies in ways that would capture for his African audiences the underlying theological ideas and values of his Christian beliefs. Michael Battle (1997) has attempted to link Tutu's *Imago Dei* theology to the idea of Ubuntu, arguing that in evoking this African concept, Tutu was attempting to bridge the gap between Western philosophy of individualism and the self-determining being, on the one hand, and African thought on personhood as a product of community, on the other. Battle argues that the power of Tutu's theological model rests on the fact that "it seeks to restore the oppressor's humanity by releasing and enabling the oppressed to see their oppressor as peers under God" (1997, 5). According to Battle, the essence of Tutu's argument is that by recognizing the image of God in others, one comes to appreciate how God creates by relating to difference. In his insistence that Ubuntu, an African value system, has the capacity to shape and transform received beliefs and the very institutions within which they are housed, Tutu seems to be making an important theological intervention. After all, if there is one persistent thread in reflections on African philosophy in its broadest sense, it is the constant will to rework and integrate indigenous knowledge into new institutional and conceptual reflections on contemporary practices and everyday experiences in Africa (Masolo 2010, 7). Tutu (2011) is aware that these two philosophical streams cannot be reconciled by simply evoking an African belief system regardless of their history and historical baggage. Elsewhere in his book, he has attempted to map an inclusive theological position that would embrace our unity in difference, to point to our common humanity beyond race, class, and religious divide. The concept of Ubuntu, rooted in relational idea of personhood—empathy for and interdependence between people—offers him a possibility for an ideal restorative and just ethical and moral principle, undergirded by our common humanity. His Ubuntu theology thus embraces the particularities of human history, while at the same time acting as a point of judgment and hope within history, for all humanity.

In drawing on Ubuntu to mediate a contemporary crisis of the moment, namely the difficult path to reconciliation and restoration of community to itself, Tutu also ran the risk of turning Ubuntu into an open-ended concept, if not a nebulous one. This risk is especially prevalent when the concept falls into the hands of politicians who appear always eager to use it to conceal their narrow nationalist rhetoric and to sidestep those very difficult questions that Tutu, as chair of the TRC, was intent on grappling with. As a concept whose strength is to be found within the moral value system in its appeal to the good or positively distinct human character, Ubuntu was never meant to be an instrument for clearing all thickets. Rather, it would enable dialogue within and between persons and communities divided by a difficult historical past, a tool for voyaging into the thickets of human relationships in order to find what binds us together as people and as human beings. Ubuntu evokes those rational or distinctly human capacities that enable persons to think or do as only someone in her or his best mindset would. To appeal to Ubuntu is to urge that, when deliberating within oneself or intervening between communities, one ought to bring out the best characteristics, such as careful use of reason, especially in matters that require recognizing the humanity of others. Ubuntu was meant to engender that process, as Kwasi Wiredu (1996) would have it, of moving from being humans to being persons. "The implications of this basic sociality of personhood," Masolo has written, "defy the boundaries of metaphysics, epistemology, or even ethics in the restrictive Kantian sense. It proposes far-reaching dimensions for a communalistic view of the world in which the project of becoming a person is always incomplete" (2010, 13).

The relational idea of personhood that I draw attention to also frames my understanding of community in the present book and, by extension, the ideal community that contemporary African sages like the Archbishop Tutu had in mind when evoking Ubuntu. The use of *community* in this sense signals the kind of society in which individuals are related to the wider groups of which they may be part, not necessarily by descent, but because individuals are inextricably related to other individuals and groups. This sense of community is necessary to attain the full realization of their humanity and also to achieve the goals of economic production and choices on how to order a society. The term *community* is used in both political

and moral senses. In the political sense, the term is sometimes used interchangeably with *society*, as in the new South Africa (meaning postapartheid
South Africa), and, when given theoretical derivation, is related to what
one school of African political thought in the 1960s referred to as "African
communalism" or "African socialism." This school of thought is closely associated with African nationalists who led the political campaign against
European colonialism in the post–World War II period, with some of them
becoming the first political leaders at the time of independence—people
like Léopold Sédar Senghor, Kwame Nkrumah, Ahmed Sékou Touré, Julius Kambarage Nyerere, and Kenneth Kaunda. Philosophically, the idea
was that socialism was a pertinent part of Africans' social fabric, which
these nationalists harnessed to inspire and underpin (with various degrees
of success) the principal social and economic arrangements of their societies. Socialism was rooted in the assumption that Africans rely on each other
because no individual is autonomous—not as a matter of fact, but rather
as a principle of organization in which individual autonomy is shunned as
an irrational value that only promotes exploitation. What the French soci-
ologist Émile Durkheim (1858–1917) once thought of as a "primitive" mode
of social organization,[1] now was turned into a new, different, and positive
expression. If Durkeim's use of communitarian form of social organization
was more ideological than philosophical in the conventional sense of the
term, recent expression of just this communal ethos has emerged in southern Africa with a significant ethical emphasis.

In the Nguni saying popularized by Tutu, "Umuntu ngumuntu ngabantu" (a person is a person only in relation to other persons), the idea is
that no individual can become a person without the role played by other individuals and by society more wholly and generally. In other words, humans
are made to be interdependent with each other. Humans realize or fulfill
their selfhood only in interplay with others as a moral and metaphysical
destiny. This interpretation may resemble how some African philosophers
like Kwasi Wiredu (1996) and D. A. Masolo (2010) conceive of personhood.
They are of the view that the realization of one's capacity to develop this
personhood can occur only in the context of living, growing, developing,
and flourishing in community. For example, although humans may be born
with the capacity for reason, actualization of a human being as a rational
animal can occur only in circumstances where the individual is condi-
tioned into a network of communicative relations with others—if not with
others of common birth heritage, at least with others already functioning

as fully developed persons. In this latter sense of Wiredu (1996) and Masolo (2010), community is seen as a universal condition for the development of personhood. Although it will naturally start with one's closest community, the family, it is the condition that drives the development of personhood in a universal community of humans. In their separate views, Wiredu and Masolo not only avoid but also strongly disavow the essentialism that characterized the version of communitarianism embraced by the political—or, as the late Kenyan philosopher Henry Odera Oruka (1990) called it, the ideological—trend of African thinkers in the years immediately preceding and following attainment of independence from colonialism. Masolo, for example, uses the thought and works of the famous Tanzanian poet and philosopher, the late Shaaban bin Robert, to buttress his idea of how communitarianism is superior to individualism. According to Masolo, Shaaban states that this superiority is not because communitarianism has long been woven into the African social fabric but rather because it is ethically a better principle for building a society with fewer and smaller differences between people; it is also more likely, therefore, to bring the greatest amount of happiness to the greatest possible number of people. (That is, as long as it is not misapplied by those who would take advantage and use it to justify the easiest or quickest way to get their needs taken care of.)[2]

All these different senses of community frame the discussions in the chapters of this book, but the reader needs to keep an eye on how the discussion of community is ultimately elevated from its ordinary senses to the philosophical ones, as just explained. As this collection conveys, specifically regarding Ubuntu, the idea of community as a network of mutuality is both the basis for and the driving force behind Reverend Tutu's now-famous aphorism, which points to a social system in which everyone assumes responsibility to others and to the shared whole as a virtue that is theologically sound because it calls everyone to see the image of God (*imago dei*) in every human being. In this sense, Tutu's view also transcends the specificity of the cultural context in which Ubuntu is the principle of everyday interaction between human people regardless of their identity or station in life, and to point to its global ethical relevance. It is only in this sense of community—as a network of mutuality—that Ubuntu could be used as an instrument in consensus building among a diverse community of people such as South Africa, and therefore truly a vehicle for reconstitution of that community. By *reconstitution*, I mean that process of putting together and restoring a broken community to itself as

Edward Said (1993, 253) would have it. Reconstitution is even more urgent and relevant in polarized communities or communities that are undergoing or have undergone conflict.

Ubuntu can serve as a universal ethical and moral concept for reordering communities beyond the confines of South Africa. It may, for example, be an apposite principle for engaging racial politics that continue to ravage the moral fabrics of Western societies such as the United States. Ubuntu may also provide answers to some of the challenges thrown up by the Black Lives Matter movement in the United States because it puts into sharp relief those structural and institutionalized forms of racial and economic discrimination that disrupt the common narrative of the American dream. It also may throw into relief the colorblindness of the United States. As Martin Luther King Jr. (America's Tutu) warned several decades back, "In these trying circumstances, the black revolution is much more than a struggle for the rights of Negroes. It is forcing America to face all its interrelated flaws—racism, poverty, militarism, and materialism. It is exposing the evils that are rooted deeply in the whole structure of society. It reveals systemic rather than superficial flaws and suggests that *radical reconstruction of society itself is the real issue to be faced*" (King and Washington 1986, 316, emphasis mine).

Reading King's words almost five decades later, one cannot help but see strong parallels between his United States and Reverend Tutu's South Africa and their insistence on a "radical reconstruction" of their respective societies ravaged by similar forms of social discrimination and violence. It is during moments of political crisis that the reconstitution of community is called for, although the radical reconstitution required cannot take place except within a communalistic ethos such as Ubuntu, which, as Kwasi Wiredu argues, "bears an important ethic of human community as such. The fundamental imperative of ethics is: adjust your interests to the interests of others even at the possible cost of some self-denial" (2001, 172). Put differently by Teodros Kiros, "Africa's communalistic societies" whose tenets inform Ubuntu philosophy "provide a sense of belonging, sympathy, and solidarity as alternatives to modernity's excessive individuality and insecurity. Communalism also provides instruments for building consensus through compromise and extended negotiations that come to an end when a working consensus is reached" (2001, 5). Consensus building is, therefore, a process of reasoned activity and not simply a suppression of disagreements, as those who oppose communalism often suggest.

This book brings together essays that represent a diverse range of voices and perspectives on Ubuntu. Collectively, these essays help elevate the debate on the concept beyond the political rhetoric to which it has been confined to date and, more important, show its links to aspects of communalistic ethos and its ethical and moral role in the reconstitution of community. It brings together for the first time the views of scholars from such different disciplines as linguistics, literature, law, theology, and philosophy and draws on these multidisciplinary perspectives to examine the concept in all its complexity. The essays approach the Ubuntu principle from its cultural origins to its growth in daily use to refer to a universal human value, which includes the mantra popularized by Archbishop Tutu. All its meanings suggest possible resolutions to contemporary conflicts in South Africa and around the world. That is, the mantra *umuntu ngumuntu ngabantu* is an aphoristic appeal to the ideal that people ought to strive to create the kind of society in which all members can find the fulfilment of their humanity.

It is understandable that, for a society such as South Africa, with its long history of trauma and grief, the search for a grammar that is both ordinary and philosophically ideal for communal healing and restoration is a compelling social and political imperative. But a failure to understand and disaggregate the language of healing and restoration for what it is presents a real danger of concealing rather than healing the fears and trauma of the community. The essays in this volume unravel the moral content of Ubuntu as a term and concept and, by so doing, elevate it above the now familiar narrow ethnic deployment. Contributors to the book are cognizant of the fact that Ubuntu cannot be a panacea for the ills of our history, but rather that it is a vehicle that enables engagement and dialogue by underscoring our interdependence, even if our history teaches us otherwise. If it is true that Ubuntu would contradict the fundamental principles on which the new South Africa is built, a South Africa founded on the assumption that social relations occur between rational and autonomous individuals as the prevalent argument goes, it would do so only partially.[3] A strong communitarian ethos continues to inform and mediate the practices of many black South Africans in their daily encounters and in various sites at which they perform those rituals that bring them together and remind them of their common experiences. Everyday life in South Africa is still in certain ways shaped by apartheid and postcolonial social architecture, and individualism is still at the very core of South African social systems, but a *mit-Sein* understanding of human agency and the desire for communal renewal also persists, and Ubuntu, as one of the cornerstones of an African philosophical practice, captures that *mit-Sein*.

We are not interested in examining Ubuntu simply as some form of high-end philosophy but as a value system that is rooted in the everyday practices of ordinary people, through their daily public encounters in institutional contexts such as the church, schools, and their cultural rituals and rites. Indeed, recent scholarship has shown that ordinary people often endeavor to grasp, deal with, and overcome alienation and trauma by turning to long-standing spiritual and cultural rites and epistemologies. The traditional African belief systems, particularly those that assert personhood, community, and ancestral veneration, offer an affirming and enriching alternative to the metanarratives and projects of the state actors, especially in a fragile democracy and a violent transition. Central to these epistemologies is the concept of personhood, which states that a person depends on others to be a person. A symbiotic relationship, even if sometimes contested, exists between the individual and the community. This sense of community is not limited to relationships between people. It is also linked to the totality of the universe, and the forces of the universe are seen as life: living energy that encompasses the material and the spiritual. Thus, a complete personhood will be connected to other persons and also to ancestors and a supreme being.

A precise definition of Ubuntu is elusive because its meaning has always incorporated local cultural nuances and global aspirations, and it will continue to do so. Like other African expressions of humanism, Ubuntu will remain the subject of contested definitions and theoretical explorations. It will remain very much constitutive of the tortured relationship between Western and African modernities—the subject, that is, of contestations between dominant Western epistemologies and African belief systems. In South Africa specifically, spiritual leaders like Archbishop Desmond Tutu have used Ubuntu in the contested terrain of sociopolitical influence in order to restore the black self by evoking both the specificity of its cultural expressions and the universality of its ethical meaning. That is why, as Leonhard Praeg argues, "to say that 'Africans have Ubuntu' is never simply to make a disinterested observation about Africans, but a statement [that] we should *feel*, *experience* and understand [it] as a challenge, as an exercise of power, as an assertion of the right of Africans to be recognised, to be present, to be a part of (not apart *from*) the conversation" (Praeg 2014, 15).

Ubuntu is also about those ethical values that have defined relationships among Africans—values that colonial value systems imposed on Africans have eroded or simply repressed. At this point in history, traditional African values are in need of rescue or radical reinstatement in order to erect a true African society rather than a postcolonial one, which already implies colonial influence. It is precisely for these reasons that some of the following chapters seek to explore ways in which we can talk about the study of Ubuntu as a project to recover a value system that has traveled through history, mutated, and continues to be mediated by a complex history of postcolonial politics itself.

Conceptually, therefore, the many voices represented in this book seek to grapple with a range of challenges that the idea of Ubuntu throws at us: Ubuntu's etymological roots, especially how it has traveled spatially, historically, and as a discursive practice; Ubuntu and the idea of personhood and agency; Ubuntu as a nonideal theory and a vehicle for self-determination; Ubuntu as underpinned by reason and rational thinking; Ubuntu and the ethic of social justice; and, ultimately, Ubuntu as a vehicle for reconstituting community. In what follows, I try to tease out themes that the chapters that constitute this volume surface and reinforce.

The first is how Ubuntu as a concept has traveled, especially the way in which its etymological roots point to its close affinity with the Bantu languages and also how the concept enters into dialogue with other discursive practices, especially received ideas that came to the African continent through colonial modernity. The linguistic roots of the word *Ubuntu* are found, in a variety of forms, in the languages and dialects of the so-called Bantu-speaking peoples of Africa. It is embedded in the very name *Bantu*. In the words of Wim van Binsbergen, "It is therefore the result of coupling the prefix generating abstract words and concepts (i.e. *ubu-*, in the Nguni languages) to the general root *–ntu* which one and a half centuries ago persuaded the pioneering German linguist [Wilhelm] Bleek to recognise as a large linguistic family all those speakers of the languages that had this root as the core of the otherwise different modifications or variations of the prefix as the 'Bantu-speaking' family: the entire group of languages, spoken from the Cape to the Sudan belt [and beyond], where the root *-ntu* stands for 'human'"(2001, 53).[4]

The idea here is not to show African social life unadulterated but rather to demonstrate that despite the slight variations, the widely shared etymological roots of Ubuntu's linguistic map point to something much larger than a regional or a South African phenomenon, as many have falsely suggested. To the contrary, the concept's footprints are likely to be found in many parts of Africa. This volume's project, though, is not one of recovery, but one that seeks to draw linguistic connections in order to surface what is constitutive of that which is "human." But this volume goes beyond the linguistic connections to point to the universality of the term, its moral and ethical principles found in societies outside the Bantu-speaking peoples and, in fact, in other parts of the world.

Besides Ubuntu's etymological and historical roots, Ubuntu's relevance for contemporary times has been its ability to enter into dialogue with received knowledges, especially those emanating from the West. This is particularly so when Ubuntu is mobilized by communities to reconstitute themselves. For example, it has been helpful in redrafting a range of theological templates closely associated with Christianity, most evidently in the work and practice of the Reverend Tutu. Values that underpin Ubuntu serve as a corrective tool to the often individualistic understanding of personhood, which is inseparable from individual human rights and free intentionality, to show that individuals cannot flourish except in certain kinds of relationships with others. In this volume, we are able to demonstrate that the centrality of Ubuntu in Tutu's thought and practice allows him to achieve three important things: one, to locate the Christian idea of love within an African context; two, to provide the foundation for the notion of restorative justice, which was so important in the workings of the South African TRC, which Tutu chaired; and three, to undergird Tutu's famous idea of a rainbow nation, which is really about the porousness of our cultures and the idea of unity in diversity that Ubuntu celebrates, or perhaps more poignantly, to see Ubuntu as a source of multidimensionality in community. Ubuntu actually helped Tutu develop a moral vision for integration, or, if you will, reconciliation, and to extend our understanding of human nature as fundamentally relational beyond Kant and even Aristotle. As Augustine Shutte (2001) has observed, the moral and ethical values of Ubuntu can serve to liberate Christianity from its baggage only if a healthy dialogue is encouraged between Ubuntu and the Christian faith.[5] Indeed, Ubuntu's capacity for mutual dialogue across cultures is proof that an African concept such as Ubuntu can travel, not simply to enter into discourse with an imported religion such as Christianity, but also to inhabit and colonize it, to render it relevant to our age. In domesticating Christianity, this African concept is able to realize its universal appeal that became most evident during the TRC in South Africa. Praeg (2014) captures this well when he writes, "To call Ubuntu a glocal phenomenon means recognising that global discourses (Christianity, human rights and so on) give a particular expression to the meaning of local traditions such as Ubuntu, but in a way that also allows the resulting Ubuntu to feed back into the global discourse as a locally based critique and expansion of those very discourses" (37).

Another point this volume raises is the manner in which personhood and agency were always central in the interventions that black intellectuals often made in the face of colonial and postcolonial experience. How Africans draw on what Anthony Appiah (1992) calls the philosophy of culture by engaging those everyday African cultural practices is central to the twining of personhood and agency here. What surfaces is a long-standing debate among African philosophers about the relevance of a philosophical practice that grounds "explanations of reality or analysis of ideas in beliefs and languages—that focuses on and stems from the structure and experience of everyday life" (Karp and Masolo 2000, 9). We draw sharp links between language, art, and Ubuntu and argue that they are fundamental in forging a united voice against dominant ideologies on personhood, especially those ideologies that were marshaled by the colonialists in their denial of the humanity of the Africans. Therefore, when black intellectuals and artists intervened, it was centrally about what it means to be human; it was to elaborate what it means to be or not to be a person in an African context. The intervention was never a reification of cultural experiences and social forms in Africa, but rather an attempt to provide a critical account of how value systems such as Ubuntu could offer a radical understanding of personhood when placed alongside those conceptions that seek to separate the individual from the community. The point about the philosophy of culture is underscored by Bheki Peterson's essay in chapter 3, which traces the ethos of Ubuntu through African art and kinship values, especially in southern Africa, and in particular among the Zulu-speaking people. It is significant, as Peterson argues after Mark Sanders, that as a moral and ethical touchstone, Ubuntu is often mobilized during moments of historical crisis and that "the strength of the concept of Ubuntu is its ability, by inventing memory in the future perfect tense, to generate stability at a time of transition and to stage recovery at a time of loss" (Sanders 2002, 120). It is not surprising then that in South Africa Ubuntu moved into the public and intellectual space with the Black Consciousness movement of the 1970s—eventually turning into a key concept on black theology in South Africa—and again in the 1990s, especially during and in the aftermath of the TRC. By looking at the contours of Ubuntu and the architecture of kinship in some of the communities in South Africa, we demonstrate how relationships were modulated and measured through human nature—especially good conduct and good nature—the humaneness that Ubuntu encapsulates.

The theme is amplified and extended further in the volume by showing how a traditional concept such as Ubuntu is reinvented and mobilized in order to engage with the broader sociopolitical discourses of our time. Ubuntu is therefore posited here as a concept embedded in nonideal theory, which seeks to engage social problems critically, particularly in contexts where society is defined by fragile democracy and conflict. In this sense, the concept addresses the need to identify the pitfalls of a leadership that has erred, or a citizenry that has detoured from the right path, thus causing society to fall short of its right or ideal objectives and goals. In this volume, Ubuntu is seen as an emancipatory ethical principle, as the likes of Tutu have argued, because it redefines our understanding of what it means to be human. As part of the people's values, Ubuntu serves to unsettle external and overly deterministic historical and cultural paths, and in the process, replace them with a belief in self-determination—a complex libertarian discourse as both Hountondji and Freire would argue (Karp and Masolo 2000, 10; Hountondji 1983; Freire 1972).

This volume's chapters advance the recognition of Ubuntu's layered dimensions, especially the need to embed both the capacity to reason and good moral conduct in the idea of Ubuntu. Doing so is important because one of the recurring critiques of relational forms of personhood is the tendency to exclude reason or rational thinking when talking about communitarian ethos. Therefore, the argument goes, since Ubuntu is relational, it has to be associated with a herd mentality in which the capacity to reason is precluded. In chapter 2, using the works of two philosophers, Alexis Kagame and Shaaban bin Robert, from Central and East Africa, respectively, Masolo draws our attention to the layered dimensions of Ubuntu as a rebuttal to some of the myths about communitarian ethos. Kagame connects the term *Umuntu* with the capacity to reason, and Shaaban's idea of "utu bora" targets moral values as the central attributes of human beings. By linking the discourses of these two philosophers, Masolo suggests that the meaning of being "properly human" is the result of a continuous discourse and a process. Examining the two thinkers in tandem reinforces the point that the linguistic and conceptual roots of Ubuntu are widely spread and can be found in East, Central, and southern Africa. Writers who work through different languages theorize about Ubuntu-like concepts whether they form -*ntu*-type constructions or not. Indeed, this comparison allows Masolo to demonstrate that Ubuntu "calls everyone's attention to the many worldwide incidences and forms of injustice" (chap. 2).

Another important theme that emerges in this volume is that Ubuntu is in fact a philosophical vehicle for reconstituting communities. Various chapters make the point that Ubuntu is in fact a discourse and practice in building relationships between the individual and community in order to deepen and extend the multidimensionality of society and to reconstitute community afresh. Thus, Ubuntu does not simply confer high importance on the community over the individual, as many have tended to assume, but rather, "it refers to the individual's experience in reintegrating into a greater community and sense of belonging to it," as Niels Weidtmann argues in chapter 4. Ubuntu is, therefore, an ethical principle that undergirds every process of communal renewal. It revitalizes those connections not just between the living, but also between the living and the living-dead (the ancestors), as well as "the renewal of its sense of community with the Supreme Being."

By endowing personhood with a rich multidimensionality, what we have here is a radical revisioning of Placide Tempels's (1959) idea of "vital force." When Ubuntu is experienced as a vital force, it becomes that ethical and moral touchstone for experiencing the multidimensionality of human reality through a continuous revitalization of community at every level. The emphasis here is on the interdependence between the individual and community and how individuals come to register their awareness of the multidimensionality of their own being only during the process of communal reconstitution in which members of the community enter into dialogue in order to build a communal consensus.

We acknowledge that a certain valorization of communal ethos persists in certain readings of Ubuntu, in which the individual agency is deleted altogether. This result is one of the dangers this volume cautions against in rebutting those scholars and lay thinkers who valorize communitarian ethos in Africa, reducing it to a practice of unanimity. And this critique of valorization is apt because of the danger of collapsing the complex experiences of communities too readily. One must realize that the very idea of community, as eloquently argued in this volume, necessarily incorporates the recognition of diversity, including good individual development, as long as all able parts of the community are engaged, by virtue of dialogical inclusiveness, in charting a path that is to some extent determined by the good or well-being of the collective as well as it can be experienced in consensus. In other words, although they are falsely confused, consensus is vastly different from unanimity, and instead "is an affair of compromise, and compromise is a certain adjustment of the interests of individuals (in the form of disparate convictions as to what is to be done) to the common necessity for something to be done" (Wiredu 2001, 174). Aspects of the volume, especially chapter 5 by Louw, is nevertheless correct in insisting that Ubuntu is a concept steeped in ambiguous discourses, often overdetermined by the context of its present use and application. Those who, for example, do not feel part of the community that espouses Ubuntu philosophy may feel excluded, even when the intension is not to exclude them, as in the South African Truth and Reconciliation Commission. But the multiple, different, and even conflicting uses of the term in different settings and by different actors mean that the term is in need of being disaggregated from its applications in order to determine what it really means. What we are attempting to do is to provide thorough analysis of what it means beyond the popular aphorism and to register its sense of pluralism and the alternative humanism it offers in the discourses of people like Reverend Tutu. Thus, in its critique of European humanism, rooted in the principle of individual freedom as the source of all rights and responsibility in the contemporary world, Ubuntu may well offer what critics like Achille Mbembe have argued is, "an enquiry into the possibility of a politics of the future, of mutuality and of the common" (2009, 35).

We argue that, in order to realize its full potential, Ubuntu philosophy will have to enter into dialogue with both complementary and competing visions of how a holistic understanding of what is humane can be realized. It is in this vein that the link between social justice—legal and economic— and the ideal humaneness are twinned here. The fundamental question raised, after the late Kenyan philosopher, Henry Odera Oruka (1997), is whether one can really practice Ubuntu without what he calls the human minimum. Odera Oruka's thesis is that humans are products of their respective societies, and thus the factors that drive individuals into crime, for example, are mainly external, and individual factors are secondary. Consequently, individuals cannot reasonably be held accountable for their crimes. Since Odera Oruka describes crimes as mainly caused by social factors, it is possible to connect his concept of punishment to his concept of justice and the need for a human minimum. The value of Odera Oruka's theory, discussed in chapter 6 in the volume, is in the sterling way in which it brings into view the link between social justice and the human minimum that he advocates for all humans, thus signaling a new ethic for Ubuntu. In other words, securing the human minimum in terms of economic needs is a necessary condition for the flowering of Ubuntu values. The argument forcefully made in the volume is the inescapable sociality of the human self by insisting that the fullness of our humaneness is possible only through belonging to, participating in, and sharing in the community.

If Amilcar Cabral (1973), talks about a return to the source, meaning active indigenous sources repressed by colonialism, this volume signals how formerly colonized societies continue to turn to an oral resource base to reconstitute themselves. We gesture toward a comparative philosophical analysis by offering a reading of Ubuntu, an African concept, alongside a Latin American concept conveyed in the expression "buen vivir." This is a classic example of comparative philosophy at work and deftly demonstrates that formerly colonized societies, or those that have experienced forms of oppression by minority groups, evoke their own traditional ideas that they believe to be effective in combating the injustices of the oppressive systems in their histories. By drawing these transcultural parallels between the two concepts, the volume is able to suggest that concepts rooted in communitarian ethos are not unique to Africa, as many have tended to argue. Even though anxieties persist about the dangers of uncritically using concepts rooted in tradition, especially when they are used to mediate contemporary problems, it has to be remembered, with Mudimbe (1988) in mind, that all societies carry their traditions with them in the present. Traditions themselves are reinvented and deliberately reworked to make them relevant in the present. For example, when in the 1980s African and Africanist historians talked of "the usable past," they were talking about this deliberate attempt to make choices about certain aspects of Africa's traditions. However, they were also intimating that the past lives on in the present, even when the past traditions are transformed, and that not all answers to our current predicament are to be found in the present or in the future. The point has been made that although Ubuntu as a concept remains active in the everyday practices of a number of African communities, its reemergence into political discourse coincided with a moment in South Africa's history when the society was groping for a new language that would engender introspection and help restore a shattered community. That kind of grammar would not be found exclusively within apartheid or in postcolonial formations characterized by divisive and repressive political structures. If there is one important point to glean from this study, it is that most repressed societies tend to turn to their own value systems, even if those remain silenced and subjugated, in order to articulate a new grammar of liberation and to reconstitute themselves time and time again. This is true for former colonized communities in Asia, Latin America, and Africa.

The essays go beyond basic theoretical elaboration of Ubuntu to examine the practical application of Ubuntu, particularly in contexts of fragile democracy in Africa. The typical trend in postconflict situations is for conventional forms of justice or institutions of justice to either collapse or be adulterated through the leadership of the same state actors whose misdeeds, or at least complicity in, causing or propagating unjust conditions were responsible for the societal disintegration in the first place. It is akin to making the perpetrators of injustice be their own prosecutors and judges against their victims, thus thwarting any possibility of vindication or fair treatment for victims before the law. Victims therefore do not trust them. Besides, by blurring the lines between protectors and perpetrators, and by failing to create a separation between victims and perpetrators because they inhabit the same space, an environment of intimidation is fostered, which makes achieving reconciliation and healing among members of affected communities difficult. In these contexts, modes of justice and reconciliation based on indigenous values and settings may often be preferred. Thus, this volume wrestles with various ways in which both perpetrators and victims of injustice enter a space where they can share their grief with the rest of the community and start a journey toward closure and healing. They also draw the rest of community into their respective worlds and share what in their view would constitute justice and, in the immutable reality of its irreversible history, reconciliation.

Studies on the Rwandan genocide and Kenya's 2007 postelection violence demonstrate the role that narrative and literature can play in contributing to reconciliation in societies that have suffered schism and collective trauma. Similarly, narratives by victims and perpetrators point to how they frame their ideas of justice and reconciliation in ways that echo back to indigenous forms of redress embedded in indigenous value systems such as Ubuntu or Utu. The values referenced in the narratives point to both religious and secular traditional modes of redress in which our common humanity and humaneness are at the heart of dialogue and privilege the need for a higher moral compass in regulating human conduct that full personhood implies in Africa.

Finally, the big question that some of the chapters in this book engage with is precisely what it means to be human and to belong. As some contributors suggest, Ubuntu discourse is also an engagement with contemporary problems; it is an attempt to think through the postcolonial moment of loss and fragmentation, one that they can return to only through imagination and as a problem for reflection. Therefore, to recover Ubuntu as a usable tool for a future community requires a major engagement with history, with how we reconcile our sense of loss with what it means to hold out a philosophical reimagining that is liberating in the present and in the future. As noted previously, a number of chapters in this book grapple with what the concept of Ubuntu may open up in this process of reimagining the multidimensionality of Africa and the rest of the world.

The approach in this book is to understand Ubuntu in all its complex manifestations by historicizing it and to register the possible ambivalences and contradictions that we have come to associate with other African humanist ideologies before it. We need to understand both past and contemporary issues that it seeks to address—and indeed to see it as a form of reengagement with modernity, to reinvigorate and redefine human connectedness—and that shape Ubuntu's grammar and values. In this sense, we are likely not simply to think of Ubuntu as a reinvented aspect of tradition but also to register its embeddedness in known traditions, on the continent and in the multiple diasporas to which the continent has extended, as a reclamation of its cultural universality. This way, we can understand how the term has traveled to become a critique of colonial modernity. Ubuntu is also a strand of African humanism whose roots and value transcend South Africa, as many have suggested. In this sense, we posit that Ubuntu is an ethical and moral principle that can be mobilized in response to a range of problems facing the continent, especially in redefining notions of justice, reconciliation, and restoration. If there is something that distinguishes this book, it is that it locates Ubuntu within the realm of the everyday practices of African communities, especially in mediating those matters that affect communities as they grapple with change and the trauma that have often characterized those difficult moments in the continent's history of colonialism, apartheid, and the postcolonial moment. Like other facets of Africa's cultural ethos, Ubuntu offers those possibilities for being mobilized in moving our many communities forward as they struggle to chart new ways of reconfiguring a humane and just society for all.

Notes

1. See *Emile Durkheim on Institutional Analysis*, ed. and trans. Mark Traugott (Chicago: Chicago University Press, 1978) for Durkeim's ideas on society and social organization.

2. I owe some of my thoughts on the idea of community to extended discussions, often accompanied with useful notes and references, that I had with D. A. Masolo during the preparation of this book. I wish to express my full gratitude for his generosity in sharing his ideas, even though I take full responsibility and ownership of how I frame the idea of community and the reconstitution of it here.

3. See Praeg (2014).

4. Mogobe Bernard Ramose (2005) argues that we should consider Ubuntu in its hyphenated form—*ubu-ntu*—to realize its full meaning. As two words, "ubu-ntu is the fundamental ontological and epistemological category in the African thought of the Bantu-speaking people. It is the invisible one-ness and whole-ness of ontology and epistemology. Ubu- as the generalized understanding of be-ing may be said to be distinctly ontological. Whereas -ntu is the nodal point at which be-ing assumes concrete form or mode of being in the process of continual unfoldment, ubu- may be said to be the distinctly epistemological" (35–36). Ramose goes on to interrogate the concept and formation of *umuntu* with the stem -*ntu* appearing again here:

> Umuntu is the specific entity which continues to conduct an inquiry into be-ing, experience, knowledge and truth. This is an activity rather than an act. It is an ongoing process impossible to stop unless motion itself is stopped. On this reasoning ubu- may be regarded as be-ing becoming and this evidently implies the idea of motion. We propose to regard such incessant motion as verbal rather than the verb. -ntu may be construed as the temporarily having become. In this sense -ntu is a noun. The indivisible one-ness and whole-ness of ubu-ntu means, therefore that Ubuntu is a verb noun. (36).

In this sense, -*ntu* may be seen as a way of being, while Ubuntu would be the act of showing or performing *ntu*.

5. We are saddened to announce that during the final preparation of this manuscript, Professor Shutte passed on. One of the pioneer scholars on Ubuntu, Shutte was a major influence on the many deliberations and colloquia that we held on the concept of Ubuntu at the University of Pretoria. We will miss his insights and remember his constant reminder that any academic project that is not in the service of humanity is worthless.

References

Appiah, Kwame Anthony. 1992. *In My Father's House: Africa in the Philosophy of Culture.* New York: Oxford University Press.

Battle, Michael. 1997. *Reconciliation: The Ubuntu Theology of Desmond Tutu*. Cleveland, OH: Pilgrim.

Cabral, Amilcar. 1973. *Return to the Source*. New York: Monthly Review Press.

Durkheim, Emile. 1978. *Emile Durkheim on Institutional Analysis*. Edited and translated by Mark Traugott. Chicago: Chicago University Press.

Freire, Paulo. 1972. Trans. Myra Bergman Ramos. *Pedagogy of the Oppressed*. London: Penguin Books.

Hountondji, Paulin J. 1983. *African Philosophy: Myth and Reality*. Bloomington: Indiana University Press.

Karp, Ivan, and D. A. Masolo. 2000. Introduction to *African Philosophy as Cultural Inquiry*, edited by Ivan Karp and D. A. Masolo, 1–18. Bloomington: Indiana University Press.

King, Martin Luther, Jr., and Melvin James Washington. 1986. *A Testament of Hope: The Essential Writings of Martin Luther King Jr*. San Francisco: Harper and Row.

Kiros, Teodros. 2001. "African Philosophy: A Critical/Moral Practice." In *Explorations in African Political Thought: Identity, Community, Ethics*, edited by Teodros Kiros. New York: Routledge.

Masolo, D. A. 2010. *Self and Community in a Changing World*. Bloomington: Indiana University Press.

Mbembe, Achille. 2009. 'Postcolonial Thought Explained to the French: An Interview with Achille Mbembe'. *The Johannesburg Salon* 1. Available at http://www.jwtc.org.za/the_salon/volume_1/achille_mbembe.htm.

Mudimbe, V. Y. 1988. *The Invention of Africa: Gnosis, Philosophy, and the Order of Knowledge*. Bloomington: Indiana University Press.

Odera Oruka, Henry. 1990. *Sage Philosophy: Indigenous Thinkers and Modern Debate on African Philosophy*. Leiden: J. Brill.

———. 1997. *Practical Philosophy in Search of Human Minimum*. Nairobi: East African Educational.

Praeg, Leonhard. 2014. *A Report on Ubuntu*. Pietermaritzburg, S. Afr.: University of KwaZulu-Natal Press.

Ramose, Bernard Mogobe. 2005. *African Philosophy through Ubuntu*. Harare, Zimb.: Mond.

Said, Edward W. 1993. *Culture and Imperialism*. London: Chatto and Windus.

Sanders, Mark. 2002. *Complicities: The Intellectual and Apartheid*. Scottsville, S. Afr.: University of KwaZulu-Natal Press.

Shutte, Augustine. 2001. *Ubuntu: An Ethic for a New South Africa*. Pietermaritzburg, S. Afr.: Cluster.

Tempels, Placide. 1959. *Bantu Philosophy*. Paris: Présence africaine.

Tutu, Desmond. 2011. *God Is Not a Christian: Speaking Truth in Times of Crisis*. London: Rider.

Van Binsbergen, Wim. 2001. "*Ubuntu* and the Globalization of Southern African Thought and Society." *Quest* 15, nos. 1–2: 54–89.

Wiredu, Kwasi. 1996. *Cultural Universals and Particulars: an African Perspective*. Bloomington: Indiana University Press.

———. 2001. "Society and Democracy in Africa." In *Explorations in African Political Thought: Identity, Community, Ethics*, edited by Teodros Kiros, 171–84. New York: Routledge.

JAMES OGUDE is Senior Research Fellow and the Director at the Centre for the Advancement of Scholarship, University of Pretoria. Until his recent appointment he was a Professor of African Literature and Cultures in the School of Literature, Language and Media Studies at the University of the Witwatersrand, serving as the Head of African Literature and also Assistant Dean–Research in the Faculty of Humanities. He is author of *Ngugi's Novels and African History: Narrating the Nation,* and he has coedited four books and one anthology of African stories, including most recently *Chinua Achebe's Legacy: Illuminations from Africa.*

1

UBUNTU IN THE CHRISTIAN THEOLOGY AND PRAXIS OF ARCHBISHOP DESMOND TUTU AND ITS IMPLICATIONS FOR GLOBAL JUSTICE AND HUMAN RIGHTS

Aloo Osotsi Mojola

THE TERM *UBUNTU* (AND ITS VARIANT FORMS, E.G., Kiswahili *Utu*) is of Bantu origin and is common to the languages and dialects of the Bantu language family. In reference to the languages and dialects of this African language family, Derek Nurse and Gerard Philippson, in *The Bantu Languages*, note that "Bantu-speaking communities live in Africa south of a line from Nigeria across the Central African Republic (CAR), the Democratic Republic of Congo (formerly Zaire), Uganda, and Kenya, to southern Somalia in the east. Most communities between that line and the Cape are Bantu. The exceptions are pockets; in the south, some small and fast dwindling Khoisan communities; in Tanzania one, maybe two, Khoi-San outliers" (Nurse and Philippson 2003, 1). Thus "communities speaking Bantu languages are indigenous to 27 African countries" and "roughly one African in three" speaks a Bantu language (1). The Bantu language family is part of the larger Niger-Congo language group, one of the four language groups found on the African continent, namely, the Niger-Congo, the Nilo-Saharan, the Afroasiatic, and the Khoi-San (Heine and Nurse 2000).

The term *Bantu* was first coined by German scholar and linguist Wilhelm Heinrich Immanuel Bleek in his classic text *A Comparative Grammar of South African Languages* (1862) to refer to the entire group of languages that use the term Bantu or share significant grammatical, morphological, phonological, lexical, and semantic features. Bleek may be considered as the Father of Bantu Philology as he pioneered the use of the term *Bantu* to refer to this group of languages. He was intrigued by the common use of the root or stem *-ntu* (or variants such as *-ndu, -tu, -to, -nto*). This root means "entity" or "object." When it is given the prefix *mu-* (or variants across the range of Bantu languages *omu-, mo-, um-, m-, <u>mo-</u>*) to become *muntu* (or its variants) it means "human being" or "person." When it has the prefix *ba-* (or variants *aba-, a-, vha-, vho-, bo-, wa-*) to become *bantu*, which is the plural form, it means "human beings" or "persons."

Some twenty-three nominal or noun classes, mostly paired and with corresponding semantics, have been identified in this group of languages. In the most common and ubiquitous noun class, class 1 (for example in Luyia, Luganda, Lusoga, Kisukuma, Kinyarwanda and others), *mu* is singular and is paired with class 2 *ba*, its plural, and usually refers to human beings, proper names, kinship terms, personifications. Noun class 7, for example, has the prefix *ki-* (or variants such as *eki-, chi-, oshi-, tshi-, se-, isi-, e-, i-*) and gives *kintu*, meaning roughly "thing" across the range of Bantu languages. Its plural class 8 has prefix *bi-* (or such variants as *ebi-, zi-, i-, zwi-, di-, izi-*), which yields *bintu*, which means "things." The semantic content of *bintu* includes body parts, tools, instruments and utensils, animals and insects, languages, diseases, and outstanding people. Not all Bantu languages necessarily have the full set of twenty-three noun classes. Katamba notes that "in no single language are all the approximately twenty-four noun classes reconstructed for Proto-Bantu. . . . The highest number of classes retained by a single language seems to be twenty-one, as in the case in Ganda. Languages with numerous noun classes are said to exhibit the canonical Bantu noun class system, while others with 'reduced' noun class systems have only a rump of the original set" (Katamba 2003, 108. See also Katamba's table 7.1 at 104 and table 7.4 at 109).

Ubuntu, which is the focus of our interest in this paper, belongs to noun class 14, whose semantic content consists of abstracts and collectives and thus has no singular or plural. Its stem, as noted above, is *-ntu* and its prefix is *ubu-* (and such variants as *obu-, u-, vhu-, bo-, wu-*), which yields Ubuntu (and variants, i.e., *obuntu, untu, vhuntu, bontu, wuntu*, etc.). As this analysis shows, the term *Ubuntu* is not limited to the "Nguni language family which comprises Zulu, Xhosa, Swati and Ndebele" (Van Binsbergen 2001, 53) or the Southern African Bantu languages, as many commentators or writers suggest. On the contrary, the term is common to the entire spectrum of Bantu languages, stretching from the Nigerian-Cameroonian border all the way to the southern tip of the African continent. Its derivation is inextricably connected with *muntu. Muntu* (or any of its variants), as indicated above, means "person" or "human." Ubuntu, an abstract noun derived from it, can therefore etymologically be said to convey the idea of personhood or humanness.

Situating Ubuntu within the African Cultural and Belief Context

Words or key terms cannot be understood in a vacuum. They are inextricably connected to their underlying sociocultural contexts and environments, belief systems, and the historical associations that affect word meanings. Ubuntu cannot therefore be fully or properly understood without a look at the history, cultures, religious practices, and philosophies of the Bantu communities who regularly employ the term.

It might be the case that Bantu communities used the term *muntu* to refer to one of their own, in other words, to a fellow Bantu. It does not seem to be so. The term *muntu* means any person, any human being, irrespective of ethnicity or race. All humans are included in its semantic content. Even though some misunderstanding has led commentators to limit the term *Ubuntu* to the personhood or humanness of members of a Bantu community or communities, the term is inclusive and embraces all of humanity. Etymologically and semantically, it clearly refers to the humanity or humanness of any human being (this follows from the fact that Ubuntu as argued above is not language specific or ethnocentric, but person or human centric).

Among the Bantu-speaking peoples and communities of Africa, Ubuntu has to do with the essence of what it means to be human, what really makes humans human. Ubuntu means humanness, personhood—a sharing and a participation in the values that constitute, sustain, and ensure the existence of human community. Placide Tempels ([1952] 1959), in his classic and well-known text *Bantu Philosophy*, made a preliminary attempt to explore how Bantu communities understood this Ubuntu. His work and life as a Franciscan Catholic missionary among the Baluba in what was then Belgian Congo from 1933 to 1962 motivated him to search for a philosophy underlying the beliefs and practices of the Baluba and of the Bantu peoples in general. In his text, he speaks of a Bantu ontology, a Bantu wisdom or criteriology, a Bantu psychology, and a Bantu ethics, among other philosophical concerns. The paternalistic approach espoused in the book is a reflection of the negative European prejudices against Africans during that era, which explains the unfavorable and negative reception *Bantu Philosophy* received, especially among African scholars. Despite the unpopularity and strong rejection that the work has encountered, it stimulated many subsequent pioneer studies, among them that of the Rwandese priest and scholar Abbé Alexis Kagame (1955, 1970, 1976). Abbé Kagame's studies of the Rwandese language and culture and its underlying religious and philosophical ideas were no doubt influenced by Fr. Tempels's work. His key text, *La philosophie bantu-rwandaise de l'être* [The Bantu-Rwandan Philosophy of Being] was an exploration and reflection on the nature of being as manifested in the Kinyarwanda language and culture. Abbé Kagame took to heart Louis Hjelmslev's dictum, "Il n'y a pas de philosophie sans linguistique." That is, the underlying philosophy of a people and culture is found in an exploration and reflection on the structures of their heart language. Thus, in *La philosophie bantu comparée*, Kagame (1976) extended his explorations to Bantu languages in general.

It is interesting to note that Abbé Kagame was the first African scholar to refer to Ubuntu in writing. Thus in his *La philosophie bantu comparée* (1976), he speaks of Ubuntu in terms of the virtue of liberality. He did not, however, pursue further the axiological aspects of Ubuntu. He concluded from his studies that the Banyarwanda and Bantu cultures in general conceptualize reality under four fundamental categories of thought, namely (1) *muntu* (plural *bantu*), human being, rational being; (2) *kintu* (plural *bintu*), nonhuman being, thing, nonrational being; (3) *hantu*, place and time, spacing and conceptualizing from being a temporal perspective; (4) *kuntu*, modality, modal being (in other words, contingency or determination). Reducing Bantu or African philosophy to these four categories is not without its challenges and questions. The influence of ancient Greek as in modern Western philosophical thinking is clearly evident here. These four categories are basic semantic categories derived from Kinyarwanda or other Bantu linguistic morphology, as a quick look at the semantic or nominal classes of Bantu languages and a reflection on them will quickly show. Janheinz Jahn, commenting on these four categories of Kagame's philosophy, writes,

> Everything there is, must necessarily belong to one of these four categories and must be conceived of not as substance but as force. Man is a force, all

things are forces, place and time are forces and the "modalities" are forces. Man and woman (category Muntu), dog and stone (category Kintu), east and yesterday (category Hantu), beauty and laughter (category Kuntu) are forces and as such are all related to one another. The relationship of these forces is expressed in their very names, for if we remove the determinative the stem NTU is the same for all the categories. NTU is the universal force as such, which, however never occurs apart from its manifestation: Muntu, Kintu, Hantu and Kuntu. NTU is Being itself, the cosmic universal force, which only modern, rationalizing thought can abstract from its manifestations. NTU is that force in which Being and beings coalesce. (Jahn 1961, 100–101)

The usage of *force* here is clearly influenced by Fr. Tempels's *Bantu Philosophy* ([1952] 1959). He states, for example, that "force is the nature of being, force is being, being is force. . . . Muntu signifies, then, vital force endowed with intelligence and will. . . . God is the great muntu, . . . (1959, 51) the great Person, that is to say the great, powerful and reasonable living force. The 'bintu' are rather what we call things; but according to Bantu philosophy they are beings, that is to say forces not endowed with reason, not living" (55).

Marcel Griaule (1970), a French cultural anthropologist, has also written for us his findings on the cosmology and religious ideas of the Dogon of Mali. His work is based on his studies and conversations with an ancient hunter and sage, Ogotommeli, in 1946 over some thirty-three days. The conversations revealed a complex system of cosmological and religious beliefs held by these ancient people. His findings were later published as *Conversations with Ogotommeli*. A number of scholars, cultural anthropologists, and students of African religions and philosophies were inspired to engage in similar studies. Among them are E. W. Smith (1950); Edward Geoffrey Parrinder (1954); Bolaji Idowu (1962, 1973); and John Mbiti (1969, 1970). These explorations and attempts to understand African belief systems and practices and their underlying values are pivotal in understanding how the idea of what it means to be human was constructed. This is central in throwing light on our understanding of Ubuntu.

Ubuntu in the Context of Some Core Values
of the African Life and World

Ernst Wendland (1990) has highlighted for us in summary form some of the core principles common to African traditional life and thought. It should be noted that the list under discussion by Wendland here is based on his own observations and inferences drawn from a lifetime of study and life in Central Africa. The terms in this list are drawn mainly from the traditional religious beliefs and practices of Central Africa, where Wendland has worked and spent most of his life. The principles he listed are widely recognized and frequently referred to in the literature by various scholars and, moreover, commonly believed and practiced in a majority of sub-Saharan African cultures and communities. A principal feature of Bantu or African traditional beliefs and practices is their being "strongly homocentric in orientation and humanized in operation" (30). Tempels ([1952] 1959) described it as follows: "The created universe is centered on man. The present human generation living on earth is the center of all humanity, including the world of the dead" (64). Other characteristic features of traditional Bantu or African cultures and belief systems include the following:[1] the principle of synthesis, the principle of dynamism, the principle of gradation, the principle of communalism, the principle of experientialism, the principle of humanism, and the principle of circumscription.

The principle of synthesis refers to "a distinct preference for a synthetic approach toward life . . . an emphasis upon searching for the relatedness of things, to include rather than to exclude" (Wendland 1990, 74). The principle of dynamism or life force "involves, in effect, a total personalization of the cosmos. Every living being possesses such a force" (83). This principle is often misunderstood and is perhaps behind the reductionist claim that traditional African cultures were or are animistic. This claim, common in journalistic literature, is a gross mischaracterization of these cultures. The principle of gradation[2] refers to the graded, hierarchical structure of reality, according to which God the creator is positioned at the top (see Tempels [1952] 1959, 61–64). The great clan of spirits or divinities come next on the ladder and include clan spirits (originators, culture heroes), ancestral spirits (forgotten in name or personality), and the living dead (both benevolent and malevolent). Humans are squarely at the center of this ladder or circle—chief, religious specialists (good or bad), elders of society, adults (with family), youth (initiated), children (those with a name), and infants. They are followed by ranks of nature—animals (and their ranks), plants (and their ranks), and inanimate objects and places (loci of spirit forces). The principle of communalism holds that "every individual, though valued in and of him/herself, is always viewed in relation to the whole of which he/she constitutes a vital part, beginning with the extended family (the fundamental kinship unit) through clan membership, and on up to the tribe as a whole. . . . Mutual sharing, or natural socialism is a prominent expression of the principle of communalism" (Wendland 1990, 93–94).

Nyerere (1968), Kaunda (1962), Nkrumah (1964), and others all have their roots in this principle. Kwasi Wiredu, a well-known African philosopher, writes as follows: "There can be little doubt that traditional African society was communitarian, unless it be a matter of exceptions that prove the rule. . . . Communalism is an embodiment of the values of traditional Africa" (quoted in Metz 2012, 392). The principle of experientialism is a kind of empiricism "firmly grounded on a synthesizing, subjective perspective that begins with the world of man . . . [and] regards the universe holistically that is, as a unified, integrated system in which man and nature live in close harmony" (Wendland 1990, 96). The principle of humanism is a sixth principle according to which "the world revolves around man, and thus regular ritual activity is organized either around the human cycle of existence (i.e. birth, maturation, marriage, procreation, and death) or on those occasions when people find themselves experiencing serious difficulties in life, whether communal (e.g. drought, famine, plague) or individual (e.g. sickness, barrenness, depreciation)" (Wendland 1990, 103). The principle of circumscription is the seventh and final principle and refers to the concept of the "limited good" or principle of delimitation, which is the idea that all resources beneficial to humans are finite and therefore need to be fairly shared and used sparingly and responsibly with a view to the common good of all. This concept stands against greed and use of resources at the expense of the community. It upholds the idea of solidarity and the principle of egalitarianism in the sharing of common resources.

The core principles summarized here define the contours or framework of a traditional African Bantu thought world. A traditional understanding of the idea of Ubuntu is arguably rooted in this matrix of values that define the ideals espoused by traditional African societies—the humanism, the communalism and human solidarity, the synthesis, the experientialism, the cosmic order or gradation, and so forth. Some of these principles have been framed in ethnophilosophical terms or as sage philosophy, as in the writings of Paulin Hountondji (e.g., 1983) or Henry Odera Oruka (e.g., 1990, 1991). There are those who have dismissed these ideas as parochial, primitive, irrational, illogical, outdated, irrelevant, inapplicable, misplaced, based on serious misunderstandings, and so on. (See, for example, Van Binsbergen 2001.) On the contrary, it could be argued that the validity of these ideas might be understood to transcend their place and time of genesis.

Moreover, all philosophy is, from a genetic perspective, ethnophilosophy. Everyone has heard of so-called Greek philosophy, German philosophy, Chinese philosophy, Indian philosophy, African philosophy, for example. In so doing, philosophy is being defined in relative and ethno-philosophical terms. The contemporary ideal of a universalistic, objective, absolute view of philosophy has been deconstructed and shown to be untenable. It is preferable to talk of philosophy as a cultural or intercultural activity relative to the time, place, and community or people.

Two Current Conceptions of Ubuntu

Christian B. N. Gade's research (2011, 2012) on the nature and meaning of Ubuntu is an eye opener. From the data collected in his research on this term, he concluded that responses to what Ubuntu is can be grouped in two clusters. According to the first cluster, "ubuntu is defined as a moral quality of a person" or "something only a person can possess, so if you are not a person, then you are not of this moral quality." According to the second cluster, "ubuntu is defined as a phenomenon (for a possible subject instance a philosophy, an ethic, African humanism, or a worldview) according to which persons are interconnected. If you are not a person, then you are not part of the interconnectedness between persons" (Gade 2012, 494).

Gade reports that the term *Ubuntu* first appeared in writing in 1846 and that "more than a century passed before the first authors began to define ubuntu more broadly than simply as a human quality" and that it was not until the second half of the 1900s that Ubuntu began to be defined as a philosophy, an ethic, African humanism, and as a worldview in written sources (Gade 2011, 309). According to Gade's rich and well-documented and wide-ranging research,

> prior to 1980, ubuntu was most commonly described as—"Human nature," "Humanity," "Humanness," "Manhood," "Goodness of nature"—"Good moral disposition," "Virtue," "The sense of common humanity," "True humanity," "True good fellowship and sympathy in joy and in sorrow," "Reverence for human nature," "Essential humanity," "The kindly simple feeling for persons as persons," "Manliness," "Liberality," "A person's own human nature," "Generosity," "Human feeling," "Humaneness," "Good disposition," "Good moral nature," "Personhood," "Politeness," "Kindness," "Real humanity," "Humanity (benevolence)," "Personality," "Human kindness," "The characteristic of being truly human," "Greatness of soul," "A feeling of human wellbeing," "Capacity of social self-sacrifice on behalf of others." (Gade 2011, 307–8)

The virtues listed belong to Gade's first cluster alluded to above. Moreover, as Gade points out, "Prior to 1980, the level of disagreement about the nature of ubuntu does not seem to have been as great as it is today: all of the descriptions cited above can be interpreted as descriptions of a human quality" (Gade 2011, 308). These attempts at describing the nature of Ubuntu are widespread throughout Africa in capturing the ideal of a good person, a virtuous person, a morally mature individual in society. Needless to say, the word may have been understood relative to the contexts of place and time.

It would appear that the term *Ubuntu*, "defined as a philosophy, an ethic, African humanism, and as a worldview in written sources," (see Gade 2012, 494) is a later development. According to Gade (2011), "it was in the period from 1993 to 1995 that the Nguni proverb '*Umuntu ngumuntu ngabantu*' was used for the first time to describe what ubuntu is" (308). This does not mean that the proverb was originally used during this period. Undoubtedly, the proverb and similar proverbs across most of Africa are timeless. The usage of the term in its secondary sense as "an ethic, an African humanism, or a worldview according to which persons are interconnected" (Gade 2011, 308) is a later development. Professor John Mbiti, a leading and renowned authority on African religions and philosophy, describes Ubuntu interconnectedness as follows: "I am because we are, and because we are, therefore I am" (Mbiti 1969, 108–9). He explains,

> Only in terms of other people does the individual become conscious of his own being, his own duties, his privileges and responsibilities towards himself and towards other people. When he suffers, he does not suffer alone but with the corporate group; when he rejoices, he rejoices not alone but with his kinsmen, his neighbors and his relatives whether dead or living. When he married, he is not alone, neither does the wife "belong" to him alone. So also the children belong to the corporate body of kinsmen, even if they bear only their father's or mother's name. Whatever happens to the individual happens to the whole group, and whatever happens to the whole group happens to the individual. (106)

It is interesting to note that Archbishop Desmond Tutu describes the idea of Ubuntu in these terms. He writes, "Ubuntu means that in a real sense even the supporters of apartheid were victims of the vicious system which they implemented and which they supported so enthusiastically. Our humanity was intertwined. The humanity of the perpetrator of apartheid's atrocities was caught up and bound up in that of his victim whether he liked it or not. In the process of dehumanizing another, in inflicting untold harm and suffering, the perpetrator was inexorably being dehumanized as well" (2013, 35).

The revered heroes and fighters against the African slave trade, colonialism, neocolonialism, politico-economic imperialism, or environmental degradation have been inspired by and have drawn on this rich fountain and heritage of Ubuntu. Among these are Kenneth Kaunda's dreams of his Zambian humanism, Kwame Nkrumah's visions conjured up in his *Consciencism* and other writings, Frantz Fanon's (1963, 1967) *Wretched of the Earth* and yearnings for a new humanity, Nelson Mandela in his struggle against apartheid and the creation of an inclusive human society, and Julius Nyerere's Ujaama villages and the search for a true human humanity characterized by Utu (the Swahili variant of Ubuntu), among others.

Archbishop Tutu's theological vision and struggle for a peaceful, loving, reconciliatory, inclusive, fair, and just society are clearly part of this narrative and history of struggle against inhumanity to fellow humans, hypocrisy and greed, brutality and violence, exclusion and exploitation, and injustice and oppression.

Archbishop Desmond Tutu and Ubuntu

Archbishop Desmond Tutu is not the originator of the term *Ubuntu*. He is, however, one of its most prominent living exponents, as well as one of the most well-known ambassadors of and witnesses to the idea of Ubuntu. He has gone further than most in understanding its true meaning and in existentially living it out in his thought and practice. Tutu (2013) writes

> In our African *weltanschauung*, our worldview, we have something called *ubuntu*. In Xhosa we say, "*Umntu ngumtu ngabantu*" . . . very difficult to translate in English, but we could translate it by saying, "A person is a person through other persons." . . . For us the solitary human being is a contradiction in terms.
>
> *Ubuntu* is the essence of being human. It speaks of how my humanity is caught up and bound up inextricably with yours. . . . The completely self-sufficient human being is sub-human. . . . We are made for complementarity. We are created for a delicate network of relationships, of interdependence with our fellow human beings, with the rest of creation. . . .
>
> *Ubuntu* speaks of spiritual attributes such as generosity, hospitality, compassion, caring, sharing. You could be affluent in material possessions but still be without *Ubuntu*. This concept speaks of how people are more important than things, than profits, than material possessions. It speaks about the intrinsic worth of persons as not dependent on extraneous things such as status, race, creed, gender, or achievement.

In traditional African society, Ubuntu was coveted more than anything else. . . . It was seen as what ultimately distinguished people from animals—the quality of being human and so also humane. Those who had *Ubuntu* were compassionate and gentle, they used their strength on behalf of the weak, and they did not take advantage of others—in short, they *cared,* treating others as what they were: human beings. If you lacked *Ubuntu*, in a sense you lacked an indispensable ingredient of being human. You might have had much of the world's goods, and you might have had position and authority, but if you had no *Ubuntu*, you did not amount to much. Today, *Ubuntu* is still greatly admired, sought after and cultivated. . . .

Ubuntu teaches us that our worth is intrinsic to who we are. We matter because we are made in the image of God. *Ubuntu* reminds us that we belong in one family—God's family, the human family. In our African worldview, the greatest good is communal harmony. Anything that subverts or undermines this greatest good is ipso facto wrong, evil. (21–24)

The statement on Ubuntu by Tutu clearly demonstrates the essential significance and centrality of this idea in his theological vision and practice. His life and work is an embodiment and open witness to Ubuntu. One might ask how or why Tutu, a Christian theologian, has grounded his life and moral vision on an idea central to the ethico-moral values of traditional African religions and cultures. The apparent convergence between the virtues espoused in the Gospel and Ubuntu is reason enough. The archbishop's upbringing and cultural roots are steeped in a culture that draws on African values of which Ubuntu is an essential part. His faith and vocation are steeped in Christian theology. This has, it would appear, led to the Christianization of the idea of Ubuntu by the archbishop. (See Battle 2000.) This is a perfect example of what is currently referred to as indigenization or inculturation, the process by which Christian values and ideas are assimilated or clothed in indigenous garb and made intelligible by means of local cultural ideas, as well expressed in local idiom.

Ubuntu as *Imago Dei*

No wonder Archbishop Tutu understands Ubuntu in terms of the *imago dei*, the Judeo-Christian belief and teaching that draw on Genesis 1:27, which states that "God created man in his own image."[3] Clearly, the statement not intended anthropomorphically. It refers to the human spiritual, moral, and intellectual nature said to be contingent on God's own nature, believed to be the source and ground of these attributes. Thus, human dignity and worth, human unity, and brotherhood and sisterhood are held to be grounded in this belief in God. All humans belong together. In Tutu's book coauthored with his daughter, *Made for Goodness*, they write,

> *Ubuntu* recognizes that human beings need each other for survival and well-being. A person is a person only through other persons, we say. We must care for one another in order to thrive. The impulse to care, the instinct for goodness, is a shining thread woven into the fabric of our being. As human beings we may tarnish the sheen or rend the fabric of our own goodness. We can act in cruel and heartless ways. But because we are human, we cannot completely rip out and destroy every vestige of the godliness by which and for which we were made. We cannot alter our essence. We are made by God, who is goodness itself. We are made like God. We are made for goodness. (Tutu and Tutu 2010, 15)

They add "We can choose to act out of the goodness that is the essence of our being. . . . We can choose goodness no matter the circumstances" (Tutu and Tutu 2010, 190).

Tutu's inclusive vision of all humans is thus rooted in his full acceptance of Ubuntu, his firm belief in our oneness, our common humanity, our being created in God's image, our interconnectedness, our common destiny. In this view, "the greatest good is communal harmony. Anything that subverts or undermines this greatest good is ipso facto wrong, evil" (224).

Ubuntu and Forgiveness, Reconciliation, and Restorative Justice

Archbishop Tutu's defense and preference for forgiveness and reconciliation, for restorative justice and communal harmony, are rooted in his vision of the human family as God's family, where each member possesses infinite worth and dignity and deserves respect, nurture, and support. (See Battle 2009; Haws 2009.) During a visit to postgenocide Rwanda, Tutu addressed "our sisters and brothers in Rwanda, and outside Rwanda," insisting that "there can be no future without forgiveness. There will be no future unless there is peace. There can be no future unless there is reconciliation. But there can be no reconciliation before there is forgiveness. And there can be no forgiveness unless people repent" (Tutu 2013, 35; see also Tutu 1999). This passionate talk of forgiveness and repentance is undoubtedly derived from Christian teaching and theology, but in Tutu's understanding, it consistent with and fully supportive of an Ubuntu ethic. And this is how Tutu fuses African with Christian visions or his indigenized faith with practice as an African Christian.

Tutu's understanding of justice is much influenced by his understanding of Ubuntu. He has "advocated that the values embodied in *ubuntu* should be given practical expression in African systems of justice" (Tutu 2013, 32). His desire is "to see a resurgence, a revival, a renaissance of so many of the wonderful attributes and values that Africa has[:] . . . a jurisprudence, a penology in Africa which is not retributive" (32). He holds that Africa "had a jurisprudence which was restorative. When people quarreled in the traditional setting, the main intention was not to punish the miscreant but to restore good relations. For Africa is concerned, was concerned, about relationship, about the wholeness of relationship" (Tutu 2013, 32). In his view, the chief purpose of restorative justice is "not punitive but restorative, healing. It holds as central the essential humanity of the perpetrator of even the most gruesome atrocity, never giving up on anyone, believing in the essential goodness of all as created in the image of God, and believing that even the worst of us all still remains a child of God with the potential to become better, someone to be salvaged, to be rehabilitated, not to be ostracized but ultimately to be reintegrated into the human community" (Tutu 2013, 42). Tutu's firm belief that "*Ubuntu* (and so restorative justice) gives up on no one" and that "No one is totally hopeless or irredeemable" (44) is what provided him with a compass and framework for his leadership and work in the South African Truth and Reconciliation Commission.

Ubuntu and the Idea of a Rainbow People

As Tutu argues in his book *The Rainbow People of God* (1994), we ought to live as "the rainbow people of God" (179–84), respecting one another in spite of our differences of opinion or lifestyle, moving together "to freedom, to justice, to democracy, to peace, to reconciliation, to healing, to loving, to laughter and joy" (176) because

> We belong in a world whose very structure, whose essence, is diversity, almost bewildering in extent. It is to live in a fool's paradise to ignore this basic fact. We live in a universe marked by diversity as the law of its being and our being. We are made to exist in a life that should be marked by cooperation, interdependence, sharing, caring, compassion and complementarity. We should celebrate our diversity; we should exult in our differences as making not for separation and alienation and hostility but for their glorious opposites. The law of our being is to live in solidarity, friendship, helpfulness, unselfishness, interdependence, and complementarity, as sisters and brothers in one family, the human family, God's family. Anything else, as we have experienced is disaster. (50)

This is the very essence of Ubuntu. It has characterized Tutu's moral vision, his life of struggle for freedom, for justice and for human rights, not only within the confines or borders of his own nation, South Africa. On the contrary, he has vigorously struggled for the practice of Ubuntu in the rest of Africa and around the world and has not shied away from controversy or confrontation in the struggle. He has come to be widely associated with the idea of Ubuntu and is perhaps one of its foremost witnesses.[4] It is not surprising that he has elevated the idea of Ubuntu to a theology. In his understanding, Ubuntu and Christian theology are indistinguishable. In a book coauthored with his daughter Mpho, we read, "Ubuntu theology is an understanding of life that values community" (Tutu and Tutu 2010, 108).

Ubuntu in the Global Arena

As we indicated earlier, *muntu* (or any of its variants) is used to refer to any human being and the term *bantu* is its plural form and refers to human beings in general. When, however, one speaks of Bantu languages or Bantu peoples or communities, what is intended are all those whose first language was a Bantu language or who belong to a Bantu community. Ubuntu, in contrast, is not so limited. Ubuntu is a moral quality of a person in its primary sense but also a phenomenon "according to which persons are interconnected." Ubuntu is at the same time an ethic, a moral imperative, a moral virtue expected of all humans wherever they are found. Ubuntu is what makes us human. It is a Kantian categorical imperative in the sense that the word assumes that every human being, every *muntu* everywhere, should be true to their Ubuntu and should be guided by the moral imperatives and demands of Ubuntu. Ubuntu may thus also be understood as a moral virtue.

Archbishop Tutu's social and political activism was not limited to South Africa. During his tenure as chair of the All Africa Council of Churches, his voice reverberated throughout the entire continent. He could not accept the "docile and quiescent" churches typical of sub-Saharan Africa. He advocated a critical solidarity that led him to activism around the continent and around the world. He has been dubbed a rabble-rouser for peace and justice and freedom. (See Allen 2006.) He deeply feels for Africa, which he describes as "a beautiful continent . . . a continent that is bleeding . . . where there is a great deal of suffering. It is a continent that is being destroyed by civil war. . . . It suffers because it has to bear such a heavy burden of international debt. It is a continent that suffers from malnutrition. It is a continent that suffers from poverty. It is a continent that suffers from gross exploitation by those who are rich. It is a continent where there is little justice" (Tutu 2013, 63).

This litany of Africa's problems and suffering is endless. His list proceeds as follows:

> You look around Africa at this time, as God's children all over Africa—the poor getting poorer, the hungry getting hungrier. You look over all Africa and you see many of God's children suffering oppression. You see God's children many times in prison for nothing. All over Africa you see God's children treated as if they were rubbish. In many parts of Africa you see God's children having their noses rubbed in the dust. You see God's children trodden underfoot by the powerful. In many parts of Africa God's children can't speak what they want to say because when they say, 'NO, this is wrong,' they are taken to prison or they are killed. Not just in South Africa. . . . There are wars here, there, everywhere. . . . And people ask, 'Where is God? Where is God when we suffer in this way?" (Tutu 2013, 69–70)

In the context of this chapter, these disturbing and brutal realities may lead one to ask, "Where is *Ubuntu*? Where are those whose conscience is still guided by *Ubuntu*? Does *Ubuntu* still exist? Has it ever existed, either in traditional African society, as many attest, or in contemporary African, let alone global society?"

Perhaps Archbishop Tutu is right in his belief that Ubuntu is an essential feature of our being human, that it is wired in our very being, that it derives from our being created in God's image, that it transcends all artificially created human barriers and binds together all humans.

Ubuntu and Human Rights

Ubuntu is about human dignity and about human rights. It is about our inalienable right to be treated and respected as persons of dignity and infinite worth before the Creator and the entire human family. It is about truth, and justice, and beauty, and goodness. It is about peace and joy and hope and love. These values are not subject to empirical proof or verification. They are a matter of faith, faith in humans and faith in the future of humanity. Or to borrow a point made by Geoffrey Robertson in reference to the fundamental rights to life, equality, liberty, and the pursuit of happiness, it could be argued that Ubuntu, like any of these values, is "not drawn from any empirical source or discovered through rational argument, they may be given by God but the proof of their existence is that we all feel and think them—they attach 'inalienably' to the human person, like a shadow. They are not the end product of philosophical discovery but the starting point for it, imposing a duty on government to order itself in a way which will maximize opportunities for individual fulfilment" (Robertson 2002, 7).

The struggles and efforts of activists and warriors for a more peaceful, more just, more caring, more loving, and more human world matter and make a difference. Everyone needs to participate and advocate acting as our brothers' and sisters' keepers. The moral vision and compass provided by Ubuntu should inspire humans to care for and protect one another, especially the weak and disadvantaged, the oppressed and exploited, the poor and sick, the marginalized and excluded. Berma Klein Goldewijk and Baas de Gaay Fortman are quite right in their insistence that "human dignity . . . needs to be brought to the centre of the international human rights debate. . . . The protection of human dignity as the basic source and fundamental standard of human rights seems often to be a forgotten element in the international human rights debate quickly" (cited in Jacques 2007, 32). Human dignity, insofar as it deals with self-esteem and the individual feeling of self-worth or affirmation by others, is intimately and inextricably connected to Ubuntu. The loss of self-worth and humiliation or depreciation by others can lead to feelings of shame, self-hatred, and even depression and suicide. All around us, our fellow human beings are deprived of their dignity and sense of worth and their Ubuntu in a number of ways. As Genevieve Jacques (2007) correctly observes,

> Reaffirming human dignity as the starting point—the cornerstone as it were—of the whole issue of human rights introduces an ethical dimension that allows us to see much more in our human rights commitments than the legal box into which they have been squeezed. Indeed when we understand that depriving people of food, health, care, education or housing is just as destructive to life and as humiliating as attacks on physical integrity, freedom of expression or religious liberty, it adds a deeper and more visible significance to the struggle against human rights violations—and makes the struggle all the more imperative. . . . It reminds us that the important thing in "human rights" is human beings: creatures who do not exist alone but only in relationships with others." (34)

Jacques explicitly acknowledges some indebtedness to Ubuntu thinking (42) and to the idea that human rights are, in the final analysis, about human beings and their relationships with other human beings, their interrelatedness, their solidarity, their self-worth and self-respect, their well-being.

Ubuntu and the United Nations Instruments
on Human Rights

The *Universal Declaration of Human Rights* rightfully opens its preamble with the "recognition of the inherent dignity of and the equal and inalienable rights of all members of the human family" as "the foundation of freedom, justice and peace in the world." It reminds us that "disregard and contempt for human rights have resulted in barbarous acts which have outraged the conscience of mankind." Article 1 of the same declaration proclaims that "All human beings are born free and equal in dignity and rights. They are endowed with reason and conscience and should act towards one another in spirit of brotherhood." Anyone who is committed to Ubuntu values will fully affirm these proclamations from the *Universal Declaration*, which affirms the universal appeal and applicability of the ideas underlying Ubuntu. Similarly, the various human rights treaties are intended to protect violations of the human rights of the world's citizens. This is no doubt in the spirit of Ubuntu. *The Rome Statute of the International Criminal Court*, which was adopted by the United Nations on July 17, 1998, was grounded on the strong belief stated in the opening line of the Preamble to this document, which opens as follows: "Concious that all peoples are united by common bonds, their cultures pieced together in a shared heritage, and concerned that this delicate mosaic may be shattered at any time." The second paragraph of the Preamble to the Rome Statute affirms its being "mindful that during this century millions of children, women and men have been victims of unimaginable atrocities that deeply shock the conscience of humanity." The *Rome Statute* takes the struggle against man's inhumanity to man to a higher level. It affirms that the most serious crimes must not go unpunished by the international community. It makes a commitment to bring an end to impunity for the perpetrators of these crimes—which include the genocide, crimes again humanity, war crimes, and the crime of aggression as defined in the *Charter of the United Nations*.

We may take it that through the internationalization or globalization of the human rights story, such instruments as the *Universal Declaration*, the various human rights treaties, the *Charter of the United Nations*, the *Rome Statute of the International Criminal Court*, and a great many other agencies, nongovernmental organizations, and individuals fighting in the trenches of the human rights war have affirmed Ubuntu as a universal value.

Notes

I am grateful to Sarah Lind of the United Bible Societies for her generous assistance in preparing an annotated Ubuntu bibliography.

1. A summary and explication of these appears in Wendland (1990), "Traditional Central African Religion," 71–112.
2. Tempels ([1952] 1959, 61) uses the term "hierarchy of forces" or *primogeniture* to refer to the same principle.
3. See also Gen. 5.1–3 and 9.6.
4. "We are true witnesses if we are on the side of the weak, the powerless, the exploited, if we have solidarity with them, if we care for the widow, the orphan, and the stranger, if we are the servants of God" (Tutu 2011, 60).

References

Allen, John. 2006. *Rabble-Rouser for Peace—the Authorized Biography of Desmond Tutu.* London: Random House.

Battle, Michael. 2000. "A Theology of Community: The Ubuntu Theology of Desmond Tutu." *Interpretation* 54:173–82.

———. 2009. *Reconciliation: The Ubuntu Theology of Desmond Tutu.* Rev. ed. Cleveland, OH: Pilgrim Press.

Bleek, Wilhelm Heinrich Immanuel. 1862. *Comparative Grammar of South African Languages.* London: Trubner and Co.

Fanon, Frantz. 1963. *The Wretched of the Earth.* London: Penguin.

Gade, Christian B. N. 2011. "The Historical Development of the Written Discourses on Ubuntu." *South African Journal of Philosophy* 30:303–29.

———. 2012. "What Is Ubuntu? Different Interpretations among South Africans of African Descent." *South African Journal of Philosophy* 31: 484–503.

Griaule, Marcel. 1970. *Conversations with Ogotommeli—an Introduction to Dogon Religious Ideas.* London: Oxford University Press.

Haws, Charles G. 2009. "Suffering, Hope and Forgiveness: The Ubuntu Theology of Desmond Tutu." *Scottish Journal of Theology* 62:477–89.

Heine, Bernd, and Derek Nurse. 2000. *African Languages: An Introduction.* Cambridge: Cambridge University Press.

Hountondji, Pauline J. 1983. *African Philosophy—Myth and Reality.* London: Hutchinson University Press.

Idowu, Bolaji. 1962. *Oludumare—God in Yoruba Belief.* London: Longmans, Green.

———. 1973. *African Traditional Religion—a Definition.* Maryknoll, NY: Orbis.

Jacques, Genevieve, 2007. *Resisting the Intolerable, guided by a Human Rights Compass.* Geneva, WCC Publications.

Jahn, Janheinz. 1961. *Muntu—the New African Culture.* New York: Grove.

Kagame, Alexis. 1955. *La philosophie bantu-rwandaise de l'être.* Brussels: Académie royale des sciences coloniales.

———. 1970. *The Bantu Concept of Space-Time.* Translated by Jean-Paul Martinon. Paris: UNESCO.

———. 1976. *La philosophie bantu comparée*. Paris: Présence africaine.

Katamba, Francis. 2003. "Bantu Nominal Morphology." In *Bantu Languages*, edited by Derek Nurse and Gérad Philippson, 103–20. London: Routledge.

Kaunda, Kenneth. 1962. *Zambia Shall Be Free*. Nairobi: Heinemann.

Mbiti, John. 1969. *African Religions and Philosophy*. Nairobi: Heinemann.

———. 1970. *Concepts of God in Africa*. London: Society for Promoting Christian Knowledge.

Metz, Thaddeus. 2012. "An African Theory of Moral Status: A Relational Alternative to Individualism and Holism." *Ethical Theory and Moral Practice* 15:387–402.

Nkrumah, Kwame. 1964. *Consciencism—Philosophy and Ideology for Decolonization*. London: Panaf.

Nurse, Derek, and Gerard Philippson, eds. 2003. *The Bantu Languages*. London: Routledge.

Nyerere, Julius Kambarage. 1968. *Ujaama—Essays on Socialism*. Oxford: Oxford University Press.

Odera Oruka, Henry. 1990. *Trends in Contemporary African Philosophy*. Nairobi: Shirikon.

———. 1991. *Sage Philosophy—Indigenous Thinkers and Modern Debate on African Philosophy*. Nairobi: Acts.

Parrinder, Edward Geoffrey. 1954. *African Traditional Religion*. London: Hutchinson University Publishers.

Robertson, Geoffrey. 2002. *Crimes against Humanity—the Struggle for Global Justice*. London: Penguin.

Smith, Edwin William, ed. 1950. *African Ideas of God—a Symposium*. London: Edinburgh House.

Tempels, Placide. (1952) 1959. *Bantu Philosophy*. Paris: Présence Africaine.

Tutu, Desmond. 1994. *The Rainbow People of God*. New York: Doubleday.

———. 1999. *No Future without Forgiveness*. New York: Random House.

———. 2013. *God Is Not a Christian: Speaking Truth in Times of Crisis*. London: Rider.

Tutu, Desmond, and Mpho Tutu. 2010. *Made for Goodness—and Why This Makes All the Difference*. London: Random House.

Van Binsbergen, Wim. 2001. "*Ubuntu* and the Globalisation of South African Thought and Society." *Quest* 15:53–89.

Wendland, Ernst R. 1990. "Traditional Central African Religion." In *Bridging the Gap: African Traditional Religion and Bible Translation*, edited by Philip C. Stine and Ernst Wendland, 1–129. New York: United Bible Societies.

ALOO OSOTSI MOJOLA is Professor of Philosophy and Translation Studies at St. Paul's University, Limuru, Kenya, and Honorary Professor as well as Research Associate on the Faculty of Theology, Pretoria University, South Africa. He is author of *God Speaks in Our Own Languages: The Story of Bible Translation in East Africa 1844–2018, Bible Translations and Culture: Critical Conversations and Interventions,* and *Issues in Bible Translations.*

2

CRAFTING IDEAL CONDITIONS

Ubuntu and the Challenges of Modern Society

D. A. Masolo

REFLECTIONS ON THE NATURE AND SIGNIFICANCE OF THE concept of Ubuntu are in line with contemporary social theory. John Rawls (1972), the US philosopher who is arguably the most influential and widely discussed social philosopher over the past four decades, identifies two categories of social theory, one that he describes as ideal theory—because, as he says, it "assumes strict compliance and works out the principles that characterize a well-ordered society under favorable circumstances. It develops the conception of a perfectly just basic structure and the corresponding duties and obligations of persons under the fixed constraints of human life" (8, 245–46). As was the case with the eighteenth- and nineteenth-century European contractarian philosophers to whom he is a formidable heir, it is understandable that Rawls views his own theory to be a rendition of how the world ought to work in ideal conditions, and he thought that it was commendable to common sense. In his envisioned society, "everyone is presumed to act justly and to do his part in upholding just institutions. Though justice may be, as Hume remarked, the cautious, jealous virtue, we can still ask what a perfectly just society would be like" (1902, 8).[1]

Rawls (1972) calls the second type of social theory nonideal. Its aim usually is to put in place the principles and measures that will need to be taken in order to protect the society in its structure and goals. For example, the theory explains the merits and demerits of opposing an unjust government, or the mechanisms of removing from office an adulterous monarch, or mechanisms of removing a president whose moral standing no longer represents the image of the ideal society as ingrained in and expected by the will of the people. Evidently, nonideal theory addresses those problems that may not be visible in the entire ideal structure but only in some parts of it, yet with the capacity to affect the people's trust in it, and thus the performance of its duties. Thus, what Rawls calls nonideal theory, the one that addresses waywardness in society, deals with what he calls "partial compliance" to expectations of the ideal. It is within this same framework— of partial compliance in relation, or in respect, to the envisioned "strict compliance" of ideal theory, that citizens may still judge their system or its rulers as just or unjust, liberal or illiberal, good or bad, to be reelected or to be kicked out, and so on. According to him, "a conception of social justice, then, is to be regarded as providing in the first instance a standard whereby the distributive aspects of the basic structure of society are to be assessed" (9).

To what extent, then, can we understand the meaning and significance of the idea of Ubuntu in relation to its general reception as a one-word social statement? In this respect, we may ask whether the pervasive uses of the term are evocations that seek to place themselves within the category of nonideal theory, or how else should it be understood? Historians among us will recall the series of events that have defined social transformation worldwide since the eighteenth century, when the general economic and political inequality caused social unrest and eventually provoked humanitarian movements seeking social reform. Many social scientists turned their attention to studying the problems of economic disturbances and social disorganization in order to arrive at solutions to the generally unsettled conditions. Several theoretical positions emerged out of this intellectual march toward understanding the "real" problem and suggesting solutions.

Some historians and social theorists suggested a laissez-faire or hands-off model that favored government nonintervention in the hope that matters would finally adjust themselves when most worthy entrepreneurs would endure while the less worthy perished. Others rejected this survival-of-the-fittest view of Herbert Spencer, preferring in its place a regulation of industry and technology that would address the needs of the poor through regulation of employment, among other regulatory schemes. Still others, like Karl Marx, directed their attention to an economic view of history to show just how much capitalists, driven by a zealous commitment to self-aggrandizement, could not have cared less about the workers whom they exploited in their quest to amassing wealth. Inevitably, he recommended the regulation of the activities of capitalists as the solution to social unrest as related directly to economic and political inequality.

Two other and closely related phenomena of this social history into the nineteenth century are racism and nationalism. Even in its appearance in romanticism, nationalism is a movement that was always built on or driven by the intensification of in-group unity. In these cases, racism and nationalism were two facets of the same state of mind: loyalty to and exaltation of one's own group. Beyond the merely discernible confluence of these two phenomena in such intellectual movements as German romanticism, they took strong enough root to influence and define some of the most fragmenting and polarizing ideologies and public policies of the twentieth century, first through the colonial domination of the world in the global South and Ireland in the North and, second, in at least two cases, continuing a legacy of racial segregation that was already several centuries old. One case was the United States of America, in the North, and the other was South Africa, in the South. But while the United States was dismantling the legal obstacles to democratic freedom and human dignity in the hope of unifying a nation long defined by a history rooted in slavery, South Africa was doing exactly the opposite, legalizing the reign of a ferocious racist minority rule.

The general similarities of the circumstances in which the term *Ubuntu* is pervasively evoked suggest that we look closely for its meaning within the broader sociopolitical discourses of the twentieth century in respect to the goals that underlie its evocation. To that end, it is worth noting that in the history of its public uses, the term occurs invariably in speeches and commentaries of all kinds that address the prevailing social, political, and moral policies as norms of public and sometimes even private conduct. Thus, although it is a term that is ordinary in its daily appearances in the dialect variations of the "M-Ba" (also called "Bantu") languages across eastern and southern Africa, its popular and political uses have their emergence in the very specific historical and social circumstances of South Africa as a state with what was then a fragmented nonexistent nationhood. Its use today has two basic aims: a nation's reminiscence, on the one hand, and a nation's hope, on the other. In religious sermons, as in political rallies and museum tours, the term is invoked both to signal the resilience of a people and to address the glare of a vacuum in the once-impenetrable apartheid system. The terms of this two-pronged public discourse therefore goes like this: "we survived because we had Ubuntu" and "the path to rectitude is Ubuntu." In these contexts, then, the object of the invocation is the obstacle to an ideal state or condition—in this case, the apartheid system as a whole, but especially the inhumane details in which its policies were implemented. What, for example, would a young tour guide otherwise mean when, in describing the strength of will and endurance of the political prisoners at Roben Island, she says: "their endurance was made possible by their Ubuntu, which their captors and oppressors did not have"? Or when Reverend Archbishop Desmond Tutu, in what he calls "My Credo," says, now famously, that "a person is a person through other persons"? Or when, in response to a simple morning greeting, "How are you?" a local Digo elder says, "*Sina Utu* (I have my humanity)"?

None of the above uses of the term is incorrect or privileged over another. Yet they render concepts that are meant to be comprehended differently on each occasion. So, while the tour guide's reference to the Ubuntu of the infamous island's political prisoners may have been intended to state their resilience and determination, and Archbishop Tutu's use intended to state the basic mutual dependency that makes humans persons, the Chidigo greeting refrain is meant to tell one's own sense of health, as is indicated by one's experience and awareness of one's integrity of being. Together, these different uses of the term Ubuntu seem to invoke the idea of a value regarded to be basic to being human. Resilience and determination anchored in the belief of that which is a basic good can keep a prisoner strong in confronting injustice, just as mutual dependency, which itself requires mutual recognition and respect as may be availed in a simple morning greeting, gives everyone the chance to experience the integrity of their humanity.

In light of John Rawls's dual (ideal-nonideal) social theorizing, Ubuntu, as used in the senses exemplified above, cannot be a concept within the scheme of ideal theory, although it emerges out of the imagination of one. In those uses, it appears in common parlance as a term of political protest or critique and invokes the view that society is, in its status quo, only in partial compliance with the conditions of an ideal state, or, in those instances, suggests that society cannot be considered to be in an ideal state when it does not embrace or use as a regulatory maxim the basic and universal values that underlie all human nature: the dignity, mutual recognition, and respect that ought to characterize all dealings between humans.

"Ubuntu" as a Critique of Unfairness

The Rwandais philosopher Alexis Kagame (1956) may have pioneered the philosophical discussion of the concept of Umuntu, a dialect variant of Ubuntu, but he certainly did not pioneer the everyday uses of the term in either Kinyarwanda, Kirundi, or in any other of the languages that belong to the same (Bantu) cluster as Kinyarwanda or Kirundi. The latter two are his vernacular, and his earlier reflections on this concept, including in his magnum opus, *La philosophie băntu-rwandaise de l'être* of 1956, are based on them. His later work, *La philosophie băntu comparée* of 1976, brought the discussion into a broader comparative perspective with other Bantu dialects in the region (of eastern and central Africa). As may be known already to many readers of African philosophy, Kagame's analysis of the term, and of the general ontological structure into which he inserts it, is pretty controversial, and that is not necessarily because of its Aristotelian rendition per se, although the use of Aristotle in the controversy ultimately becomes important. In *La philosophie băntu-rwandaise de l'être*, Kagame raises the question of conflating socioethnological categories with those of philosophy (Kagame 1956, 17–24). He refers specifically to the relation between the popular reference to the kings of Rwanda as gods and the philosophical order of being that he intends to propound. The controversy as defined in this critical view (expressed in the dialogue by the interlocutor Kama) is that if god is considered the supreme being and creator, then, as pointed out by Gama in the dialogue, there is a problem, and the proposed solution—namely, that from a purely philosophical standpoint, god is not an *être* (being)—leaves Kagame trapped into admitting in a poor argument that while sociocultural beliefs and orders do change over time, such as has happened to the attributes once given to the king, principles established by philosophy are, by contrast, permanent. This too is false, of course, but his intent here is to claim that because the idea of god as established by philosophy is permanent, that of "kingship" is not permanent, and so cannot be philosophical. The catch here is that Kagame was not interested in propounding the philosophical concept of god in Kinyarwanda or Kirundi in the first place, but rather that of being, which, by virtue of the argument, while owing its existence to the creator, places *muntu* at the top of the order.

Kagame's controversy is further complicated by his use of the phrases like "race *băntu,*" or "les princes de race *băntu,*" all of which appear to be used in the text in reference to "the Hamites," the ethnic group that migrated into the region from the Horn of Africa to the northeast around the end of the fourteenth century. The statements here indicate that Kagame uses these terms to refer to a cultural group that is distinct from the Hamites, whose arrival, he says, "modified how the princes of the *băntu* race were conceptualized" (1956, 18). Definitely, there is no equality between kings and princes, as the latter do not possess ultimate authority; their status is designated, presumably by the former. In effect, Kagame appears to observe, with a sense of resignation to the natural force and effects of social dynamics, that the new social order that resulted since the arrival of the ethnic Hamites in the region was part of how nature works: new groups sometimes succeed in overthrowing the previous order and establish themselves as the beneficiaries of the new and hierarchized order. In this historical case specifically, he refers to the Tutsi royal system as transforming the preceding princely system of the "*băntu* race." He then remarks, again with a sense of resignation to and endorsement of history as the dialectical process of being's "self-proof," that the arrival of Europeans later provoked similar destabilizing effects on the status of the Hamite kings themselves (1956, 18). I have said elsewhere (see Masolo 2018) that this Hegelian way of analyzing the character of being in sociohistorical terms is troublesome because it raises suspicion about naturalizing inequality and domination.

Kagame's reference to races (1956, 18) in the context of a discussion of modes of being raises legitimate questions about his stand on how his distinctions can avoid implications that they correspond to differences in intellectual and moral capacities between members of the distinct races. To be fair to Kagame, and unlike Hegel, he does not explicitly conflate social ranks with moral hierarchies. It does not become clear, therefore, that his position, which undeniably is clearly and dangerously racialist, espouses racism. But it is not clear either, at least in light of the absence of a critique, that he stands free or clear of such charges. After 1994, the literary, historical, and philosophical work of ethnic Tutsi intellectuals further strengthened the perception among members of the Tutsi community that their privileges were entitlements and their political domination was self-justifying.

From a methodological standpoint, Kagame believed strongly in cultural pluralism that manifested itself in expressive varieties, especially in language, without sacrificing the universality of both reason and the object of reason. His belief can be found in his analysis of the universality of the concept of "substance," which concretely is experienced only in its various modifications (1956, 80–101). Similarly, the universality of humanity (being with intelligence) is real only through the modifications of social structures and encounters with space. While both reason and substance remain universal in both form and metaphysical subcategories, how they are experienced assumes many and ever-changing varieties.

If we step aside from the controversial sociopolitical trajectory of his categories, it is obvious that Kagame distinguishes the category of Umuntu (Ubuntu or Utu in other variations) from the others by attributing to it the virtue of intelligence, whether this is in act, as is usable by living *abantu*, or merely as an attribute abstractly associated with the very nature of what it takes to be an entity that belongs to this category (see Kagame 1956, 204–46). In Kinyarwanda, Kirundi, and even in Kiswahili noun formation, *u-* gives a noun its abstract form, as in "the nature of," or "to be (something)." Sometimes it takes a descriptive form in action nouns in the singular, as in *uuwaji* (the act of killing), whose plural form is *mauaji* (the killings). The *u-* put before the *m* in *muntu* in Kinyarwanda and Kirundi, or before the *m* in *mtu* in Kiswahili, gives the abstract form to the real *muntu* or *mtu*, "a human being" or "a person." The difference, then, is that while Kinyarwanda and Kirundi retain the first letter *m* of the word or term when it is abstracted, Kiswahili replaces it with the *u*, so we have *Utu* rather than *Umtu* or *Umuntu* in Kinyarwanda and Kirundi or *Ubuntu*, as is the case with the dialect variations farther south and central.

What, then, are the other virtues identified by Kagame? They seem to arise from the primary one, intelligence. Kagame's use of this attribute needs to be seen in terms of "capacity for reason" rather than as a skill, which the use of *intelligence* could suggest in some instances (1956, 216–22). A being with intelligence, or a rational being, can be entrusted with responsibility because of her or his ability to deliberate and to make choices. The controversy that surrounds this analysis—namely, that Kagame's choice of words was deliberately meant to lend support to the stratified social form in Rwanda and Burundi in which the ruling Tutsi alone possessed intelligence while the majority Hutu could legitimately be relegated to serfdom—is not about the untruth of all this, but rather about the fact that it privileges an existing social structure preferred by Kagame because he was a member of the privileged elite. His critics saw his analysis as a philosophical narrative that aimed at perpetuating a structure of power and domination.

From Saint Augustine to the eighteenth-century European social contract theorists, putting humans at the top of creation was meant not only to explain how they differed from the rest of creation but also to justify why they deserved special treatment from each other. Topping this placement was the view that humans, all humans, sat at the top of all creation as a result of their rationality and, therefore, ability to manipulate and dominate the rest of nature, almost *à la* Placide Tempels. This position of humans at the top of the rest of nature—as indicated in most conceptual expressions to be found in the languages of the Lacustrine region—is indicative of distinctive concepts of *muntu* that separate him or her from existents in lower categories. This distinction implies that when some terms are used commonly to describe both humans and animals, one must seek an understanding that such terms—such as, for example, *Muya* or *Moyo* in ChiLuba—reference to animals is only by analogy rather than in the same sense (Kagame 1976, 227–30). Almost invariably, in most of the languages from this region, Kagame argues, the indication is that a clear distinction is made between a sensible spirit (*l'âme*) and a properly human spirit. Although the former perishes at the instance of physical or bodily death, the latter survives; it is immortal. Citing the Kiswahili verb *kuona* (to see) as example of the ambiguity of ordinary language, Kagame defends his comparative-analytic method for arriving at the proper conceptual content of terms as used to describe metaphysical attributes of existents. To say in Kiswahili that "*Naona kuna kiti hapa* (I see that there is a chair here)," or, as in Kagame's own example, "*Naona madyi* [*sic*] *hayo baridi sana* (I see that the water is very cold)," does not carry the same meaning of the verb *kuona* as in "*Naona mambo hayo [ni]mabaya sana* (I see that things are very bad)" (237). The former use is sensual, but the latter is purely mental or conceptual and refers to an understanding. Hence, although ordinary languages may often use the same terms to refer to a vital principle in both animals and humans, the meaning of such terms shifts significantly in the case of their uses to describe human attributes—in this case, different senses of "perceiving," one sensory, the other mental. Thus, humans, insofar as they are animals of a definite or specific category—with intelligence—will always possess all the same capacities—mostly only biological—as lower animals do, but, in ontological distinction from them, they also possess reason, hence some of the terms ordinarily used to describe sensory experiences may actually be describing mental or emotional experiences like "understanding," "a feeling," and so on.

Kagame's (1976, 256–67) rich linguistic analysis of the various Bantu languages is done in search of an understanding of *muntu* and his or her proper place within the order of nature. The focus on *muntu* is unmistakable, whether they are living or dead—the latter ascending, according to local beliefs, to the rank of minor deities of sorts, a position from which they carry on their protective relations with the living. Through their memory or other forms of invocation, the interconnectedness between the ontological orders of *muntu*—*bazima* and *bazimu*, the living and the dead, generally speaking—remains unbroken.

The center of Kagame's (1956, 1976) exposition of Bantu philosophy of being is palpable. The idea is that humans, *bantu*, or beings in the ontological category of *muntu*, have a moral status that transcends any social or cultural differences there may be between them. Part of the results of the comparative linguistic analysis is that despite differences in expressive cultures of the Bantu, there is a common and universal understanding of the unique status of *muntu* within nature. No *muntu*, in life or death, is, in thought or treatment, reducible to the category of lower beings, especially that of a thing, *kintu*, or *kitu*. Like organisms, Kagame's expository scheme unveils, humans sustain themselves through processes of integration and functional interrelationships that extend beyond the boundaries of change and transformation such as those that occur at death. Living relationships shift to imaginary inclusiveness by which the dead are reintegrated into the social order (within their respective family and lineage systems) as historical markers of a moral continuum.

The focus on the value and welfare of the human race as found in Kagame's exposition counters the racism and nationalism of the nineteenth century (Kagame 1956, 204–46; 1976, 227–304; and Balibutsa 1985, 83-175). Emphasis on social and moral integration over the uniqueness of the expressive models of every community points to what is good for the cultivation of an ideal human condition—namely, the derivation of a sense of self from a network of relations with other humans, both vertically and horizontally, as extended into the realms of *bazimu* and *bazima*, respectively. In Kagame's view, the following are the qualities all humans share: a connection upward to their respective ancestors and horizontally to all those with whom they immediately associate and share the living social space. All humans, without exception or exclusion, are defined by this common network. Thus, to dichotomize the network in exclusion of some is to interfere with a natural order.

How does one transition from *muntu* to Umuntu? As we saw earlier, when placed before or in place of the first letter of the concrete noun, the *u-* gives the word its abstract form. Thus, when considered or addressed in the abstract in Kinyarwanda, Kirundi, or in any similar Bantu vernacular, the act, character, or qualities of being a *muntu*, a "human being" or "person," becomes Umuntu, "the act of being a human," or "humanity," or "human-being-ness," or "personhood." In Kiswahili, on the other hand, *u*- replaces the first letter of the term being transformed into the abstract, *mtu* becomes Utu, or in another example, *mzima*—an adjective meaning "alive" or "healthy" or "whole," or even "grown; adult"—becomes *uzima* in abstract form, meaning "life," "health," "wholeness," or "adulthood." Similarly, *mkora*, meaning "an untrustable person," becomes *ukora*, "untrustworthiness"; "*kubwa/mkubwa*," meaning big/senior, becomes *ukubwa*, meaning bigness, size, or, in social senses, "seniority." In the group of languages spoken in central, eastern and southern Africa and clustered together as Bantu, the abstract form signifies all the attributes or expectations that define or are associated with the concept. The attributes describe, as in the example Umuntu or Utu, what it means to be a person or human being, or what is to be understood in statements like "*Okelo ni mtu* (Okelo is a person)" or "*Okelo ni mtu mzima, siye mtoto* (Okelo is an adult, not a child)," or "*Okelo ni mzima kabisa* (Okelo is in very good health)." In these instances, Utu, or humanity, *uzima*, adulthood, but also wholeness or completeness, *utoto*, childhood or childishness, and *uzima*, well-being, are the types, or indicators, against which real and specific states are judged. In the same way, the adjective *bora*, perfect, is transformed into the abstract noun *ubora*, perfection, by adding *u*- before the first letter of the adjective term. We shall see below how the philosopher Shaaban bin Robert creates the concept of human perfection by coining the phrase "*Utu bora*," perfect humanity or human perfection. He names the main protagonist of his essay on this topic "Utubora" by forming a single term, the name, out of the descriptive phrase.

Kagame (1956, 204–45; 1976, 227–304) is right, then, when he lists the attributes that describe what kind of being *muntu* is as distinguishable from other beings. And since the debate here is about attributes that separate humanity from the rest of nature and also justify a specific manner in which they ought to be treated, let us make comparison with a study on a similar subject from another African tradition of thought farther afield. Because he is well known for his analysis of the concept of negritude as an articulation of African humanism, Senghor (1977) has an interesting philosophical take on this. Articulating his thoughts in a commentary on the Dogon myth about the rise of *Nommo*, he says (302) that, contrary to the Western conception of the origin in which all things preexisted in god's contemplation, to the Dogon only two original *hommes* issue from god. One of them rebels against *Ama* and, as punishment, is turned into a fox. The other, *Nommo*, later dies but resurrects and is equipped with the power and art of the word, which, together with techniques, he is charged to teach to the rest of the universe, especially other humans. According to Senghor, the nucleus of the Dogon myth resonates with what he has always proposed about negritude: "that it is a humanism, and it is modern" (302). He observes that the nucleus of the Dogon myth is that humans are constantly making themselves, a process, as suggested in the Dogon ideas about *Nommo*, that takes place dialectically in the reciprocal and mutually dependent relational development between mind (spirit) and body, especially with the latter's sensory organs and parts. Mind and body, each activates the other, causing thought and technique to develop in tandem. We know from Marcel Griaule (1965) that Dogon people, through Ogotemmêli's masterful narration, believe that the universe, both wholly and in its various parts, is sustained by a dialectic balance of opposites in a continuous mode that Bergson once referred to as "creative evolution." Senghor affirms, above all, that this focus on *Nommo* in the Senegalo-Guinean languages agrees with the nominal classes analyzed from the Bantu languages. He refers to Tempels specifically (303), but it can be assumed that insofar as Kagame inherited the core of Tempels's project, reference is therefore made to Tempels too by extension.

In Senghor's view, the sense of humanity in Umuntu is not just about the attributes of the human race as a collectivity. While this is true because Umuntu, like *Nommo*, expresses precisely the qualities that distinguish humans collectively from other forms of life and beings in general, they are to be dissociated from a system of thought or belief that places it at the center of concern and focus for human thought. The belief systems as narrated by Ogotemmêli, and that he and Kagame analyzed, are expressions of humanism. "Because we are dealing with a system, not always logical but coherent, Negro-African philosophy places man at the center of creation, therefore of the entire universe, as both object and subject, as the end and the means" (Senghor 1977, 305).

Human Perfection in the Moral Idealism
of Shaaban bin Robert

Besides Kagame's ontological analysis, the concept of Umuntu, or Utu in its Kiswahili variant, has been the subject of explicit reflection by few others, among them Shaaban bin Robert (1968b), the famous Swahili poet, essayist, and philosopher from Tanga. As his title suggests, the work is dedicated to philosophical reflections on the ideal or desirable qualities of personhood.[2] Among these qualities he ranked righteousness (*adili*) or justice (*haki*) highest—the most important of all virtues—because they are the highest regulators and keepers of social order. Others are moderation (*kipimo*), courage (*shujaa*), kindness (*hisani*), peace (*amani*), trust or faith (*imani*), learning (*elimu*), love (*mapenzi*), and intelligence (*akili*). (See bin Robert 1969, 17–19.) To be virtuous (*kuwa mwadilifu*) is to be someone who not only applies his or her best reason to understanding what is presented to them for counsel but also acts with moderation, who practices courage and kindness and also keeps the peace and their faith. Thus, the inevitable theme of another book, *Adili na Nduguze* (bin Robert 2010) is the search for this balance of virtues both within oneself and in one's application of them in guiding her or his conduct and relations with other people.

I now will direct my attention to another of bin Robert's always interesting books, *Utubora Mkulima* (1968b). This multilayered story is about a young man, Utubora, who lost his father at an early age, forcing him to abandon the Islamic school he was attending so he could get a job to find the means to take care of himself and his mother. A family friend who was a clove merchant on the island of Zanzibar takes him under his wing and hires him as a store clerk with a decent pay for his age. He takes his childhood nanny with him to take care of his house while he focused on work. He was a diligent and exceptionally disciplined young man unlike any other and seemed in everyone's view to be one lucky young man with a promising future, but he is enlisted into the army during World War II and shipped out to Burma. He learns many lessons as a result of these travels, among them the virtues of courage and self-discipline. Armed with them, he withstands many temptations. In today's language, he dodges the effects of the traumatizing experience of being in a war.

One day, after his return from service in the war, although his employer was happy to have him back, he suddenly announces his resignation from that job and his intention to return to the village on the mainland. Neither his employer's appeals nor his mother's sudden death back home move him to change his mind. His nanny, being far older and like a mother to him, scolds him for being rash and immature in his ways, but he won't listen to any of it. His mind was made up: freedom was a greater good than the material goods of the new monetary lifestyle desired by many whose thinking did not go far enough. He was decidedly different and wanted to bring to the awareness of other people a different and critical way of thinking about the kind of values that give human life its real worth.

In his firm belief that no good comes without courage and sacrifice, he moves back to the mainland with his nanny in order to start anew in a life built around the values of freedom, self-determination, and moral good. Because both his parents had died, Utubora chooses to settle in Busutamu, where he purchases a virgin parcel of land in order to start his new life on his terms. According to Utubora (or to Shaaban, as the plotter of the story), it is hard to be good in a world in which material accumulation has become the center of attention. For those who are focused on the right values, no good comes without major sacrifices, including losing some close friends or being shunned by those whose thinking is slow or just based on the wrong values. In the end, Utubora's moral virtues bring him rewards of many kinds and, ultimately, happiness. After rejecting the ordinary concept of material success, Utubora puts in place a type of self-realization that emphasizes the rational and moral self as the essence of humanity or, in Kiswahili, *utu bora*.

Neither the title of the book (*Utubora Mkulima*) nor the name of the main character of the story (Utubora) nor its lesson is a matter of every ordinary person's awareness or belief. Although they are understood as native Kiswahili speakers, residents of Utubora's new neighborhood in Busutamu,[3] a small village on the mainland across the channel from Zanzibar, become curious about their new neighbor's identity, especially since his name is so unusual—they had never heard it anywhere before. They seek answers to their curiosity through indirect knowledge, a medium whose familiarity can be gained relatively more easily. The wife of the local headman (Mke wa Liwali) seeks to get information from Utubora's nanny, Bihaya,[4] a sensual person whose values were almost always in sharp contrast to those of Utubora. She was relentlessly opposed to Utubora's radical decision to resign from his job and to abandon the urban life in Zanzibar with all its worldly attractions based on material comforts that satisfied the cravings of the body. By contrast, even if he earned a reasonable salary as an employee, Utubora found the life of dependency on others to be oppressive and material comfort hardly a source of happiness. And, above all, the life of employment is only marginally in line with the fundamental human purpose on earth: to transform the world and oneself (20). Focus on wealth and other worldly goods can be a distraction from this fundamental moral vocation—to seek that which is in line with the moral dignity of humans. "True blessings and fortune," says Shaaban, "make visits from time to time to those who are brave, but rarely to those who are weak in thought and commitment to doing that which is good" (20).

In addressing Utubora's nanny Bihaya, the wife of the local headman says, "allow me to ask what the occupation of this person you talk about might be, for even his name is so extraordinary. He himself must be an ideal [or perfect] person as his name suggests; is he?" In response, Bihaya says, "He does not have a steady occupation right now, but I assume for now that it will be farming. But regarding his name, I must say that I have never seen anyone else whose nature was so precisely just like his name says, as this man and his name" (21). In turn, and apparently to emphasize that farming is not necessarily beneath a person so well regarded as a model of human nature, the wife of the local headman says, "Farming is certainly one of the most important occupations, and so I hope we can have a farmer among us. Above all, we are delighted to hear that the person you describe is just as his name says, and I hope you will not find me to be overbearing in saying that nothing could be worse than having someone whose conduct is so bad that he is closer to being a beast than a person" (21).[5]

According to Shaaban bin Robert, virtuous conduct tops the list of the dispositions that make a person attractive and desirable, and when those dispositions are absent, one becomes beastly and repulsive. Shaaban's concern here appears to be not just with the humaneness of human conduct that protects their (human) lives from being short and brutish, but with virtues as specific human attributes. Humans are definable by their moral attributes—*homo moralis*, not as a separate dimension, but as a central part of her or his social attribute (*homo socialis*). When inculcated and exhibited consistently as the basis of conduct, moral virtues separate humans from lesser beings. As indicated by Shaaban, it may be hard, especially in our current world, for most people to possess all or most of the listed virtues, and that is precisely the basis of the uniqueness of those who, like Utubora, strive to live virtuously.

In Shaaban's view, intellectual virtues are more basic than most others, especially moral ones. One cannot perform good deeds unless she or he knows what good deeds are and why they are considered to be so. Utubora had wisdom that was rare for a young man his age. His wisdom enabled him to rationalize and to free himself from many temptations that could have come easily to people of weak minds. He overcame temptations to cause physical harm to himself despite possessing the means to do so easily (11).[6] Knowing what is the right thing to do is partly derived from historical awareness. As Utubora puts it, "we ought to succeed where our ancestors failed, otherwise we will not be worth being their descendants and heirs, for the benefit of coming later, like descendants do, is to perform better than our ancestors did. We do so by working harder at everything we undertake to do, [hence] we will become farmers at my mother's birthplace because success is about collaboration and sharing a vision" (14).

For philosophers, there is quite an interesting dose of moral theory in *Utubora Mkulima*, not just an articulation of the essence of selfhood as built on the virtues of good reason and right moral conduct. First, Utubora labors through the moral principle that a good deed must be good in itself, and not in expectation of any gains that may accrue to the agent for performing the good act. To demonstrate this, Utubora commits to cleaning up BiMkubwa's neglected compound and to bringing her back to community engagement by showing her acceptance and understanding her state of depression from the deaths of her child and grandchild. He performs these services largely without being seen by BiMkubwa and asserts firmly to her one day that his objective is the good that will result from his actions, not the pay or the rewards that might be disturbing her conscience. In Shaaban's view, moral good must issue out of what a person is made of, not the result of calculations of material or other gains or interests. The only variation of Shaaban's view from the German characterization of the law of the good as an intuitive inclination (propounded by both Kant and Marx)—but a crucial one—is that the idea of the moral good is a product of relational contexts and aided by a person's individual standards refined out of life experiences by a sharp and critical mind. It is in respect to these qualities that Utubora differs not just from the general populace he finds in Busutamu, but also from someone like Makuu (unpopular deeds) who was knowledgeable by virtue of having attended the same institution for Islamic studies in Zanzibar with Utubora. Shaaban gives the name Makuu to a character whose deeds are outstandingly unpopular because they are counter to expectations for good knowledge and judgment about how society ought to work. In contrast to Utubora, as his name is carefully chosen to suggest, Makuu is narcissistic and selfish and believes that everyone should be left to their own fate undisturbed. His ideals are antisocial. Others may have the inclination to do good to those in need, but they lack the mental fortitude and courage to carry out their beliefs. Society cannot change or improve if it relies on such people: they are ineffective.

While one bad person does not spoil a whole society, one ideal one can transform it in previously unheard-of directions. The path of human progress is paved by heroes, not by villains. We have seen the doom of villains in such characters as P. W. Botha and those who preceded him (for example, Marais Viljoen and Balthazar Johannes Voster) and their contrast with such personalities as Nelson Mandela and Mohandas Karamchand Gandhi. In his own lesson of contrasts, Shaaban polarizes Utubora from Sheha, his one-time fiancée. While the wayward manners of Sheha do not represent all women, despite many men's illogical tendency to think otherwise, the exemplary deeds of Utubora will become a marvel to every resident of Busutamu.[7]

The more direct contrast between good and evil is portrayed in the contrasting personae of Sheha and Radhia. Narcissism and selfishness are not as solid foundations of life as they may seem to those who embrace them. Their rewards are limited and often short-lived. This is how the pursuit of material well-being as an end unto itself fails to deliver happiness or success for Sheha. Her marriage, defined primarily in terms of access to wealth, ends quickly in divorce, and her attempts to inherit her father's business also ends in disarray because of her deception and desire for revenge, which Shaaban portrays as vices of egoism. Radhia, on the other hand, suffers sadness for the misfortunes of others. To counter her fiancé Makuu's view that everyone should be left to live out their individual fates, Radhia states firmly that "living without caring about other people's welfare cannot be right! We are created to rejoice in our own and other people's successes, but also to feel sad about our own and other people's misfortunes. I believe that we are created to care for and to share and collaborate with each other in every way" (28). She finally cancels her betrothal to Makuu, whose status in the community depended disproportionately on the fact that he was materially well off although he lacked inner moral good. Radhia extricates herself from this embodiment of narcissism and selfishness in order to follow the guidance of her mind that it is the inner qualities of a person that make him or her respectable and lovable. So she falls in love with, and finally marries Utubora. It is this union of caring about and service to others that becomes indicative of Shaaban's idea of perfection—namely, that the pursuit of human perfection brings together inner qualities of one's moral uprightness and an altruistic perspective that views work primarily as service to others in society, especially to those who cannot help themselves.

Since the book is fictional, every bit of it is carefully crafted as either direct statements and arguments for, or metaphorical allusions to refutations of, bad moral qualities or defenses of good ones as they may relate to the concept of ideal personhood. One is called on to read Radhia's words as a direct statement of the communitarian ideal of human nature, while reference to BiMkubwa and the state of her compound, on the other hand, is allegorical. Withdrawal into the isolation and privacy of the self is likely to lead to loss of a sense of the good; it is comparable to living by oneself in the bush separated from a dialogical comprehension of the worth of life and other values that make life desirable. Philosophers are likely to be reminded here of Thomas Hobbes's now famous dictum in his description of "the incommodities of such as war [as prevails in a state of nature]": no commodious building; . . . no society; and which is worst of all, continual fear, and danger of violent death; and the life of man, solitary, poor, nasty, brutish, and short" (1962, 100).

Shaaban's view is that society and its utility to the dignity of the individual has incontestable priority over egoism and solitude. But, in his view, society does not emerge from the ground as mushrooms do. It is contractual, formed by agreements between people both formally and informally. In the formal order, society is a structure of social roles and hierarchies aimed at the protection of the rights of citizens. Among them are their right to the ownership and integrity of their property. Aware of her rights, BiMkubwa threatens Utubora with possible charges and prosecution for trespassing on her property and interfering with it (bin Robert 1968b, 45–47) and invokes the intervention of those who hold public offices in the village, like *Liwali* (village councilor), the imam (religious leader), and the *hakimu* (the judicial officer). Informally, the fabric of society is constituted out of the goodwill of the people themselves, the will to do what is good and uplifting of the dignity of all humans. Yet this is not automatic: the tacit contract between citizens implies a continuous discourse about what it means to be properly human (42–43). The admiration for the quality of personhood manifested by Utubora indicates that despite failures and shortfalls in aspirations, people have quite a good sense of what an ideal (accomplished) human character (*uanadamu uliokamilika kwa mtu huyu*) should look like, and they thought it was fairly well manifested in the character of Utubora (43). As they say, you know what it is when you see one. It (*Utu bora*) may be rare or unusual, but that is precisely the manner of what is ideal. Unlike most people, Utubora symbolized in his moral character the *homo* without the *lupus* (wolf). In other words, perfection is borne by those who serve other people, not by those who prey on them like wolves, even if they may come from strange places previously unfamiliar to them.

Shaaban appears to be deeply concerned about the relationship between morality and the law, and Utubora is deeply disturbed by the prospects of finding himself on the wrong side of the law despite his conviction he is acting to bring about some kind of good, a moral or societal good, a good of human well-being. On the one hand, then, the question is, How can focus on a moral good take precedence over the law? How can morality trump justice, which is the object of law? On the other hand, the wonder is how the law can protect what society considers to be evil. What does one do with the laws of an evil government? While Shaaban appears to leave the door open to reflection on these matters, there is no doubt in the text that what matters to him is the need to reflect on the presuppositions of both morality and the law. In the end, BiMkubwa and Utubora, the law and morality, appear to find a compromise. Although she makes it clearly known that even though Utubora might be on the wrong side of the law as it is understood, she decides to leave Utubora to pursue his goals and even rewards him for the good he brings back to her life and world. As a result of Utubora's actions, BiMkubwa is reembraced by the community and she becomes respectable again because her compound is rendered worthy of being a human abode.[8]

Utu Bora and Social Theory

"*Wa miguu miwili huwaje wa minne* (How does a person turn into a beast, literally: how does this two-legged person turn into a four-legged beast?)?" (bin Robert 1968b, 21). Take note of the similarity of this remark in Shaaban's work to the remarks made by Archbishop Tutu, Simphiwe's mother, and his widow at the Amnesty Hearings of the South African Truth and Reconciliation Commission (TRC) proceedings in reference to the moral character of the brutal apartheid era. Separated by several decades as well as by the specific sociopolitical circumstances, the remarks powerful lesson lines: any form of domination is morally and legally wrong, and violations of human rights have no room in any society because they are contrary to the expectations of reason. It is now pretty clear that Shaaban's view is that we show what we are made of by means of our conduct, which, without saying, is our public conduct. We know now that it was not enough for him to be human or to have human nature (*wa miguu miwili, au uanadamu*), in contrast to beastly nature (*wa miguu minne, au unyama*). Accomplished human nature is manifested in the character of the bearer. In other words, our self-regard and treatment of others indicates whether we have the habits necessary for the ideal human nature and how accomplished we are in that regard. Conceptually, this is what Shaaban intends by the term *Utu bora*. To capture its sense of an all-around moral character to be viewed as ideal or necessary for everyone, he presents it as an embodied possibility, Utu-bora. *Ustaarabu* is the Kiswahili term for a condition of life predominantly guided by the knowledge of things necessary for a civilized life, but Shaaban, for obvious reasons, does not use it even once in *Utubora Mkulima*. Instead, he chooses to show that when we cultivate the proper moral character, we can, through the agency of all persons, effect the desirable kind of society for the normative kind of Utu (*Utu bora*) exemplified in the fictional Utubora in the text *Utubora Mkulima*.

There is an implied sense of equality in Shaaban's idea of *Utu bora*. It is not one's station in life that defines their Utu. Everyone owes everyone else the treatment that all humans deserve regardless of the jobs they perform, the amount of wealth they possess, the faith they profess, or the level of education they have. In *Kusadikika*, a book on the concept of justice, Shaaban (1966, 1–6) indicates from the beginning that neither physical attributes, nor race, nor class or social status give us virtue. In his view, one would still be empty of *utu bora* if one had the attributes of beauty, or if one had wealth but lacked righteousness as a principle of daily practice. In *Siku ya Watenzi Wote* (bin Robert 1968a), his book on democracy, Shaaban, always visualizing a world of happy citizens, describes a world in which all citizens engage in activities that augment the qualities of their own incarnation of ideal personhood (Utu). Such achievements, according to Shaaban, are possible only when there is collaboration between citizens toward a common purpose. He thought of love as the virtue that made collaboration and attainment of its objectives possible. He calls love "the preservative salt of personhood (*chumvi ya hifadhi ya utu*)" (1968a, ix). Hatred, on the other hand, causes personhood to rot.

Siku ya Watenzi Wote cannot, and should not, be read in isolation—which reveals how hard it is to read Shaaban, not just because of the sometimes impenetrable complexity of his language, but also, and I believe more fundamentally, because his works run into and out of each other as if the corpus of the work itself is a running poem. *Siku ya Watenzi Wote* proposes an era of liberty and democratic space in which everyone assumes personal responsibility in the collective task of bringing about the desired society. All citizens would become doers, in contrast to the passivity of life under domination. Together, then, *Utubora Mkulima, Kusadikika*, and *Siku ya Watenzi Wote* make a trilogy in Shaaban's social theory. They articulate the essence of selfhood as grounded in the virtues of reason and moral principles that dictate that not only are all humans equal but also their equality ought to be reflected in their being treated with justice, which entails duties and rights. In *Kusadikika* specifically, Shaaban criticizes discrimination by race, gender, or class.

Ideal Theory and the Invention of *Subpersons*

The ideal world envisioned by Shaaban is not what world history has unveiled, especially since European expansion and occupation of territories abroad since the fifteenth century. The concept of human equality enshrined in the European enlightenment theory of social contract as the basis of democratic principles did not prevent colonization under which sociopolitical spheres were created and administered without contractual agreements with, or participation of, indigenous populations. The contract did not apply to non-European people. Otherwise, how, then, would European colonizers justify treating their non-European subjects in the colonies differently and simultaneously claim to believe in the principles of the social contract, specifically that all persons are created equal and free, on which their own nations and governments were founded? This is the question that Charles W. Mills (1997), the Caribbean-born Canadian philosopher teaching in the United States—and perhaps one of the best critics today of the European social contract theory and its enforcement in the making of the modern world—seeks to understand about the European concept of the contract. Mills argues that this tradition of thought, of which John Rawls is one of the most recent and most vociferous representatives, was not and was never intended to be fully a social contract in the universal sense of the term. Noting that the eighteenth-century theory was constructed between two waves of European expansionism, Mills argues that it could only have been meant for those to whom it was intended to apply: white people who considered themselves to be equal and free and to possess civic and legal rights that the contract confers on them under the collective general will.

It was a racial contract. In the practical realm, policies derived from the racial contract led to segregation, as inequality became the norm in multiracial societies administered under white domination. They created the ghettos and neighborhoods in the United States and Bantustans and townships in South Africa. In all colonized territories, whites and nonwhites lived in separate spaces and led parallel lives. The formal name for these separations mattered little, whether it was segregation in the United States or apartheid in South Africa. Common about them was the false assumption that the phrase "separate but equal" was a morally sensible combination of terms. It is strongly refuted by Shaaban in *Kusadikika*. But the idea is even stronger in the thoughts of Utubora that no one is human enough who does not make by himself or herself right and rational choices in life. The denial to nonwhite sections of society the rights that belong to personhood defined colonialism generally and the racism of racial segregation and apartheid. In other words, colonization and its informal appearances in segregation and apartheid rob their victims of their Utu and thereby all the means by which they could pursue their *Utu bora*, ideal personhood or their possible human perfection. Such pursuit, according to Shaaban, can happen only by means of rational choices and decisions, the exercise of which requires freedom. As a result, then, neither colonialism nor any one of its manifestations can be rationally or morally justifiable.

Even more rationally and morally alarming is the fact that, in the African case, besides South Africa, the scramble for and formal colonization of the continent would be carried out by the same regimes that had proclaimed abolition of slavery many decades earlier (in 1794 by the French, 1834 by the British, and 1863 by the Dutch). Only in South Africa was this period only a continuation of a system already in place for centuries past. In all these systems, the treatment of black people by white people was no less inhuman or inhumane under colonialism than it was during the period of slavery. Works of art, like Joseph Conrad's *The Heart of Darkness*, or the recent and critically acclaimed film *Twelve Years a Slave*, have tried imaginatively to capture some of the horrors that defined the experiences of black people under these conditions: a black person had no right to claim his or her freedom. In the eyes of white people, being black and being free were contraries, so to utter them affirmatively in the same sentence would be a contradiction. To claim being black and free at the same time, or that one was both black and had knowledge, were all criminal utterances punishable by law. From a moral standpoint, they were considered to be against nature itself, and so they would be seen only as either childish or insane because they just could not be true. In other words, not only was a black person believed to be irrational, but it also was irrational, a contradiction, to claim that he or she was not irrational. Behind Utubora's resilience and persistence in following his own and carefully considered decisions is the salient confrontation of the racist belief passed down through the hegemony of Islamic education and Arab culture that natives could not be self-determining and flourish by their own thoughts and planning.

The marks of the atrocities of the apartheid era in South Africa are still felt like raw wounds in the bodies and minds of its victims and their relatives and the population of apartheid victims at large. To date, racial discrimination remains rampant in various parts of the world, even if largely only informally. In the Unites States, in South Africa, and in many cities of Europe, racial discrimination continues to be a major hurdle to the attainment of justice, and focus on it remains a key component and theme of critical social and political theory. The apparent gross contradiction between, on the one hand, a commitment to an egalitarian society built on the principle of equality assumed under the concept of the social contract, and, on the other hand, a continuing and systematic racial discrimination of nonwhite people in the practices of institutions, both public and private, and in the attitudes of ordinary folk in their interactions with their fellow citizens or residents of different racial roots, warrants address. It is not alarming, then, that it was only recently, on December 20, 2018, that the US Senate finally passed a bipartisan bill—the Justice for Victims of Lynching Act of 2018, introduced by the black California senator Kamala Harris—to make lynching a federal crime; the successful act follows two hundred previous attempts at similar legislation and was passed sixty-three years after the fourteen-year-old Emmett Till was murdered in Mississippi by two brothers who kidnaped, tortured, and shot him after falsely accusing him of whistling at one of their wives. The two brothers were acquitted by a jury of six white men. Even today, both the judicial and law enforcement systems treat black people with unjustifiably disproportionate harshness while police brutality against black people, often bordering on crimes against humanity, goes unchecked because of the composition of juries or of those in supervisory roles. In apartheid South Africa, as the TRC confessions revealed, scores of black South Africans went missing without a trace, and their killers went unpunished either because they fled the country in the wake of liberation or because of the terms of the confessions at the TRC.

Charles Mills (1997) observes that the history of European expansionism has exposed the racial particularism of the European social contract theory that is sometimes but falsely heralded as universal. About the racial particularism of the contract, he says, "though based on the social contract tradition that has been central to Western political theory, [it] is not a contract between everybody ('we the people'), but between just the people who count, the people who really are people ('we the white people'). So it is a Racial Contract" (3). Thus, for him, while the social contract can be a useful conceptual lens for looking at society and its governance, its obfuscation with the ugly realities of group power and domination make it a profoundly misleading account of the way the modern world actually is and came to be. The structures of conquest and colonization or other forms of domination exclude the conquered and colonized from the contract that, in its original rendition, was meant to be between equals, those whose humanity was attributable directly to their common origination in god's creation as proclaimed by the architects of the contract theory such as John Locke, who, in his second *Two Treatises of Government* (2002), emphasizes the importance of good government with such vigor that he says that resistance to a tyrant is not the right of just "the Body of the People," (T II. Xiv. '168: 379–80) but of everyone or any individual (T II. Xviii. '208: 404), thus sanctioning tyrannicide as one possible form of resistance to tyranny (T II. Xix. '241:426-27). It can be argued, then, that in distinguishing between a lawful ruler and a tyrant, and in identifying the ends of government with the use of political power for the common good of all the people, and in tracing the origins of political authority to the consent of the people by contract where the people are viewed as a corporative entity, Locke's theory of resistance preserves and is structured around a core of traditional political ideas in their assumption of who these contracting individuals are, both individually and as a corporative body in their collective actions—they are persons; they have rights, above all to be treated equally with other persons, and that the government owes its authority to them and hence is answerable to them.

By contrast, Mills (1997) observes, the colonized or otherwise dominated is stripped of these fundamental claims of personhood. He argues that this methodical and justified stripping is not merely a violation—as when we break a law knowing well that we are deviating from the norm. Rather, he writes, "the Racial Contract is real and . . . apparent racist violations of the terms of the social contract in fact uphold the terms of the Racial Contract" (5). In other words, Mills finds a contradiction in Rawls's concept of "ideal theory" because Rawls assumes it to address an ideal social contract. The ideal theory addresses what Rawls deems to be a "nonideal/naturalized" contract, one that assumes that the assumed equality that gives contracting agents a stake in the civil society applies only to the dominant group whose stance at the hypothetical 'original position' is defined by a racial similarity as white people and excluded all non-whites. If, therefore, those who are excluded from the ideal contract as defined, but in reality in a nonideal contract under whose spatial cum jurisdiction space they abide, it must be on the basis of a nonideal identification—namely that they are not real *persons* as those assumed under the ideal contract. They are *subpersons*, meaning that the agents of the ideal contract bear no obligations toward them as they do toward each other as required by the terms of the contract binding between them. Here is a long quotation from Mills (1997) elaborating on the racially discriminatory nature of the contract as it is conceived and applied (discriminatorily) to the regulation of polities understood to be either all-white, or white-dominated, and hence exclusive of nonwhites and, until 1930's, also of white women:

> The Racial Contract is that set of formal or informal agreements or meta-agreements (higher-level contracts about contracts, which set the limits of the contracts' validity) between the members of one subset of humans, henceforth designated by (shifting) "racial" (phenotypical/genealogical/cultural) criteria C 1, C 2, C 3 . . . as "white," and coextensive (making due allowance for gender differentiation) with the class of full persons, to categorize the remaining subset of humans as "nonwhite" and of a different and inferior moral status, subpersons, so that they have a subordinate civil standing in the white or white-ruled polities the whites either already inhabit or establish or in transactions as aliens with these polities, and the moral and juridical rules normally regulating the behavior of whites in their dealings with one another either do not apply at all in dealings with nonwhites or apply only in a qualified form (depending in part on changing historical circumstances and what particular variety of nonwhite is involved), but in any case the general purpose of the Contract is always the differential privileging of the whites as a group with respect to the nonwhites as a group, the exploitation of their bodies, land, and resources, and the denial of equal socioeconomic opportunities to them. All whites are beneficiaries of the Contract, though some whites are not signatories to it. (11)

On November 2, 2018, a white man was arrested for allegedly fatally shooting two black people at a Louisville, Kentucky, grocery store. According to eyewitness reports, when the shooter was confronted by an armed fellow white man in the parking lot, he said: "You will not shoot me. Whites don't

shoot whites." The question of power and domination, and how the phenomenon of dark ontologies fares in it does not start with the *particulariza-
tion of the universality* of the social contract in the eighteenth century. It
stretches back a long time, including, among other episodes, the infamous
Papal Bull *Terra Nullius* that gave the Capuchin missionaries the right to
claim the Angolan coast for Portuguese explorers and, later, colonizers in
the fourteenth century, but also used in the justification of the occupation
of native lands elsewhere. These episodes raise pertinent questions about
the concept and nature of persons or, if you wish, of personhood, in relation
to its historical uses to justify the differential distribution principle that accorded members of one or some groups rights considered inalienable from
the fact of being human, while denying the same to others, just as we have
said above.

Shaaban and "Ubuntu": A Conclusion

In one sense, both *Kusadikika* and *Utubora Mkulima* are works in ideal
theory and, in that regard, differ significantly in their objectives from *Siku
ya Watenzi Wote*. Both former texts are works that spell out the ideal conditions (of a just society, as in *Kusadikika*) or forms (of rational and moral
virtues as foundations of ideal human character, as in *Utubora Mkulima*).
Their objective is not just to spell out these conditions but to urge and evoke
in the reader or listener the vision of what it takes to attain a desirable selfhood and a desirable society. To use Rawls's language, they both call for
strict compliance with the conditions as a requirement for achieving the
objective of a just society. This is not what occurs in *Siku ya Watenzi Wote*,
or in the public invocations of the idea of Ubuntu as part of a continuing
political discourse today in South Africa and the world. In *Siku ya Watenzi
Wote*, Shaaban's objective is to correct an anomaly within a particular sociopolitical sphere: in preparation for the impending period of Uhuru, he
wants to exorcize the sense of apathy and feelings of alienation that he felt to
be prevalent in the attitudes of the colonized. In the realm of sociopolitical
freedom—by which it appears Shaaban meant the absence of the burden of
foreign domination—locals are expected to assume awareness of a different
and collective sense of responsibility, namely to retake charge of their own
affairs and destiny. Everyone becomes a doer or agent in the making of
one's own self and own country. The call for this awareness is corrective or
restitutive measure. It is a nonideal theorization of what actions are likely

to put in place or, where there had been a breach, to bring back the desirable order.

In another sense, however, both *Kusadikika* and *Utubora Mkulima* may be regarded as examples of nonideal theory. Written with two imperial systems—Islamico-Arab system as embodied in the Omani empire headed by the sultan, and European colonial system represented by the British governor—as backdrops, they present alternative, rebellious views of a truly just polity in which indigenous people enjoy recognition and respect of their dignity and the socio-political space that accords them the freedom of choice at the individual moral level, as well as the political freedom for self-determination. It is Shaaban's view that these choices ought to start with the recognition of agriculture ("Ukulima" in Kiswahili), as the mainstay of economic future. In these senses, *Utubora Mkulima*, embraces the moral message of Ubuntu in central and southern Africa as a rejection of serfdom suffered or experienced under any imperial power, be it Arabo-Omani, British, or Boer. Utubora's message? The pursuit of the good is everyone's right, but the teaching of it as a moral imperative is a task to be borne and exemplified by those who have the understanding and courage to reject the status quo and implement change.

As complex and varied as they may be, the public discourses that evoke or employ the concept of Ubuntu belong to the nonideal type of theory. Fortunately, in contrast to Shaaban bin Robert's moral idealism in *Utubora Mkulima*, the invocations of Ubuntu in the domains of everyday discourse are not about perfect expectations, even if those who invoke it may well be aware of the ideals or aspirational visions toward which they approximate the demands when they make the invocations. Here is an example: a worker who complains to an employer about unfair pay for the job the worker performs may be aware of the best level of pay that the specific type of job and their level of performance should fetch. That may be different from how the employer understands the matter, and the employee might know that too. Furthermore, they may be realistic enough to assume that no one ever gets the pay most commensurate with the job and job performance. But let us say that the same employee knows that her colleague with similar experience and at the same level or rank, but with a poorer performance rating, gets better pay than she does. So when she goes to the employer and says, "What you are doing to me is not consistent with Ubuntu," she might not be demanding what she believes to be the perfect pay she deserves, even if it might be the perfect thing for the employer to do. Rather, her invocation of

Ubuntu could be taken as reference to the minimum expectation of respect for her humanity, namely equal treatment with all those who are accorded the most reasonable treatment as would be given to any human being in similar circumstances. At the same time, her invocation of Ubuntu in such a circumstance would be calling the employer out on the employer's moral shortcoming in terms of the employer's failure to act as would be expected of someone with moral reasoning and possibly legal judgment to practice justice. As we saw from Shaaban, the appeal to moral reason is superior because, on the legal side, although equally unacceptable, the employer could justify his or her actions by easily claiming to act in conformity to a law, a very bad one in this case, and so be legal in their action while being a total moral failure. Indeed, Shaaban shows in *Utubora Mkulima* that it is far nobler to be righteous than to obey a law that is rotten by virtue of its disregard of a section of the citizenry as subpersons. He writes, "Nothing in the world could be worse than to see [him or her] who appears to be a human being to be so different in their conduct that they resemble beasts due to the evil nature of their conduct" (bin Robert 1968b, 21).[9] Although it is expected of human nature that every person mature in his or her thinking by the age of thirty years, Utubora had attained such a level of moral and intellectual maturity much earlier than many and thus had already discarded at an early age all senses of hatred for others, nor did he distrust or have a low opinion of women the way many men with bad upbringing do (19). The notion of conscientious objection that came to prominence in public discourse in the 1960s—choosing to disobey unjust and inhuman laws in favor of what is morally right—has encouraged and justified the actions of liberation heroes worldwide, as we saw in the courageous ideas and actions of the antiapartheid heroes. The objections are about minimal but crucial expectations. But big things come from humble beginnings and, as Utubora declares (12), no change happens for a person who does not act.

To invoke Ubuntu is to call attention to one's freedoms and rights, such as the right to freedom of thought and its expression, freedom of congregation, freedom from arbitrary arrests and torture, freedom from discrimination based on one's race, gender, ethnicity, age, sexual orientation, or religious affiliation—all civil rights and freedoms as defined in the new South African constitution and rightly interpretable therefrom—the right to a fair trial in a court of law, the right to bid for and lawfully own property anywhere in my country or anywhere in the world, the right to live anywhere in my country or anywhere in the world. Because these are the freedoms and rights that enable all healthy people to act in pursuit of their interests and to attain their Utu, it is Shaaban's view that when they are denied, he or she to whom they are denied is thus being treated like an animal, and he or she who denies them to others is conducting himself or herself as a beast, as if they should be walking on four rather than on two legs. The invocation of Ubuntu in various contexts and circumstances is thus more than just a reminder of the moral imperative it stands for. It is to evoke redress, when one is denied any number of such freedoms and rights, on claims of suspected injustices to which they claim to have been subjected. Adopting the principles of Ubuntu rehumanizes both perpetrator and victim of injustice. It reconciles duties and rights.

According to Shaaban (1968b), good deeds add to one's Utu and bad deeds subtract from it (42).[10] Commenting on why he had collapsed upon hearing a former police officer confess to the murder of Simphiwe, that the police had previously killed Simphiwe with rat poison prior to burning his body on a bonfire while they roasted meat for their lunch on the side, Reverend Desmond Tutu said, "I was completely beyond shock about how low we had descended in our disregard for human life. We had come so low that someone would be burning the body of another human being while he himself roasted his lunch by the side at the same time." Compare this to the remarks by Shaaban's Mke wa Liwali (1968b, 21) earlier: "*Hapana jambo baya duniani kama kuona kiumbe mwenye umbo la mtu amebadilika kuwa kama mnyama kwa uovu wa matendo yake. Wa miguu miwili huwaje wa mine* [literally: Nothing in the world is more horrifying than to see a person conduct himself or herself as if they were a beast. How does this two-legged person turn into a four-legged beast?]" (25). Despite being separated by several decades and by different circumstances, these remarks not only point to the universality of the moral imperative but also reveal the universality of the principle that lies at the core of the contraction theory—namely, the transition from the state of nature, like beasts, to that of persons, meaning rational, moral beings. Here is the difference: for Shaaban, like for Reverend Tutu, reason and moral responsibility, or reciprocity with others, is just human nature; it does not arise by contract. In other words, *Mtu* ought to exercise reason and conduct himself or herself in manners endowed by having *Utu*. The very idea of *Mtu* evokes this basic moral principle on which others are built. Likewise, this same *Utu* endows on them inalienable rights that Others, *Watu*, ought to recognize in the way they conduct themselves toward him or her. It is this reciprocity that becomes the basis of civil society.

We cannot, and must not, in our conduct towards others, descend to the state of nature.

Even at the interview, which was conducted several days after the bonfire incident, the Reverend Tutu was still visibly shaken. Back at the testimony itself, the police officer was unfazed by all the outpouring of emotion around him, including the loud burst into wailing and subsequent fainting by the late Simphiwe's two children seated in the audience. My comment while teaching this piece is that Reverend Tutu and the police officer were not talking about the same entity from a metaphysical point of view. They were inhabiting two contrasting conceptual spheres and so were talking past each other. While Reverend Tutu was overcome with disgust at the treatment of the body of a person in manners that were usually accorded a chicken or the carcass of some other animal or bird in the food category, the policeman was a member of a culture to which black people were not persons in the way they themselves were. Black people were subpersons and so could be treated like objects. In a world where the killing of nonhuman animals by cruel methods is illegal, the black person in apartheid South Africa was less than these nonhuman sentients. They were subpersons and hence not worthy of any form of dignified treatment in life, much less in death.

We cannot lose sight of the timing of this undertaking of inquiry into the idea of Ubuntu. The reason it presents itself as a component of nonideal theory in contemporary sociopolitical discourse is to be found in the sociopolitical condition of the latter decades that defined the state of our nations. The South African apartheid system was not just one of these conditions in the continental or even global stock of brutal regimes defined by racial hatred, it was its epitome. It is in this context, I believe, that the idea of Ubuntu emerges as a call to corrective measures in many domains of the social fabric in South Africa and the world at large. Because there is no "African" as an adjective or other type of qualifier in Ubuntu (humanity), it calls everyone's attention to the many worldwide incidences and forms of injustice.

Let the now famous essay "Whose Fourth of July?" by Frederick Douglass, the African American slave who bought his freedom and became an abolitionist, become the anthem for those who continue to struggle for recognition of the most fundamental reality of their existence—their humanity, Ubuntu! We all ought to ask with them, on every independence day, whose freedom is being celebrated on these days when so many people are still denied their freedoms and the other rights that come with it. Is it because freedom belongs to humans, which they are not? Or are they just not human enough to deserve it?

Notes

1. Rawls refers here to Hume (1902), sec. 3, pt. I, para. 3, 184.

2. The adjective *Bora* can be read in this context as connoting "the best," "excellent," or "ideal" in regard to quality or value. *Ubora*, then, is "excellence in quality or value," "first-rate or highest value," "nobility" or "noblesse." There are, then, two ways of reading what Shaaban has in mind with this title: one, it can be read as "ideal state of being human," "the best value of humans," or as is also suggested in its own Kiswahili rendition, "Ubora wa Utu," the ideal characteristic or value in being human or a person, or *Utu bora*, ideal personhood. It can be assumed, then, that when possessed, those characteristics that are considered ideal for being properly or truly human make us ideal persons. He or she who possesses these ideal characteristics not only is an ideal person, especially in moral senses, but also has on that basis ideal personhood. In his trademark linguistico-conceptual creativity, Shaaban creates a name out of this concept and makes the bearer of the name the chief subject of what ought to be emulated by others. Thus, to make his reader follow how this virtuosity is expressed, "Utubora," becomes the bearer and manifestation of "ideal personhood." Shaaban says in the foreword to *Utubora Mkulima* (ix) that "although translations may have their value, writing in the vernacular carries the advantage of revealing the moral habits, discipline, and inclinations of the native speakers of a language that are often and easily lost in translations. On the other hand, capturing the spirit of a people through their vernacular requires correct knowledge and use of the canonical literary style of the language in question in its purity and originality." He believed that *Utubora Mkulima* was characterized by such stylistic elegance while also delivering the underlying spirit of the people (their philosophy). In other words, the effectiveness of a language as a medium of communication lies in both its literary elegance and its conceptual expressiveness. His essays, therefore, need to be read together with his *Pambo la Lugha* in which he captures the elegance of Kiswahili in its poetic form.

3. Shaaban coined this name, which means "sweet embrace," to indicate that in contrast to the gloomy urban environment of Zanzibar, this mainland village was one that offered a different social atmosphere in which residents sought out and cared for each other. It was a place of social cohesion.

4. Again, to serve his conceptual goals, Shaaban coins this name from the Kiswahili word, *Haya*, which means "shame," a state of mind or attitude that arises when one realizes that one may be unworthy or may have done something that is not rewardable or not considered in good standing, such as not being very intelligent or thoughtful. The name means Binti Haya, or Bibi Haya, probably the latter, because of her age relative to that of Utubora.

5. "Nadhani hutaniona mjuba nikisema kuwa hapana jambo baya duniani kama kuona kiumbe mwenye umbo la mtu amebadilika kuwa kama mnyama kwa uovu wa matendo yake. Wa miguu miwili huwaje wa minne!"

6. Worn out physically and mentally both from experiences as a soldier in World War II, and from abandonment by a fiancée who ran off with a rich man while he was away at war, Utubora, in possession of a loaded rifle upon his return from war, had many temptations

to think that nothing was left worth living for. But he quickly reasoned that suicide was for those who lacked fortitude of mind and ability to think straight and critically. This discussion by Shaaban is particularly interesting in light of contemporary medical diagnosis of war-related mental illnesses and disorders that afflict those returning from wars. Generally referred to as posttraumatic stress disorder (PTSD), the exact nature of these afflictions is still under research and study, but many victims of PTSD, real or merely claimed by subjects, are on record as committing unusual acts, generally involving violence on themselves and on other people, including family members and acquaintances. That Shaaban refers to such a possibility in his description of his imaginary subject Utubora is an indication of his critical consideration of human conduct or mental experiences under various circumstances even before these problems were widely recognized as medical issues, let alone being addressed. Although some situations in life may cause reason to experience some struggle, it must overcome emotion.

7. Busutamu, "sweet embrace," may have been coined to indicate Shaaban's idea of "living in harmony." If there was not already harmony among the residents when Utubora arrived there, then, as we shall see, his ideal moral character and exemplary lifestyle of altruism helps to spur the village's transformation from Bususumu (bitter embrace), which it had become, back to Busutamu, which it was when Utubora's mother was born, lived, and grew up there. For Shaaban, then, the goal for humans should be the creation of those conditions that can enable humans to attain their perfection. On the other hand, those conditions can only be if people, citizens, live righteously and virtuously. Not only is his name unusual, but his character is too. His belief in and practice of selflessness is a Muslim virtue, which is that a true Muslim needs to understand work as service to others, to those in need. Also, in a general sense, that it is not enough to believe in good deeds; one ought to practice them for the betterment of society.

8. It is unclear what Shaaban's goal is here, but it is reasonable to argue that he is dissociating the idea of a good person from obedience to the law. According to Shaaban, a good citizen is not only a law-abiding person, for there can be bad laws, unjust laws, and so on, and he or she would not be obliged to follow them. We saw that according to John Locke, too, citizens bear the right to rise against a bad ruler, like a tyrant. But Shaaban would differ from Locke on at least one account: Locke's position on slavery was unsteady, that although he appeared to hate absolutism and slavery as a matter of principle, his involvement with policies and gains that encouraged colonization. Locke's *First Treatise* begins: "Slavery is so vile and miserable an Estate of Man, and so directly opposite to the generous Temper and Courage of our Nation; that 'tis hardly to be conceived that an Englishman, much less a Gentleman, should plead for't" (Locke 2002, T I. '1: 141). Yet he supported slavery as punishment for some crimes, apparently putting enslavement at the same level as capital punishment. Then there are two other factors in Locke's life. One, in 1672–73, when he worked as personal secretary to Shaftesbury who had been appointed by King Charles II to head England's Council on Foreign Plantations, Locke was paid for his work with stocks in the Royal African Company, the entity that rant the African slave trade for England, but he sold them in 1675. Two, in 1669 Locke wrote *The Fundamental Constitutions of Carolina* in which he stated, "Every freeman of Carolina shall have absolute power and authority over his negro slaves." Shaaban on the other hand, views freedom as a natural right, not a value that is conferred by others as a pact, in which case it can be modified, withdrawn, or totally denied (see also Frederick Copleston, *A History of Philosophy*, book 2, volume 5 [New York:

Doubleday Publishers, 1985], 67–78; Robert M. Hutchins, ed., *Great Books of the Western World, Encyclopaedia Britannica*, vol. 35 [Chicago: University of Chicago Press, 1952], chap. 5, 29–30; Vere Chappell, ed., *The Cambridge Companion to Locke* [Cambridge: Cambridge University Press, 1994]). Utubora himself worries about his possible legal fate, which suggests that Shaaban's goal is intentional; the law may be good in its protection of people's rights, such as their right to property, but neither obedience to the law nor its mere protection of rights can by themselves be the source of self-worth or of the kind of happiness that is generated by one's relations with other people in the community. Note that BiMkubwa lived a solitary life of despair when neighbors like Makuu withdrew into their own respective private lives.

9. Mke wa Liwali: "hapana jambo baya duniani kama kuona kiumbe mwenye umbo la mtu amebadilika kuwa kama mnyama kwa uovu wa matendo yake."

10. In the Truth and Reconciliation documentary directed and narrated by the famous American documentarist Bill Moyer, there is a scene in which a survivor and recovering victim of the police torture squad faces and asks his former torturer whether he ever thought of himself as a human being while he was engaged in torturing him, which included giving him (the victim) electric torture in his anus. In another scene, the mother of the late Simphiwe, clasping in her hands a lump of hair, the only remains of her son to testify to how he was treated, finally asks the police officer, "What are you? I don't know how to think of you, whether you are a real human being, or a beast." At this point in the scene, the Reverend Desmond Tutu collapses in shock and is carried out of the hall.

References

Balibutsa, Maniragaba. 1985. *Les perspectives de la pensée philosophique bantu-rwandaise après Alexis Kagame*. Butare, Rwanda: Editions Universite Nationale du Rwanda.

Bin Robert, Shaaban. 1966. *Kusadikika: Nchi Iliyo Angani*. Diwani Ya Shaaban, No. 2. London: Evans Brothers.

———. 1968a. *Siku ya Watenzi Wote*. Nairobi: Thomas Nelson and Sons, 1968.

———. 1968b. *Utubora Mkulima*. Diwani Ya Shaaban, No. 8. London: Evans Brothers.

———. 1969. *Koja la Lugha*. Nairobi: Oxford University Press.

———. 2010. *Adili na Nduguze*. Dar es Salaam: Tanzania Publishing House.

Griaule, Marcel. 1965. *Conversations with Ogotemmêli*. London: Oxford University Press.

Hobbes, Thomas. 1962. *Leviathan. or, The Matter, Form and Power of a Commonwealth Ecclesiastical and Civil*. Edited by Michael Oakeshott. New York: Collier.

Hume, David. 1902. *An Enquiry Concerning the Principles of Morals*, 2nd ed. Edited by L. A. Selby-Bigge. Oxford: Oxford University Press.

Kagame, Alexis. 1956. *La philosophie băntu-rwandaise de l'être*. Brussels: Académie Royale des Sciences Coloniales.

———. 1976. *La philosophie băntu comparée*. Paris: Présence africaine.

Locke, John. 2002. *Two Treatises of Government*. Edited by Peter Laslett. Cambridge: Cambridge University Press.

Masolo, D. A. 2018. "Self-Constitution and Agency." In *Ubuntu and Personhood*, edited by James Ogude, 11–37. Trenton, NJ: Africa World Press.

Mills, Charles W. 1997. *The Racial Contract*. Ithaca, NY: Cornell University Press.

Rawls, John. 1972. *A Theory of Justice*. Oxford: Oxford University Press.

Senghor, Léopold S. 1977. *Liberté 3: Négritude et civilisation de l'universel*. Paris: Éditions du Seuil.

D. A. MASOLO is Professor of Philosophy at the University of Louisville. Masolo is author of *Self and Community in a Changing World* (a finalist for the Melville Herskovits Award for the most important scholarly work in African studies in the English language in the preceding year, 2011) and *African Philosophy in Search of Identity*. He is editor (with Ivan Karp) of *African Philosophy as Cultural Inquiry*.

3

THE ART OF PERSONHOOD

Kinship and Its Social Challenges

Bhekizizwe Peterson

T HE REGULAR OCCURRENCES OF EXCLUSION THAT TYPIFIED THE
relationship between colonial modernity and black people in South Africa precipitated a number of existential crises, in addition to the dilemmas
and hardships that were caused by sociopolitical and economic inequities
and inequalities. All the latter ultimately amounted to the denial and ef-
facement of the humanity of Africans. It is not surprising, therefore, that
the question of what it means to be human and the attendant quests for
personhood—as themes and tropes on lived experiences—are shot through
much of the creative and discursive interventions undertaken by black artists and intellectuals in South Africa. This is in recognition of the capacity
that ideology and the arts have to produce and even recast knowledge and
experience and serve as catalysts for social action to displace or unsettle colonial discourses and projects, especially those that reduce Africans to the
status of being infrahuman. Ubuntu, arguably, represents one of the most
salient and resonant indigenous moral concepts that African artists and intellectuals have wrestled with in attempts to think through the complexities
of personhood, particularly in the aftermath of colonialism. It is probably
also one of the most used and abused terms in South Africa's public and
political lexicon.

It is instructive that the most recent and sustained public recuperation
of the notion of Ubuntu can be traced to the early 1990s, particularly in
relation to the establishment of the Truth and Reconciliation Commission,

its hearings, and its outcome (Tutu 1999). It was also much touted by adherents of the African Renaissance that was championed by President Thabo Mbeki.[1] Before then—particularly since the emergence of Black Consciousness in the 1970s—it was a key concept in much of black theology in South Africa (Boesak 1984, 20, 56). The specific evocations of Ubuntu as being at the core of deliberations on personhood and (after apartheid) restorative justice profoundly spoke to the deep challenges that past injustices and brutalities (all a denial of the humanity of others) posed to the present and whether, as part of transitioning to a better future, other forms of healing, accountability, and redress could be achieved without further retribution (more violence and inhumanity).

Despite its contemporary valences, it is worth mentioning that the earliest written iteration of Ubuntu that I have found dates from circa 1859, that is, two decades before the colonial conquest of the Zulu nation in 1879 (Grout 1893). Today, arguably, Ubuntu is one of the most contested notions in postapartheid South Africa. In the present discussion, I would like to explore its significance and scholarly responses to it by reflecting on the concept and its implications for understanding personhood. Because of its various conceptual and linguistic renditions, it does not serve much purpose in South Africa to become obsessed with tracking its earliest recorded manifestations; such a move, in itself, would be to predicate the existence of African ontology on writing or, in other words, the colonial archive or library. It is important, however, to be able to map the ways in which it is deployed across the centuries by ordinary Africans, colonial historians, generations of the African intelligentsia, and contemporary actors from various constituencies and discourses. Perspectives on its claims and meanings are of less significance than the *work* across epochs that the idea of Ubuntu can do or the uses it is being put to.

The most common enunciation and association of Ubuntu today is in its glossing through the often-cited proverb, *umuntu ngumuntu ngabantu*— a person is a person through other persons. In the first instance, the proverb will be used to introduce the notion of Ubuntu and to show that its ambit extends beyond interpersonal interactions into a range of related relations between humans and nature that are fundamental in Nguni cosmology. Second, the proverb will help elucidate the ethical and hermeneutic challenges that the notion of Ubuntu presents. The ethos of Ubuntu can be discerned in numerous related proverbs, such as *inkosi iknosi ngabuntu*, "a king is a king because of people" (Nyembezi 1974, 125), and numerous other formulations on African humanism. David Coplan, reflecting on the SeSotho equivalent of the proverb, *Morena ke batho*, aptly describes the maxim as expressing "the idealized balance between hierarchy and reciprocity in these patron-client relationships" (Coplan 1994, 34).

What is crucial in the postulation of Ubuntu is the emphasis on the notion that personhood, identity, and morality are not innate but are achieved in relation to and through social interaction based on ethical conduct with others, especially in conditions that are marked by imbalances in social and personal power. Such a desired outlook and behavior are meant to affirm and reward goodness (respect/honor) and circumvent and punish wrongdoing. All people—irrespective of their race, gender, status, beliefs, and so on or their background, context, or circumstances—are regarded as morally equal. The good or the bad in their morality and actions can therefore be assessed in relation to the precepts of Ubuntu. Tellingly, the highest form of praise and castigation is in the conferment or denial of the idea of being human. This is apparent in expressions such as *u nobuntu* (she or he is human) in contradistinction to *akana buntu* (she or he is not human).

Consequently, it is crucial to grasp that Ubuntu, as a metaphysical concept or moral theory (and even as a sociopolitical one), is not a given or straightforward or singular. Kai Kresse (2007), in an illuminating discussion of the East African equivalent of Ubuntu, Utu (and which is also captured in the saying "*mtu ni utu* 'a human being is humanity'" (Kresse 2007, 139), emphasizes that we must remain aware that "the descriptive abstract quality of being human, in addition to the normative quality of being humane, . . . needs to be proven each time through concrete performance" (Kresse 2007, 142). In order to achieve the desired attributes of, among others, love, kindness, and reciprocity that are central to the realization of an ideal world requires that one has to "act as if one were already a part of it" (Kresse 2007, 168). The distance between the ideal and less-than-perfect existence that we inhabit and lead can be navigated only through "our *moral imagination*" (Kresse 2007, 168, emphasis added). It, finally, means that Ubuntu "can be forfeited, just as it must be earned" (Kresse 2007, 150).

The elaboration of personhood, then—whether in cosmologies and epistemologies, material culture or the arts—is best broached as, at least, an attempt to define, apprehend, and instill the desired morality and conduct among people. In the first instance, this is particularly so with regard to the challenges to kinship that poverty and urban life has been seen to represent. Mark Sanders has suggested that the proclamation of Ubuntu occurs "at times of historical crisis" (120) and that "the strength of the concept of ubuntu is its ability, by inventing memory in the future perfect tense, to generate stability at a time of transition and to stage recovery at a time of loss" (Sanders 2002, 120–21). Sanders, furthermore poses the following question: "What will render the call for ubuntu, which is typically inextricable from the lamenting of its loss, concrete? Paradoxically perhaps, it is the literary that does so" (Sanders 2002, 121). In other words, to extend Sanders insight, it is in the arts or in the realm of ideology or consciousness that Ubuntu will, predominantly, be articulated and contested in the public sphere. Artists are tasked with the responsibility of being moral barometers by exploring the instances of moral good or decay in society. The manifestation or practice of Ubuntu in socioeconomic and political spheres is another, long-term and more vexed, matter. The complex articulation between thought, social being, and living is one that requires careful consideration and practice, as Ernest Mancoba insightfully cautioned, "Our history has brought about, little by little, this dichotomy between abstraction and figuration which provokes, more and more, a terrible atomization in the very essence of life. In no domain more than the arts has this systematic dichotomy caused such destruction of the very foundation to the human identity, as both belonging to nature and sharing in the essence of an ideal being" (Mancoba 2010, 381).

Consequently, the wrestlings with alienation and the search for personhood and ethical conduct provide the overarching and over-determined thread or through-line of much of what will be explored in this discussion. Apart from serving as framing templates, personhood and ethical conduct also, because of the layered textures and problematics that they bring into relief, need to be understood as multiple and complex intercessions. They are explorations of the self (particularly in relation to experience, need, and desire). At the other end, they are also attempts at disrupting and displacing colonial discourses that rationalize the denigration, oppression, and exploitation of Africans on the basis of race.

The Poetics of Orature

Since much of the discussion on Ubuntu tends to occur as if the notion has no genealogy before its postapartheid iterations, it is needful, in the following two sections of this discussion, to chart the long-standing exploration of the idea of Ubuntu in black South African art and thought, although I will be predominantly drawing on orature here. Doing so also requires that the citations of black intellectuals and artists be somewhat generous in order to appreciate their different reflections and cadences. Orature constitutes a foundational part of the creative expressions of African individuals and communities.[2] Three primary orature genres can be identified in southern Africa and that, in their generic and stylistic articulation and cross-fertilization, allowed for large range of uses, permutations, and practices. The primary forms are *izibongo* or oral poetry (praise poems of royalty and individuals—*izithakazelo*, for instance, being a variant in which exaltations of the genealogy of a kinship group is mapped through the invocation of the surname[s], *izibongo* of key ancestors); songs (*ingoma*); and oral tales (narratives—*izinganekwane*—encompassing legends, myths, folktales, fables, myths, and folklore (proverbs, riddles, and idioms).[3]

As artistic practices, these oral genres and their encoding in indigenous performance (particularly song and dance) allowed for the conceptualization, rehearsal, and enactment of personal and social experiences, as well as a range of sensory and aesthetic needs and pleasures. Performances—whether at the king's or *umnumzane*'s (homestead head) court or on the paths between destinations—formed part of the individual's, homestead's, and clan's sensual and reflective interactions and deliberations (or publicness) whether conducted under the banner of religion, culture, creativity, or recreation.

I would briefly like to add a reminder of the significance of orature—as encoded in a proverb—in the construction of worldviews and aesthetic strategies that are meant to serve as the cultural and moral arsenal with which to negotiate the challenges of colonial and postcolonial experiences. It is important to bear in mind that the symbolism in proverbs spans aural, performative, plastic, and written encodings. Oral language, in other words, "is both complemented and inter penetrated by multi-sensory products and practices" that encompass "the seeping boundaries between the written and unwritten" and these are "issues of fundamental import for humankind" (Finnegan 2007, xi).

The significance of the complex articulation between senses of personhood and aesthetic practices can be gleaned in the role and perception of praise poetry in Zulu society. The informants that James Stuart interviewed for his archives[4]—starting from the mid-1890s until his departure for England in 1922—give considerable detail and reflection on the quotidian and ontological ways in which praises were embedded in the daily lives of commoners and kings in the Zulu kingdom. What is also striking is the regular attention to aesthetic criteria and appreciation that they demonstrate. The performative qualities of various *imbongi*s are often referred to and in a manner that suggests that the best poets were revered not only for their historical knowledge or compositional prowess but also for the performative skills that they mastered. The closest term in Zulu that approximates the idea and skill associated with the designation "artist" is *uchwephesha*: to "act with ease, skill, and dexterity" particularly "in speech or action." (Doke and Vilakazi 1972, 118). Magolwane ka Mkatini was acknowledged by most as "a great imbongi" (Webb and Wright 1986, 4:71; Vilakazi 1935, 21). Magolwane plied his trade during the reigns of at least four Zulu kings—Shaka (circa 1816–28), Dingane (1828–40), Mpande (1840–72), and Cetshwayo (1872–79)—and he became the principal *imbongi* of Mpande. Magolwane's son recalls that so enamored was Mpande with his father's recitals that "Mpande would not allow my father to go and live at home. He would allow him to go off in the winter for only two months; he would return in the third." This was because

> He would praise him by making mention of events that had taken place *in a way* that no one else had done. He would surpass them in composing praises for the king. When the king heard them he would let out a whistle. When Magolwane had finished, the king would order him to repeat those which he had himself composed. The king would then say, "Come closer, Magolwana. Come and speak at close quarters, for these praises are sweet to my ear. Speak softly." He would proceed to do so, speaking softly, saying the praises to the king. (Webb and Wright 1986, 4:140–41)

A similar observation about the intrinsic articulation between form and content; past, present, and future; reflection; and anticipation can be made in relation to what may be regarded as the most miniature forms of narrative, proverbs. Although it is impossible to date the origins of proverbs, their evolution and elevation to the status of being accepted as such is contingent on two achievements. First, the perceived wisdom of a proverbial saying and, second, its rendition in a pithy form that, itself, according to Rubusana, "*ukuteta ngamaqálo . . . kuvakaliswa inyaniso ezinkulu nezinzulu ngenteto emfutshane kakúlu*" (Rubusana 1911, 141), that is: proverbs are appealing and pleasing because of their choice of words and utterances. It is no wonder then that aphoristic statements are regarded as foundational elements of folk wisdom and lore. They are also often cast as constituting the archive of experience or the repositories of indigenous knowledge systems, some of which, according to Nyembezi, "have been learned the hard way" (Nyembezi 1974, xii). Or, put differently, proverbs as discursive notations on "human events and human fortunes" have been "reified into the tokens of an experience everybody knows and recognizes in advance, in a tacit collective experience that need not be explained." Also, their "resonance fans out into many other dimensions, from ethics and politics to psychology and aesthetics" (Jameson 1999, 168, 173) and, as a result, their multivalence means that "proverbs are *not* absolute or universal truths. . . . Proverbs only make sense in a given situation or context" (Mieder 1993, ix–x). The latter qualification does not preclude their resonances with other experiences and environments, hence the frequency with which one finds equivalent proverbs in other languages and cultures.

It is not surprising that, because of proverbs' perceived experiential and archival significance, many early black intellectuals placed great store on "preserving what will soon be buried in the past" but also because, as Wauchope—who published commentaries on praise poetry and proverbs in the newspaper *Imvo*—argued, a significant number of proverbs "bring out the ethical aspect of Native life. . . . There is the tendency in the Native mind to regard civilized moral standards as foreign and strange. My object is to show that corresponding moral standards exist in chrystallized [*sic*] forms in their National Mottoes, and that by living up to these they would not fall far below the civilized standards of morality" (Wauchope 2008, 29).[5] Sol Plaatje held a similar view, as is clear from the fact that his own collection of proverbs included what he regarded as their European equivalents, implying that African beliefs, cultures, and polities were—despite their distinctiveness—equally imbued with integrity and sophistication (Plaatje 1916). Later African scholars have concurred that African folklore is central in understanding African "axiology, that is, its system of values" and that genres such as proverbs, myths and narrative, "can be utilized as a source of philosophical thought in Africa"[6] (Gyekye 1987, 15). Other African philosophers—following Paulin Hountondji (1996)—while not disputing such perspectives, have expressed sharp reservations about what has been termed "ethnophilosophy."[7] Ironically, the proponents of ethnophilosophy, especially in the African diaspora, have not taken heed of the cautionary observations by Cheikh Anta Diop (1991), whose important work they rightly hold in high esteem. Diop's position was that African cosmology, in the precolonial era when it was "intensely lived," can be regarded as "self-conscious philosophical thought" but that subsequently "they have become degraded, fossilized," leading him to conclude that "this system of thought, of which its upholders are hardly aware, cannot be considered to be philosophy in the classical sense" (322–23). The irony, of course, is the definitional power that is accorded to "the classical sense" by proponents on either side of the divide. The musings of Placide Tempels (1959), Alexis Kagame (1989), John S. Mbiti (1969), and others (very much in line with advocates of "oral literature") and their adversaries (proponents of "philosophy in the classical definition") seem oblivious to two elementary challenges. First, there is the need to evacuate the "West," the "classic," "the canon," or whatever forms of coloniality that remain as the normative policing standards against which African ideas and practices are seen as needing to be validated or measured against. The "Afrocentric" view tends to suggest that Africans share a singular worldview and metaphysical system and one that is based on a rather static sense of the continent and its traditions. Paradoxically, in order to assert the rationality and coherence of African thought systems, there is the tendency to establish similarities between African worldviews and European ones or between African religious thought and aspects of Christianity. Second, inasmuch as continental comparable principles and practices can be found, the diversity that also typifies the continent needs to be recognized. The recognition is crucial in order not to efface the distinctions and differences in premises and emphasis that also characterize specific communities and creative movements. In such cases, acknowledgments of the indigenous are neither a gesture to the primordial nor authentic. The challenge, as Valentine Mudimbe (1988) observed, is whether analysis can move beyond "using categories and conceptual systems which depend on a Western epistemological order" (x). Otherwise, the premise would be "that African *Weltanschauungen* and African traditional systems of thought are unthinkable and cannot be made explicit within the framework of their own rationality" (x).

A method that transcends these predicaments is one that broaches culture (as a sum of human experience and as expressed through and in language, art, religion, and science, among others) as an important dimension in the production of various forms of meaning and knowledge (including philosophy) by individuals, artists, and scholars. In such a perspective, "philosophical knowledge is not a separate form of knowledge, but is present in each particular symbolic form in so far as a critical and self-reflexive discourse (including a focus on the interrelation to all other symbolic forms) is generated and expressed within and through it" (Kresse 2007, 22).

Furthermore, "This approach has the advantage of not only explaining but even anticipating an 'internal pluralism' of competing philosophical discourses not only among cultures, but potentially within every culture" (23). Before discussing Ubuntu in the light of these caveats and its contemporary appeals or dismissals, it is important to start with a brief consideration of its genealogy and meaning.

The Contours of Ubuntu and the Architecture of Kinship

Reverend Charles Roberts in his *English-Zulu Dictionary*—with a first preface dated February 9, 1880—defines Ubuntu as human nature (Roberts 1902). In their *Zulu-English Dictionary*, which first appeared in 1948, Doke and Vilakazi, also define Ubuntu as human nature, and they further regard it as denoting "humaneness, good disposition, good moral nature. *Benziwa ubuntu babo* / They are urged on by their humane feelings" and "One's real self, character. *Ubuntu bomuntu butholwa ezenzwenizakhe* / A man's real self is revealed in his deeds" (Doke and Vilakazi 1948, 608). In the latter deeds can be included hospitality, compassion, and reciprocity. In one of the narratives collected in Rubusana's pioneering anthology *Zemk'inkomo Magwalandini* (Your cattle are gone, cowards), which appeared in 1911, a groom, after experiencing elements of the latter qualities during the *Ukuhlolela* (marriage deliberations), praises his future in-laws by declaring, "*Ubesitho-ke a ncome ubuntu babazali be ntombileyo* / He praised the good human nature of the parents of the girl" (Rubusana 1911, 184).

A striking and recurring concern in the works of the first two generations of mission-educated African artists in South Africa are the reflections on the changes and alienation wrought by colonialism and urbanity, particularly in their diminishment if not obliteration of compassion for those who are experiencing hard times. Even more fascinating is the fact that such dismaying acts are being leveled against the *kholwa* (Christian converts) by its members. Tiyo Soga, in two essays published in *Indaba* in June and October 1864, "*Amahrestu nenkosi zelilizwe* / Christians and Chiefs" and "*Amakholwa na-MaXhosa angaphandle* / Mission People and Red People," observes that there is consternation among sections of the *kholwa* that converted Africans are displaying signs of disrespect to chiefs and that such negative attitudes against traditional authorities are further extended toward nonbelievers ("reds" or "pagans"). What is alarming for Soga is that "we people of the Mission stations are said to be notorious for lack of hospitality to strangers." He cites a case where a traveler was denied shelter on a cold night because none of the *kholwa* in the village were willing to host a nonbeliever. He concludes by recalling a popular proverb that cautions that "the foot does not sniff, that is, you may land where you never thought you would ever be" (Soga 1983, 175–77, quote on 172). Rubusana (1911, 141) has it as his second proverb, to wit, "*Unyawo aluna mpumlo.*"[8] Matthews (1934) argues that "one of the commonest results of the contact of cultures is social disintegration" because of "modern society and its aggressive individualism" (3). Unless the conflict of cultures is resolved, "native society will be in constant danger of collapse, and all the best elements of Bantu culture—of *ubuntu* (humanity as conceived by the Bantu)—will be irretrievably lost" (4). Jordan (1973), commenting on Soga's second essay, argued that Soga is disconcerted because "the converted has lost *ubuntu* (generosity, respect for man irrespective of position)."

It is telling that Nyembezi in his *Zulu Proverbs* (1974; first published in 1954) starts his list of proverbial categories with a section entitled *Ubuntu* and he notes that "this word in Zulu covers a very wide field. It means humaneness, good disposition, good moral nature. It will, therefore, include proverbs dealing with treatment of people, good and bad behaviour, pride, ingratitude, and such bad traits as obstinacy" (Nyembezi 1954, 46). Nyembezi further observes that "[many of the proverbs deal with hospitality. Experience has taught people that a stranger is grateful for any little act of kindness. From experience they have realized that it pays to be liberal rather than tight-fisted" (11) and "People notice that doing good is usually appreciated, and often results in the good turn being reciprocated" (40).

There are other literary examples from the first two decades of the twentieth century of the refusal to extend reciprocity that Soga bemoaned. Wauchope, in one of his essays, writes, "*Ukuba kuko nto singade sizidle ngayo tina Maxhosa kukuvela na nomtu onentswelo, otshelwe sisiceko.* / One thing we Xhosa can pride ourselves on is compassion for the destitute, for someone whose puddle has dried up" (Wauchope 2008, 273, 274). In the article "Native Customs / Amasiko Emvelo" for *Imvo* in 1903, Wauchope deploys the metaphor of a dwelling (using as symbols elements such as *pillars, rafter, roof, door,* and *decoration*) to argue that customs are a crucial foundation of any culture: "*Onke lamasiko angeniswang uTixo kuma nyange uku zekugcineke ubuntu. Yimizi yoku bopela ukuze uhlanga lungapalali.* / All these customs were introduced by God to the ancestors to preserve humanity. They are the rushes that bind the nation so that it does not fall apart" (Wauchope 2008, 324–25). S. M. Molema ([1920] 1963) settled on a less divine summation of the pivot of morality in Bantu society: "Utilitarianism. The greatest happiness and good of the tribe was the end and aim of each member of the tribe. Now utility forms part of the basis of perhaps all moral codes. With the Bantu, it formed *the* basis of morality. . . . It was utilitarianism. This was the standard of goodness, and in harmony with, and conformity to, this end must the moral conduct be moulded. The effect of this, of course, was an altruism, narrow and restricted, it is true, as extending no further than the tribe" (116). There are three significant suggestions in Wauchope's argument. The first is the emphasis on a very subtle and expansive intimation of the idea of *humanity*, one that encompasses senses of self (identity), experience (history) and the need to preserve our moral uprightness or goodness. All these deeply desired but intangible attributes are, second, physicalized for us through the recourse to the metaphors of the home. Last, implicit in Wauchope's symbolic architecture is the relationship that should exist between the constitutive elements that make up the dwelling. With regard to the makeup of the clan, we can summarize them as essentially based on cultural configurations of the relationship between the individual and the group: "customs . . . are the rushes that bind the nation so that it does not fall apart" (Wauchope 2008, 325). Concepts of kinship form an important thread in Nguni social organization and allow for an intricate configuration of a patrilineal and segmentary lineage system that established relationships between immediate relatives and the extended family arranged as homestead, age set, clan, and nation. It has been noted that "the classificatory nomenclature provides every Zulu with a number of fathers and mothers and a very large circle of brothers and sisters, the individual family, consisting of a man and his wife and children, [and] is no whit less important than among Europeans and must be considered the most important unit in Zulu society" (Krige 1965, 23).

Each precolonial homestead was, to a significant degree, self-sufficient, and surplus was achieved through the management and control of familial labor power, agricultural production, pastoralism (primarily based on the herding of cattle), and bridewealth (through marriage): all of which were contingent on access to land (which was communally owned) that was conducive to farming, grazing, and hunting. "Equally important was a network of social practices which knitted the production complex together, regulated its relations with other homesteads, and ensured its reproduction.

These included polygyny and lobola" (Slater 1980, 154).[9] Or, in line with Molema's perspective, "No race or society is really, entirely communalistic, and we find that even among the Bantu, private property—such as cattle—existed side by side with communal property, such as land" (Molema [1920] 1963, 115).

Apart from internal consumption, each homestead allocated part of its surplus to the subsistence of the head of the homestead. In essence, "through the exchange of surplus from the process of reproduction and production (daughters and cattle), the process of reproduction and production was continued" and consequently, "the correlation between the kinship and lineage systems and the way in which social production was organised is striking":

> Production groups and lineage and kinship groups were virtually conterminous: the production community consisted of a father, his wives and their children; production units within the community consisted of ranked segments of wives and their children; wives were introduced into the homestead through exchange of the homestead's surplus cattle; the homestead (production community) had been a lineage segment (production unit) within a previously existing homestead and each homestead contained incipient production units. The laws regulating the distribution amongst segments within the homestead and inheritance when these segments became production communities, were defined in terms of the segmentation of the patrilineal lineage. (Guy 1982, 114–15)

In respect to polygyny and lobola, it is worth emphasizing, as historians of Nguni societies have observed, the centrality of cattle in Nguni societies. Chiefs and lineage heads who controlled cattle exercised crucial economic, cultural, and social power. Bridewealth and lobola ensured the incorporation of women from the outside and depended on the circulation of cattle (Marks and Atmore 1980, 10). The social standing and wealth of men was measured through cattle[10] (Krige 1965, 185) and, as is not surprising, cattle served as crucial cultural and aesthetic symbols that, again, emphasized the continuities between aesthetic practices and senses of personhood. Cattle "were the pliable symbolic vehicles through which men formed and reformed their world of social and spiritual relations" (Comaroff and Comaroff 1991, 1:145). Furthermore, they are an example of the layers of intricate connections and responsibilities (spanning the environment and animals) that, beyond human relationships, were associated with and symbolically encoded in and regarded as foundational to personhood.

As Harriet Ngubane (1977) persuasively argues in her magisterial monograph, "The Zulu believe that there is a special relationship between a person and his environment, and that plant and animal life somehow affect the environment" (Ngubane 1997, 24). Furthermore, "a Zulu conceives good health not only as consisting of a healthy body, but as a healthy situation of everything that concerns him. Good health means the harmonious working and coordination of his universe" (Ngubane 1977, 27–28). When balance is lost, order is restored through *ukuzilungisa*: "It means to restore order where there has been disorder. In other words, I am using the English word 'balance' to mean 'moral order' in the symmetrical sense in relation to the position of people vis-à-vis other people, the environment, the ancestors and other mythical forces that produce pollution. 'Balance' in this sense should be understood to mean 'symmetry' or 'order' rather than, as usual, the central pivot in a counter-poise situation" (Ngubane 1977, 27).

Cattle can, then, be regarded as a resonant example of the intersections between material culture, the arts, and sensually symbolic expressions of personhood. Over and above their social and economic roles, the high esteem accorded to cattle extends to their status as aesthetic subjects. Zulu has more than a hundred names to denote the myriad of characteristics of cattle, their horns, and colors. According to Krige (1965), "in the days of the great Zulu kings" (187), aesthetic pleasure was derived from sculpting the horns into various ornamental shapes. It is no wonder that men's willingness to bow down in deference to the majestic Nguni cattle is captured in the adage, *Ubuhle bendoda izinkomo zayo*, that is, the beauty of a man is in his cattle.

The motif of cattle has persisted in the arts even among urban dwellers (Haire and Matjila 2010). The sociopolitical and spiritual significances of cattle were noted in texts such as Wauchope's (2008) incendiary challenge, uttered in 1882 in a poem, that "*Zimkile! Mfo wohlanga*" / Your cattle are plundered, compatriot" (165), and so "take up the pen/Seize paper and ink / That's your shield" (169) and in Rubusana's *Zemk'inkomo Magwalandini* (1911). Later generations of black South African artists were still conjuring cattle as primary markers of indigenous senses of self and culture. This can be glossed through a sample of titles such as the songs "Jol'inkomo" by Miriam Makeba and "Yakhal'inkomo" by Winston Mankuku Ngozi, the poems "Yakhal'inkomo" by Mongane Serote, and "Jol'inkomo" by Mafika Pascal Gwala. These songs and poems also greatly inspired the visual artist Dumile Feni, whose early masterpiece *African Guernica* has cattle as central figures.

Testing the Limits of Kinship

Colonialism marked the further complication of the limits and possibilities of Ubuntu. Capitalism further exacerbated matters. Initially, researchers who advanced the articulation of modes of production theory argued that capitalism and the colonial state in South Africa developed segregation and labor policies that relied on maintaining reserves (former independent African polities with neotraditional forms of governance such as chiefs) as dependent enclaves of colonialism. The reserves served as the suppliers of cheap and unskilled migrant labor that was paid low wages, and second, the reserves subsidized agricultural production and other social needs such as healthcare and education.[11] Subsequent historiography has noted the systematic nature of colonial methods and has offered more specific and nuanced case studies about the complex dynamics that informed the competing relations between African polities, mining and industrial capital, and colonial farmers. It has been suggested that, for instance in Natal, "the forces of colonisation were weak and had to come to terms with existing structures, utilising pre-colonial forms and ideology for its own purposes of surplus extraction, but not totally restructuring it, which led to the development in Natal of a policy and ideology of segregation which were to provide late nineteenth-century policy-makers with useful precedents" (Marks and Atmore 1980, 19).[12]

More important for our purposes is the fact that the emergence of the state and industrial society meant that "other juridical and organized principles displace kinship from the central place it occupies" in precolonial society. In the new colonial conditions, systems of kinship, though now subordinate, continued to ensure production and subsistence but did not control the surplus produced. A few important consequences include the recasting of previous patriarchal patterns into more expansive forms of male domination. The latter is further translated into novel forms in which traditional structures and authorities and new elites (in collaboration and competition) reconfigure kinship ideology and relations in attempts to respond to colonial subjugation and exploitation. The integrity of kinship and lineage are further challenged by the capitalist mode of production. Ultimately, proletarianization undermines the communal aspects of labor, family, and kinship and people engage the state and each other as individuals, as migrant workers, and as fragile families (nuclear families increase as urban settlements become more permanent). Despite all these pressures, the networks, ideology, and reciprocity of kinship remained "enabling metaphor(s) which infuses ... new social arrangements with the legitimacy of traditional communal forms" and increase the possibilities of support and survival (Katz and Kemnitzer 1985, 252–53).

Plaatje (1916) is one of the earliest texts to articulate the double jeopardy of colonialism and capitalism. The passing of the Native Land Act of 1913, which reserved 13 percent of land for African occupation, reduced the African to "not actually a slave, but a pariah in the land of his birth" (21). Plaatje's evocations of "roving pariahs" (96) signaled the devastation of people's lives, families, livelihoods, cultures, spiritualities, and futures. The dispossession of land was exacerbated by the fact that people's foundational subjectivities, along with the required equilibrium between people and nature, were thrown into disarray. The expansive suffering experienced is captured in the recurrent trope of cattle. The loss of cattle is important because "cattle have been the natives' only capital, or the natives' 'bank,' as they truthfully call them" (Plaatjies 1982, 177). Furthermore, the cruelty to animals foregrounds the question of what it means to be human. For Plaatje, as Swart contends, it is clear that "compassion for animals was a significant move toward an objective compassion for the sufferings of other humans" (Swart 2014, 703).

The import of all the perplexing and paradoxical developments unleashed by colonial modernity is that whatever their configuration, they tested kinship in general and the articulation of the relation between the individual and the group in particular. Even if it is conceded that "in Bantu society it is always the group, seldom the individual, that is important" (Krige 1965, 36),[13] it remains equally relevant that the lineage system (particularly in its mapping of social production and relations) was based on the articulation between collective and individual senses of self. Ernest Mancoba was of the opinion that "comeradeship in Africa is determined by the Age-groups which hold together throughout life so that at no stage of one's existence does one find oneself alone. At the same time one does not lose individual freedom of action and initiative" (reproduced in Miles 1994, 93).

Kwame Gyekye (1987) has correctly observed that "the concept of communalism in African social thought is often misunderstood, as is the place of the individual in the communal social order," (154) and he has elaborated one of the most persuasive responses to such misunderstandings. It is not surprising that the relationship between self and group in Ubuntu has led to similar misreadings of Ubuntu and charges of communalism in it.[14]

Drawing on his knowledge of communalism in Akan philosophy, Gyekye (1987) suggests that the "intricate web of social relationships" (157) that inform communalism are structured in ways that privilege the assumption that "the success and meaning of the individual's life depend on identifying oneself with the group. This identification is the basis of the reciprocal relationship between the individual and the group" (156). Gyekye suggests that at the core of disagreement is the tendency to conflate and confuse the key differences between the idea of the individual and the exercise of individuality and agency in communal society and the Western understanding and practice of *individualism* and the rights of the individual.[15] The emphasis on communalism in Akan thought, Gyekye argues, "does not do so to the detriment of individuality. . . . [It] does not overlook individual rights, interests, desires, and responsibilities, nor does it imply the absorption of the individual into the 'communal will,' or seek to eliminate individual responsibility and accountability" (160–61). Therefore, "Akan social thought attempts to establish a delicate balance between the concepts of communality and individuality. Whether it succeeds in doing so in practice is of course another question" (161).

When and where an individuals experienced disaffection they could express their disagreement, amendment, opposition or rejection. This suggests that the "communal structure cannot foreclose the meaningfulness and reality of the quality of self-assertiveness which the person can demonstrate in his actions" (Gyekye 1992, 112).

"A Living Politics"

Notwithstanding the strategic possibilities for the individual that Gyekye notes, it is crucial to emphasize that precolonial African polities were riddled with horizontal and vertical divisions, differences, and conflicts that informed, among others, age, gender, lineage, and clan relations.[16] The ethos of Ubuntu is but one social ideal for negotiating individual and collective tensions and contradictions. The challenges to its realization precede conquest, but there is no doubt in the perspectives of early African intellectuals that colonial modernity compounded the limits and possibilities of its achievement even at the level of the political imaginary and moral imagination. Then, and now, the limits and possibilities of Ubuntu extend beyond its possible historical, cultural, or philosophical veracities or postulations and whose political implications (especially between the potentialities of conservatism and egalitarianism) can be pursued, deferred, or obfuscated either theoretically or politically. One of Ubuntu's key litmus tests, then and now, is the status and treatment of women. In this regard, an apposite difficulty resides in reconciling the contending expectations and claims of traditional kinship and conjugal relations informed by Christian tenets and ideas of the nuclear family. Ato Quayson (2000), reflecting on the complex entanglements between kinship and nuclear families in urban areas, highlights why and how instances such as economic arrangements and life-cycle rituals play into a dualistic mode where the nuclear form dominates at home while the extended family holds sway when it comes to the performance of traditional rituals and customs. One end result of such bifurcated arrangements (or "contradictory modernity") is that the agency and rights of women as a social group are deeply limited. Quayson acknowledges the significance of the extended family and especially in African identity construction but correctly emphasizes that the extended family and its many rituals "from child betrothal practices to rituals of wife 'abductions' and rituals that women are exposed to after the death of spouses, actually conceal serious issues of coercion, consent and freedom" (Quayson 2000, 130). In South Africa, similar tensions and concerns about women's access to land, security of tenure, legal action, and inheritance are being undermined in the wake of attempts to bolster chiefs and traditional authorities through the passing of legislation about spousal and familial estates. As a result, legal actions are being pursued with regard to acts such as the Traditional Authorities Act, Traditional Courts Bill, and the Restitution of Land Rights Amendment Bill.

Undoubtedly, the accentuated sociopolitical crises that are typical of many postindependence states on the continent further call into question the kinds of claims that can be mounted under contemporary discourses of Ubuntu. Yet such tests are best moderated into appropriate perspectives and strategies if one remembers that Ubuntu was and is a metaphysical beacon and not a given. It gestures toward the possibility of communitarian relations and ethos; it does not presuppose them. In its proverbial formulation "it would be only a slight exaggeration to affirm that it is structured so as to be usable only here and in this particular place, and not elsewhere" (Jameson 1999, 179). Consequently, not only is it subject to specific and distinct moral and social elaborations and contradictions, but it can also serve widely different purposes for very different sociopolitical projects and constituencies. A refrain that underpins both the defenders and dismissers of

Ubuntu are the challenges presented by poverty, urbanity, and individualism. Yet since the idea of Ubuntu is premised on ethical conduct and moral equality that is not contingent on context and circumstance, some of its most profound progressive effects have been found among the poor and marginalized.

Mxolisi Khuleka, a mine worker,[17] started a vegetable garden to feed his family. Khuleka's garden became "the main source of food for him and his neighbours": "When the workers were not paid the first month, they saw the vegetables and wanted to buy them. I told them we are all in trouble, they could have them for free" (Monama 2014). Khuleka's evoking of the idea of Ubuntu, his generosity, itself a hope for possible future reciprocity, is a profound attestation to Ubuntu's moral presence and power. Similarly, the struggles and ideologies of Abahlali base Mjondolo (a social movement formed by shack dwellers in 2006 in KwaZulu-Natal) are instructive. The participants' understanding of their purpose is farsighted: "For us the most important struggle is to be recognized as human beings" (Zikode 2006, 7). This demand is not sought as sociopolitical benevolence or largesse from the state or the upper classes but one that is informed by their "cultural beliefs. It is common sense that everyone is equal, that everyone matters, that the world must be shared" (Zikode 2009, 34). This view is buttressed by two further principles. The first is the insistence on the moral equality of persons: the "full and real equality of everyone without exception" (Zikode 2009, 39). The second is the acknowledgment of "the universal spirit of humanity. Obviously this starts with one human life. We know that if we do not value every human life then we would be deceiving ourselves if we say that there is a community at all" (40). It is on the foundation of these two principles that *Abahlali* grasp their own responsibilities and commitment and to advocate a very new spirit of Ubuntu as

> the spirit of humanity . . . the understanding of what is required for a proper respect of each person's dignity. . . . Our movement is formed by different people, all poor people but some with different beliefs, different religious backgrounds. But the reality is that most people start with the belief that we are all created in the image of God, and that was the earliest understanding of the spirit of humanity in the movement. Here in the settlements we come from many places, we speak many languages. Therefore we are forced to ensure that the spirit of humanity is for everyone. We are forced to ensure that it is universal. . . . From this it follows that we cannot allow division, degradation— any form that keeps us apart. On this point we have to be completely inflexible. On this point we do not negotiate. (Zikode 2009, 37–38)

Consistent with such nuanced and radical readings of their humanity and class position, *Abahlali* have been active and vocal in their criticism of xenophobia and refuse to simply explain it as a manifestation of the struggle for scarce resources among the poor, as many analysts prefer to do:

> It is acceptable for everyone in the world to live freely without boundaries, without any colour or any other restrictions. Obviously if you were to talk about a just society then it is the human culture, *ubuntu*—that makes a complete human being. The culture, where a person comes from, the colour—this does not count. There it was clear for Abahlali that we have to take a very strong side in defending human life—any human life, every human life. It is acceptable and legitimate that one person protects another. It is as simple as that. . . . This is a very big challenge for South Africans who have lived most of their life during apartheid, whose teaching was about boundaries, segregations—that not everyone was a human being. At the stage only whites were considered to be human. (Zikode 2009, 43)

In the arts, then, since its invocation by the likes of Soga, Ubuntu is rarely evoked as some primordial essence, a changeless and immemorial culture or the nostalgia for pastoral innocence and bliss. In the articles and the literature where the idea of Ubuntu is evoked, most often it marks a *loss* and, at times, a profoundly melancholic one at that, a guiding light that flickered dimly at the best of times. In the sound bites of today's black political elite, it may be commodified and in political science it may present itself as a critique of whiteness, but in much of black intellectual art and intellectual traditions, it is a cutting self-reflexive observation on the limits of our selves and our human potentials. It is also important to acknowledge that its current crisis of legitimacy—between its intention and realization—is no different from those faced by other concepts and ideologies in contemporary society. For example, with regard to liberalism's and rights activists' often marshaled disenchantment with communitarianism, I am inclined to agree with Masolo's conclusion that the critique of liberal individualism in contemporary African thought is "not a rejection of the value of individuality; rather, it merely envisages an alternative way of pursuing it in the human community." Furthermore, the criticisms that African thinkers have leveled against individualism "compare well with [Alasdair] MacIntyre's (1984), [Charles] Taylor's and [John] Keke's (1997) critiques of the Western liberal idea of autonomy as a failure and an escape from having to address the prevalence of evil" (Masolo, 2003, 495–96).

The notion of Ubuntu, then, is an ethos aimed at negotiating the respective needs and responsibilities of personal and communal imperatives, in all their permutations, and at achieving desirable consequences.[18] This requires the interpellation (in the Althusserian sense of being 'hailed' into being as a possible subject (Althusser 2001, 116–19) into at least two (or for our purposes) identitarian categories: those of the self and group in the ontological sense. In other words, individual persons grasp their senses of self in relation to their identifying with specific norms, practices, and attributes (glossed as culture) that define a collective community (lived through kinship), both deeply conceptualized and experienced through the (desired) ideas of being human and of humanity (not in the biological senses). The contingent achievement of reciprocity, compassion, and humaneness are at the center of the possible conferment of personhood.

The subtle and profound ethos of Ubuntu lies in its pointed insight that the greater good is contingent not on the straightforward privileging of the welfare of the individual or the group but rather on the invocation of a very distinct moral order that includes but supersedes the interests of particular individuals or groups. In some ways, it is analogous to the relationship between players in a jazz group. Players are valued for their soloing, but the true measure of their individual contribution is assessed in relation to how it blends with and enhances the composition and the unit.[19] Mancoba perceived a similar relation among dancers. He remarked, in an interview with Miles, that "dance is a symbol of you as individual and you as individual belonging to the organic whole. . . . You feel all alone and yet you feel part of the whole. All you have to do is to survive and live on this earth" (reproduced in Miles 1994, 56).

Ubuntu is a moral template that invites us to strive, measure, and experience good in our potential to be empathetic, kind, and compassionate with others, in short, that our humanness is primarily affirmed and present in the empathy with and treatment of others, especially those who are less fortunate than we.

Notes

1. For a representative sample, see Mbeki (1998) and Makgoba (1999).
2. Coplan (1994) regards orature as an inadequate appellation and prefers auriture: "What 'orature' does not overcome . . . is the conceptual separation of verbal, sonic, and rhythmic elements of expression, a separation uncharacteristic of African performance. . . . Additionally, 'auriture' places emphasis on the ears of the hearers, who include both

performer and audience, and hence, properly, on the intended and experienced aesthetic transaction between all participants in a performance event" (8–9).

3. For more extensive discussions, see Kaschula, "Contextual Analysis," Maake, "'I Sing," and Maake, "Praise, Politics, Performance," all in Attwell and Attridge (2012).

4. For discussions of the archives, see Wright (1996); Cobbing (1988); and Hamilton (1995, 2011).

5. The poem was published in *Imwo* on December 3, 1891.

6. See Gyekye (1987), chapter 2, for a fuller discussion of this argument and also N. K. Dzobo (1987, 112), and Leshoai (1977).

7. Key texts in this debate include Hountondji (1996); Wiredu (2004); Appiah (1992); Masolo (1994); and Gyekye (1987).

8. It is not surprising that Nyembezi (1974, 51) includes the same proverb in his list as "*Unyaw' alunampumulo* / The foot has no nose."

9. On the lineage system, see Guy (1982), chapters 1 and 2, and Bonner (1983), chapters 1 and 2.

10. On the importance of cattle, see Beinart (1982), chapters 1and 2; Guy (1982), 23–27, and "The Destruction and Reconstruction of Zulu Society," 170–71.

11. Influential texts on the topic include Wolpe (1972) and Legassick (1974).

12. See also Harries (1982) and Bonner (1980).

13. According to Molema (1963, 115), "The village was a co-operative society between whose members inter-dependence was a *sine qua non*. . . . In this tribal union there was real brotherhood and the nearest approach to social and economic equality. . . . In the Bantu tribal system, services were not paid for, nor did anybody expect it. While there was food anywhere in the village or tribal domain, nobody need starve, for the rich gave freely to the needy, hardly recognising that they were giving alms anymore than the poor imagined themselves objects of charity. . . . Individualism, as understood in the Western World, could not thrive." Molema finds affinities between Bantu moral conduct, Rousseau's conception of the ideal social compact, and Montesquieu's ideas on politeness; see Molema (1963, 116, 134, and 136).

14. For a snapshot of local debates, see Metz (2011) and, in response, Oyowe (2013).

15. For a prescient overview of these questions, see Masolo (2003).

16. Zikode (2009) understands "a living politics" in the following terms: "we are all human beings and so our needs are all, one way or another, similar. A living politics is not a politics that requires formal education—a living politics is a politics that is easily understood because it arises from our daily lives and the daily challenges that we face" (34).

17. Khuleka was one of the participants in the five-month strike that led to the August 16, 2014, massacre of thirty-four mineworkers at Marikana by South African police.

18. Guy makes the salutary acknowledgment that "to establish the connections between the productive process and ideology in a social formation, or between social being and consciousness in an individual, is the most formidable of the historian's task" and, often, that empirical resources are inadequate (117–18). See Guy (1980), 10–11.

19. In a different but still evocative context, Jameson (1999) draws on André Jolles's description of metaphysical proverbs as reminiscent of an emblem. The emblem "does not incorporate the meaning of the whole in the mode of its content, and of the whole *qua* whole, but rather, dramatizes the way in which meaning of this whole can be grasped only as a coexistence of distinct unities" (179).

References

Althusser, Louis. 2001. *Lenin and Philosophy and Other Essays.* Translated by Ben Brewster. New York: Monthly Review Press.

Appiah, Anthony K. 1992. *In My Father's House: Africa in the Philosophy of Culture.* New York: Oxford University Press.

Attwell, David, and Derek Attridge, eds. 2012. *The Cambridge History of South African Literature.* Cambridge: Cambridge University Press.

Beinart, William. 1982. *The Political Economy of Pondoland 1860 to 1930.* Johannesburg: Ravan.

Boesak, Allan. 1984. *Black and Reformed: Apartheid, Liberation and the Calvinist Tradition.* Johannesburg: Skotaville.

Bonner, Phillip. 1980. "Classes, the Mode of Production and the State in Pre-colonial Swaziland." In *Economy and Society in Pre-Industrial South Africa*, edited by Shula Marks and Anthony Atmore, 80–101. London: Longman.

———. 1983. *Kings, Commoners and Concessionaires: The Evolution and Dissolution of the Nineteenth-Century Swazi State.* Johannesburg: Ravan.

Cobbing, Julian. 1988. "A Tainted Well: The Objectives, Historical Fantasies, and Working Methods of James Stuart, with Counter Argument." *Journal of Natal and Zulu History* 11:115–54.

Comaroff, Jean, and John L. Comaroff. 1991. *Of Revelation and Revolution: Christianity, Colonialism, and Consciousness in South Africa.* Chicago: University of Chicago Press.

Coplan, David B. 1994. *In the Time of the Cannibals: The Word Music of South Africa's Basotho Migrants.* Johannesburg: Witwatersrand University Press.

Diop, Cheikh A. 1991. *Civilization or Barbarism: An Authentic Autobiography.* Translated by Yaa-Lengi M. Ngemi. New York: Lawrence Hill.

Doke, Clement M., and Benedict W. Vilakazi. 1972. *Zulu-English Dictionary.* Johannesburg: Witwatersrand University Press.

Dzobo, N. K. 1987. "African Symbols and Proverbs as Sources of Knowledge." In *An Essay on African Philosophical Thought: The Akan Conceptual Scheme*, edited by Kwame Gyekye and Kwasi Wiredu, 73–84. Washington, DC: Council for Research in Values and Philosophy.

Finnegan, Ruth. 2007. *The Oral and Beyond: Doing Things with Words in Africa.* London: James Currey.

Grout, Lewis. 1893. *The IsiZulu: A Revised Edition of a Grammar of the Zulu Language.* Boston: American Board Commissioners for Foreign Missions.

Guy, Jeff. 1980. "Ecological Factors in the Rise of Shaka and the Zulu Kingdom." In *Economy and Society in Pre-Industrial South Africa*, edited by Shula Marks and Anthony Atmore, 102–19. London: Longman.

———. 1982. *The Destruction of the Zulu Kingdom.* Johannesburg: Ravan.

Gyekye, Kwame. 1987. *An Essay on African Philosophical Thought: The Akan Conceptual Scheme.* Cambridge: Cambridge University Press.

Gyekye, Kwame, and Kwasi Wiredu, eds. 1992. *Person and Community: Ghanaian Philosophical Studies.* Washington, DC: Council for Research in Values and Philosophy.

Haire, Karen, and Daniel S. Matjila. 2010. "The Cattle Motif in Sol T. Plaatje's Publications in English: Re-storying the African and Batswana Sensibilities." *Journal of Black Studies* 41:207–17.

Hamilton, Carolyn. 1995. "'The Character and Objects of Chaka': A Reconsideration of the Making of Shaka as Mfecane Motor." In *The Mfecane Aftermath: Reconstructive Debates in Southern African History*, edited by Carolyn Hamilton, 183–211. Johannesburg: Witwatersrand University Press; Scottsville, S. Afr.: University of Natal Press.

———. 2011. "Backstory, Biography, and the Life of the James Stuart Archive." *History in Africa* 38:319–41.

Harries, Patrick. 1982. "Kinship, Ideology and the Nature of Pre-colonial Labour Migration: Labour Migration from the Delagoa Bay Hinterland to South Africa, up to 1895." In *Industrialisation and Social Change in South Africa: African Class Formation, Culture and Consciousness 1870–1930*, edited by Shula Marks and Richard Rathbone, 142–66. London: Longman.

Hountondji, Pauline J. 1996. *African Philosophy: Myth and Reality*. Bloomington: Indiana University Press.

Jameson, Fredric. 1999. *Brecht and Method*. London: Verso.

Jordan, Archibald C. 1973. *Towards an African Literature: The Emergence of Literary Form in Xhosa*. Berkeley: University of California Press.

Kagame, Alexis. 1989. "The Problem of 'Man' in Bantu Philosophy." *Journal of African Religion and Philosophy* 1 (1): 35-40.

Katz, Naimi, and David M. Kemnitzer. 1985. "Kinship" in *A Dictionary of Marxist Thought*, edited by Tom Bottomore, Laurence Harris, V. G. Kiernan, and Ralph Miliband, 251–54. Oxford, UK: Blackwell.

Kresse, Kai. 2007. *Philosophising in Mombasa: Knowledge, Islam and Intellectual Practice on the Swahili Coast*. Edinburgh: Edinburgh University Press.

Krige, Eileen J. 1965. *The Social System of the Zulus*. Pietermaritzburg, S. Afr.: Shuter and Shuter.

Legassick, Martin. 1974. "South Africa: Capital Accumulation and Violence." *Economy and Society* 3: 253–91.

Leshoai, Bob. 1977. "The Nature and Use of Oral Literature." *New Classic* 4 (1): 1–11.

Makgoba, Malegapuru W., ed. 1999. *African Renaissance*. Sandton, S. Afr.: Tafelberg.

Mancoba, Ernest. 2010. "An Interview with Hans Ulrich Obrist." *Nka: Journal of Contemporary African Art* 18:373–84.

Marks, Shula, and Anthony Atmore, eds. 1980. *Economy and Society in Pre-Industrial South Africa*. London: Longman.

Marks, Shula, and Richard Rathbone, eds. 1982. *Industrialisation and Social Change in South Africa: African Class Formation, Culture and Consciousness 1870–1930*. London: Longman.

Masolo, Dismas A. 1994. *African Philosophy in Search of Identity*. Bloomington: Indiana University Press.

———. 2003. "Western and African Communitarianism: A Comparison." In *A Companion to African Philosophy*, edited by Kwasi Wiredu. London: Oxford, 483–98.

Matthews, Z. Keodirelang. 1934. *Bantu Law and Western Civilization in South Africa: A Study in the Clash of Cultures*. Master's thesis, Yale University.

Mbeki, Thabo. 1998. *Africa: The Time Has Come.* Houghton, S. Afr.: Tafelberg.

Mbiti, John S. 1969. *African Religions and Philosophy.* London: Heinemann.

Metz, Thaddeus. 2011. "Ubuntu as a Moral Theory and Human Rights in South Africa." *African Human Rights Law Journal* 11 (2): 532–55.

Mieder, Wolfgang. 1993. *Proverbs Are Never Out of Season: Popular Wisdom in the Modern Age.* New York: Oxford University Press.

Miles, Elza. 1994. *Lifeline Out of Africa: The Art of Ernest Mancoba.* Cape Town: Human and Rousseau, 1994.

Molema, S. M. (1920) 1963. *The Bantu Past and Present: An Ethnographical and Historical Study of the Native Races of South Africa.* Cape Town: Struik.

Monama, Tebogo. 2014. "Miner's Veggie Garden Kept Him Alive." *The Star*, June 25. https://www.iol.co.za/news/south-africa/north-west/miners-veggie-garden-kept-him-alive-1708913.

Mudimbe, Valentine Y. 1988. *The Invention of Africa: Gnosis, Philosophy and the Order of Knowledge.* Bloomington: Indiana University Press.

Ngubane, Harriet. 1977. *Body and Mind in Zulu Medicine: An Ethnography of Health and Disease in Nyuswa-Zulu Thought and Practice.* London: Academic.

Nyembezi, C. L. Sibusiso. 1974. *Zulu Proverbs.* Johannesburg: Witwatersrand University Press.

Oyowe, Anthony O. 2013. "Strange Bedfellows: Rethinking Ubuntu and Human Rights in South Africa." *African Human Rights Law Journal* 13 (1): 1–22.

Plaatje, Solomon T. 1916. *Sechuana Proverbs with Literal Translations and Their European Equivalents.* London: Kegan Paul, Trench, Trübner.

Quayson, Ato. 2000. *Postcolonialism: Theory, Practice or Process?* Cambridge, UK: Polity.

Roberts, Charles. 1902. *An English-Zulu Dictionary with the Principles of Pronunciation and Classification Fully Explained.* London: Kegan Paul, Trench, Trübner.

Rubusana, Walter B., ed. 1911. *Zemk'inkomo Magwalandini.* Frome–Somerset, UK: Butler and Tanner.

Sanders, Mark. 2002. *Complicities: The Intellectual and Apartheid.* Scottsville, S. Afr.: Natal University Press.

Slater, Henry. 1980. "The Changing Pattern of Economic Relationships in Rural Natal, 1838-1914". In *Economy and Society in Pre-Industrial South Africa*, edited by Shula Marks and Anthony Atmore. London: Longman.

Soga, Tiyo. 1983. *The Journal and Selected Writings of the Reverend Tiyo Soga.* Edited by Donovan Willams. Translated by James R. Jolobe. Cape Town: A.A. Balkema.

Swart, Sandra. 2014. "'It Is as Bad to Be a Black Man's Animal as It Is to Be a Black Man'— The Politics of Species in Sol Plaatje's *Native Life in South Africa*." *Journal of Southern African Studies* 40 (4): 689–705.

Tempels, Placide. 1959. *Bantu Philosophy.* Translated by A. Rubbens. Paris: Présence africaine.

Tutu, Desmond. 1999. *No Future without Forgiveness.* Parktown, S. Afr.: Random House.

Vilakazi, Benedict W. 1935. "UBhambatha Ka Makhwatha." *Ikondlo KaZulu.* Johannesburg: Witwatersrand University Press.

Wauchope, Isaac W. 2008. *Selected Writings 1874-1916.* Edited and translated by Jeff Opland and Abner Nyamende. Cape Town: Van Riebeeck Society.

Webb, Colin De B., and John B. Wright. 1986. *The Stuart Archive.* Pietermaritzburg, S. Afr.: University of Natal Press; Durban, S. Afr.: Killie Campbell Africana Library.

Wiredu, Kwasi. 2004. "Knowledge as a Development Issue." In *A Companion to African Philosophy.* Edited by Kwasi Wiredu. Oxford, UK: Blackwell.

Wolpe, Harold. 1972. "Capitalism and Cheap Labour-Power in South Africa: From Segregation to Apartheid." *Economy and Society* 1:425–56.

Wright, John. 1996. "The Making of the *James Stuart Archive*." *History in Africa* 23:333–50.

Zikode, S'bu. 2006. "The Third Force." *Journal of Asian and African Studies* 41(1/2):185–89.

———. 2009. "To Resist All Degradations and Divisions: An Interview with Sibu Zonke." *Interface* 1 (2): 22–47.

BHEKIZIZWE PETERSON is Professor of African Literature at the University of the Witwatersrand, South Africa, and Director of Natives at Large Film and Television Production Company. His publications include *Missionaries and African Intellectuals: African Theatre and the Unmaking of Colonial Marginality*, *Zulu Love Letter: A Screenplay* and *Sol Plaatje's Native Life in South Africa: Past and Present* (coedited with Janet Remmington and Brian Willan). He is writer and producer of internationally acclaimed films, including *Fools*, *Zulu Love Letter*, and *Zwelidumile* (all directed by Ramadan Suleman) and *Born into Struggle*, *The Battle for Johannesburg*, and *Miners Shot Down* (all directed by Rehad Desai).

4

THE PHILOSOPHY OF UBUNTU AND THE NOTION OF VITAL FORCE

Niels Weidtmann

IN THE LAST TWO DECADES, THE CONCEPT OF Ubuntu has attracted the attention of scholars from a variety of disciplines, among them law, politics, sociology, and philosophy. This is particularly because the concept of Ubuntu was seen as capable of playing a significant role in the process of reconciliation after the end of apartheid in South Africa and in the aftermath of the first free elections in 1994. In this chapter, I will approach the concept of Ubuntu from a philosophical point of view. For this reason, I will start with some brief reflections on the meaning of philosophy in African traditions. Obviously, it cannot be claimed that there was something like a homogeneous understanding of philosophy in all African traditions.[1] With the development of interest in Western philosophy by African scholars of philosophy at the end of the twentieth century, however, it became clear that some features are common to many African philosophical traditions—features whose cultural affinity may have hindered the acknowledgment of genuine African philosophies by Western intellectuals. In order to better understand the meaning of the concept of Ubuntu, it may be helpful to reflect on some of these features.

Henry Odera Oruka from Kenya started a sage philosophy project in 1974. He interviewed sages, collected their sayings, and classified some of them as being philosophical. His tragic death in a car accident prevented him from completing his project.[2] Nevertheless, Odera Oruka has shown that a genuine African philosophy existed in the past. Although I do not agree with his distinction between what he calls "philosophical sages" versus "folk sages," I still believe that in sage philosophy we encounter the traditional form of African philosophy. The international community of philosophers has not acknowledged sage philosophy mostly for the following two reasons: First, sage philosophy has not been written down but has been passed on by word of mouth. Therefore, no critical distance has been built between the original sayings and philosophical reflection on them by later scholars of philosophy. Orally transmitted wisdom was either taken for granted or it was not handed down to the next generation anymore. In short, the orality of sage philosophy did not allow for the formation of a philosophical discourse on sayings across generations even though each generation of sages may have critically reflected on them and changed them in one way or the other. Second, the sayings of the sages were not meant to express timeless insights in an absolute truth. In fact, the idea of an absolute truth most probably had not even existed in African cultures at that time (this idea may even be a Western concept, as we will see later). Rather, sages helped people who came to them for advice. Therefore, the sayings of the sages may be understood as having been advice given to the folk by the elderly and wise men. That means that the sayings have been deployed in particular situations to which their meaning was restricted while they have not been meaningful in a general sense.

The fact that the meaning of the sayings is bound to particular situations on the one hand and the orality of traditional African philosophy on the other hand are two important reasons, among others, that are responsible for the persistent perception that Africa does not have a valuable tradition of philosophy in its own right. Up to today, many African philosophers continue to engage exclusively in the Western tradition. Since the beginning of twentieth century, a scholarly group has emerged that tries to point to the value of the African philosophical tradition even though it might not have known philosophical discourses comparable to those of the Western tradition. With black movements like the Harlem Renaissance in the 1920s in the United States and *Négritude* from the 1930s in France, and later also in Africa, a critical reflection began on the peculiarity and the rank of African thought as compared to that of the Western world. While nationalists like Senghor and Césaire were eager to emphasize the otherness of African thinking—Senghor even claimed that African thinking was intuitive while only Western thinking was logical—a group of African and Western researchers have analyzed African languages, and to some extent also traditional African daily life and oral traditions, in order to unravel what is particular in the worldview implicit in the languages and oral traditions. By this they meant to make explicit an African philosophy that has always existed and formed the African understanding of humanity and the world in the past but that has never been spelled out by genuine philosophers. That is to say, they have acknowledged the existence of a philosophical worldview guiding the life of traditional African societies but at the same time argued for the necessity to get this worldview rationally systematized by modern philosophers.

To differentiate these two meanings of philosophy, Claude Sumner (1974) has coined the notion of philosophy in the "strict" and in the "broad sense" (100). The philosophy that is implicit in languages and oral traditions does only make up a philosophy in the broad sense while the notion of philosophy in the strict sense is restricted to mean the critical analysis and rational systematization of such implicit thoughts. Therefore, many have argued that while there was no philosophy in the strict sense in the African past there very well may be found philosophy in the broad sense, which today can be analyzed in order to reformulate traditional African philosophy in the strict sense.

An early work that systematizes what was meant to be a philosophy implicit in language and expressed by the people in their daily life rather than in a philosophy in the strict sense is Placide Tempels's *Bantu Philosophy*, originally published in 1945 (Tempels 1969).[3] Tempels at the time was a Belgian missionary in the Congo. In his book, he uses an analysis of Bantu languages and draws on his own observations and the experiences he has had with the Bantu peoples. The key notion that he coined to pinpoint what he believed to be the essence of the Bantu worldview is the notion of "vital force." According to Tempels, everything in the universe is seen to be a vital force by the Bantu, no matter whether it is inanimate minerals or animate plants, animals, and human beings; even the dead, ghosts, gods, and the creator himself are thought to be vital forces: "Force is the nature of being, force is being, being is force" (Tempels 1969, 51). To find a force at the basis of ontology has some interesting consequences, the most prominent of which is that it allows a single being to exercise influence on all other beings of lesser vital force. By this, Tempels intends to explain the belief in something like an evil eye, which in the past has been thought to sometimes be responsible for sickness and even death. Nothing in the world happens without a vital force causing it. Vital forces can also increase or decrease, which, for instance, explains why the Bantu (as well as many other African peoples) respect an elder person more than other age groups; the vital force of a person most often increases with age. On the other hand, it is not possible for a vital force to vanish altogether. Therefore, even the ancestors are seen to be vital forces and, thus, remain part of the community of the living. An ancestor may even be a stronger vital force than living persons. According to Tempels, his systematization of the Bantu worldview around the notion of vital force is able to explain the lifeworld of the Bantu peoples, their rites, and their beliefs, which up to then were often interpreted as mythical and prelogical.

Tempels intends to show that the Bantu worldview can be translated into a system of philosophy in the Western sense, which then may well count as philosophy in a strict sense, to use Sumner's terminology once again. In order to explain why the Bantu peoples have not explicated their philosophical insights by themselves, however, Tempels had to assume a weaker intellectual ability among these peoples than among Western thinkers. This assumption should perplex us, to say the least, and make us cautious when reading Tempels's Bantu philosophy. In fact, being a missionary himself, Tempels at first intended to draw a picture of the Bantu worldview that fit well into Christianity. This intention becomes very obvious when he states that "the internal and intrinsic growth of being, in the way in which the Bantu teach it, is precisely what is taught by the Christian doctrine of Grace, founded on the assured rock of Revelation" (Tempels 1969, 185).

Tempels obviously has interpreted the Bantu worldview along his own—that is, Christian—categories. This must lead us to raise a couple of critical questions about his work. While Tempels seems to have been struck by the peculiarity of Bantu worldview and to have developed some respect for its own validity, in his attempt to systematize it and to write it down, he heavily relied on Western concepts. As a result, some contradictory statements occur in Tempels's outline of Bantu philosophy. He argues for a fluid continuum of vital force that allows for the increase of vital force at one point and its decrease at another, but he still speaks of the individuality of the vital forces that make up the particular essence of every single being. Do forces have individuality? How would that be compatible with the fluidity of vital force? Although Tempels realizes that vital force must not be interpreted as meaning just the same as being in the Western tradition but has to be understood dynamically, he nevertheless assumes a hierarchical system of vital forces, each belonging to a particular entity. The assumption of a hierarchical system, however, seems to contradict the dynamic character of vital force.

Paulin Hountondji has been one of the most critical voices on Tempels's work, as well as on many works of others who have followed Tempels in the attempt to find a philosophy implicit in African languages.[4] He has labeled these works "ethnophilosophy" because he argues that they make a philosophy out of ethnographical data (Hountondji 1983, 34). Thus, Hountondji claims that even though the ethnophilosophical works themselves may count as being philosophical, doing so does not change the fact that the traditional worldviews analyzed in these works remain unphilosophical and prelogical.[5] Odera Oruka (1981) has named philosophers like Hountondji and others "professional philosophers" because they restrict the notion of philosophy to the Western tradition as it is taught at the universities.

In the last two decades, however, the strict antithesis between "ethnophilosophy" and "professional philosophy" has at least partially been overcome by the attempt to reflect on African traditions and to make some of these traditions fruitful for an African approach to modern philosophy without arguing for the need to systematize traditional thoughts. The idea no longer is to unravel a philosophy implicit in languages and oral traditions but to reflect on African traditions in the light of modern philosophy as well as to reflect on contemporary philosophy against the background of African traditions. In the context of this discourse between tradition and modernity, which intends to generate something like a genuine African voice in philosophy, the concept of Ubuntu seems to be particularly interesting.

The notion of Ubuntu has become most prominent in the process of reflecting on precolonial traditions in South Africa in order to search for a concept common to a diversity of peoples in South Africa that may help to constitute a postcolonial and postapartheid South African community. When President Nelson Mandela set up a Truth and Reconciliation Commission (TRC) in 1996, he did so in the name of Ubuntu. Bishop Desmond Tutu, who presided over the TRC, also referred to Ubuntu continually in order to bid for the acceptance of the TRC by South African society. They did so because Ubuntu usually is interpreted as meaning the African understanding of humanness. The idea of the TRC has been that the disclosure of crimes that had been committed against South African people since the 1960s would allow for reconciliation. Victims in this process have been offered financial amends and offenders were guaranteed exemption from punishment. Although the international community has seen the TRC to be a great success (which is why Bishop Tutu was awarded the Noble Peace Prize) and for some time even as being a new prototype for solving conflicts, many South Africans have criticized it because they do not think the essence of Ubuntu has been realized in the work of the TRC. I will come back to this point later.

Ubuntu is a notion of Nguni languages, which are widespread in all southern parts of Africa (Ramose 1999).[6] It usually is translated as being the African understanding of humanity or humanness. The African understanding of humanity, in turn, usually is seen to be based on the particular meaning and importance that is given to the community in all African societies. Ramose, who has published intensively on the notion of Ubuntu (for example, Ramose 1999 and 2002), interprets the concept of Ubuntu from three proverbs, the first of which is saying that a human being becomes fully human only by its relations to other human beings (Ramose therein follows Samkange and Samkange 1980, who were first in explaining Ubuntu by means of these proverbs).[7] The proverb, which Shutte (1990) cited first and which has been recited in this context ever since in order to point out the African understanding of community: "Umuntu ngumuntu ngabantu" which can be translated as "a person is a person through other persons" (Shutte 1990 and 1993, 46). The other two proverbs Ramose refers to in order to illustrate the meaning of Ubuntu are closely related to the first one. The second says that the well-being of others is more valuable and more important than personal wealth, and the third claims that the king is given his authority by the people. It can easily be seen by these explanations of the meaning of Ubuntu that the notion does have a normative character. Ubuntu says what humanity should be and how human beings should act in order to become human in the full sense of the word.

The communal understanding of humanity that is linked to Ubuntu has often been contrasted with the problematic Western concept of competitive individualism. This contrast has been challenged by both Western and African philosophers. Kwame Gyekye (1997), for instance, has pointed out that while the community indeed is of particular importance to all African societies, nevertheless, a strong value on individuality has always existed as well. By the same token, Heinz Kimmerle (2007) reminds us of the importance that the community level has in Western societies as well. A prominent example may be the idea of human rights, which goes back to the Virginia Declaration of Rights in 1776 and which, in light of crimes committed against humanity during World War II, particularly by the German Nazis, has led to the formulation of the Universal Declaration of Human Rights in 1948. The idea of human rights is based on the belief that all human beings are of the same value and belong to a universal human community. From this belief a few normative demands may be deduced (even though such demands are not part of the declaration itself), such as the respect for others, the obligation to help people in need, the responsibility for children and elder people, and so forth. It is quite close to what sometimes is claimed to constitute particular African values. Thus, it is not correct to understand African societies as community-based and Western societies as based on individuality only. Rather, individual and community seem to coexist in African societies in a way that guarantees the community a more prominent position than it holds in Western societies. Therefore, in order to really understand what Ubuntu is all about, we first need to understand the relation of individuals to the community in African societies.

In what follows, I will briefly discuss the way in which the individual and the community are related to one another in African societies, taking Wiredu's plea for "consensus democracy" as an example. Wiredu argues for a nonparty system of democracy because it implies the chance to realize consensus (Wiredu 1996).[8] He explicitly argues not only against the multiparty-system as it is practiced by the West but also against the one-party system as it was practiced by some African leaders, such as Julius Nyerere in Tanzania and Kenneth Kaunda in Zambia once their countries had become independent. According to Wiredu, the one-party system has been corrupted and misused in order to ensure the power of a single ethnic group.

For the concept of consensus, Wiredu refers to the African tradition in which decisions usually have been based on consensus. By drawing on this tradition, Wiredu and others intend to revive and strengthen democracy in Africa (Wiredu 1996; Wamba-dia-Wamba 1992 and 1997). In traditional societies, each lineage sent its head as a representative to the council of a village; the councils of all the villages in a region sent representatives to the regional council, and all regional councils sent representatives to the national council. Representation, therefore, has been organized along regional lines rather than along political parties. According to Wiredu, this has had the advantage that councilors represented communities of people who shared daily life together rather than interest groups, as in the case of a party system—though, at some levels of representation, members of these communities in fact may have been only loosely related and may have shared little in their daily life. Within each council, decisions have been made by consensus. Each council had its chairman, but he did not have the power to make his decisions against the will of the councilors. So, how was consensus achieved?

In Western societies, we know of at least two ways in which a group of people may reach consensus:

The first is by compromise; each person gives up part of her position in order to get a little closer to the positions of others; this process has to be continued until all members agree or compromise. So, by compromise a common position may be found that represents something like the smallest common denominator of all positions.

The other way is described in discourse theory as it has been outlined by Karl-Otto Apel, Jürgen Habermas, and others (Habermas 1987).[9] In their theory, Apel (1988) and Habermas argue that people searching for a common decision should continue discussing the best decision until someone comes up with an argument that everyone believes to be true and that thereby overrides any previously discussed position. The measurement by which people value all the various arguments and finally agree on the true one is the reasonability of these arguments. As long as all people engaging in the discourse are rational human beings, they will end up with an argument that they all consider to be true. This then is a consensus.

Wiredu, however, is referring to something else. The consensus he has in mind still allows for differences among the views of individual people. But he does not intend a compromise either. Wiredu explicitly states "that ultimately the interests of all members of society are the same, although their immediate perceptions of those interests may be different" (Wiredu 1996, 185). What is it that is responsible for the fact that these interests are shared by all members of the society? Eze (1998) has suggested religious and mythical narratives to have constituted common interests in traditional societies. I do not think that this is the whole story, however. Rather, we need to have a look at the way a consensus has been found in traditional societies.[10] In an attempt to achieve consensus, the individual members of a community came together and discussed a problem until they found an agreement and were able to speak with one voice. Each member of the community was allowed to contribute to the discussion, the young as well as the old, female as well as male. For sure, they have had different opinions, so that in the beginning each one spoke for his own interests. That, however, changed in the course of the discussion. During the discussion, individuals may have realized that the problem they wanted to resolve did look different when viewed at the community level as opposed to the individual level. It is only then that a consensus could be found. Thus, even when a consensus was achieved at the level of the community, a multiplicity of different individual opinions remained.

But why did individual members of the community start arguing at the level of their individual opinion and end up standing for the interests of the community? The answer is very simple. During discussion, the communality becomes renewed and the community thereby reconstituted. In the process of the discussion, the disputing persons are reminded of all that makes up a community, which includes but is not limited to shared beliefs and values, as well as the common history represented by the ancestors. During the discussion, these values and beliefs not only come into mind again but are also adopted anew. Thus, the disputants do not just become aware of their community, but the community is revived and renewed in the process of the discussion. Ernest Wamba-dia-Wamba (1985, 40) therefore states, "La palabre est donc une *lutte* qui doit restaurer l'*unité* de la communauté." (The discussion is a fight that needs to restore the unity of a community.) Once the individuals start to view the problem at the community level, they accept new standards for the evaluation of arguments. Arguments that represent a broader communal view become stronger than those representing individual perspectives at this point of the discussion. That is the reason arguments referring to the common ancestors and thereby referring to the common history of that community may have a special force and appeal. This consideration is what led the people to appoint "the most senior, but non-senile, member of the lineage" as their representative at the council, as Wiredu reports (Wiredu 1996, 184). The most senior member of the lineage is able to represent the interests of the community better than any other member because of long experience within the community. Accordingly, starting from a multiplicity of individual opinions, to reach a consensus always requires the actual reconstitution (revival, renewal) of the community.

How does this review of consensus help us to understand Ubuntu? The way in which a consensus is achieved—that is, by the revival of the community—points to the fact that it is not correct to assume the community has a somehow higher ontological status than the individual. It is not the community in itself that forces consensus but rather the process of the renewal of that community in the discussion. The renewal allows the disputants to *experience* their belonging to a community anew during the process of discussion. The individual thereby makes the experience of being part of a life that transcends her own life; this experience may give her new power for her own life since her life becomes meaningful from being part of the community. If, on the contrary, the achievement of consensus was forced by the mere fact of the existence of the community in itself, then there would not be any need for discussion. Consensus is only achieved, however, after intense discussions. The process of consensus finding requires that each individual experiences himself as being reintegrated into and affirmed by the community.

Ubuntu does not refer to the particular high importance the community often seems to have in African societies, but rather it refers to the individual's experience in reintegrating into a greater community and sense of belonging to it. The reconstitution of the community is not restricted to the process of consensus finding but can be shown to be an important feature in all areas of African social life. In fact, the process of reconstituting the community is not even restricted to individuals reviving their social cohesions but also takes place at the level of the community itself. The community as a whole, from time to time, seeks to revive the connections it has with its ancestors and its yet unborn members as well. And, above all, the community strives for the renewal of its sense of community with the Supreme Being. In traditional African societies, such a renewal can be found in the ecstatic dances of healers and sorcerers in which they try to become possessed by goddesses who were seen to be part of the greater community. In fact, the overall striving for the renewal of any kind of communal level in order to experience the reinforcement of the individual by this community may well be understood as constituting the ecstatic moment of African societies. Ecstasy in this sense means reaching out for higher dimensions of human life, which at the same time make up deeper dimensions of reality. At least in traditional African societies, there has been a deep—if often experienced— feeling for the multidimensionality of human reality. My thesis thus is that the concept of Ubuntu refers to the experience of the multidimensionality of human reality rather than to the importance of community life in itself. On the contrary, the importance of community life that we find in African societies is a consequence of Ubuntu, but Ubuntu is not its origin. Also, the proverb saying that "a person is a person through other persons" may well be interpreted in the way I propose to understand Ubuntu here. A person is a person through other persons because only together can individual persons create (constitute) a new dimension of human reality.

While in Western philosophy reality is understood as being one universal context—that is, *the* world or *the* being—and while therefore Western philosophy strives to explore this context, the Ubuntu understanding may pay more attention to the multidimensionality of human reality. Ubuntu philosophy, therefore, may seek to realize this multidimensionality and to gain a deeper understanding of reality rather than to explore an abstract universal aspect. Western universal knowledge is powerful, but from an African perspective it might not be able to explain the reality of our life worlds. The universal context, that is, *the* world or *the* being, cannot be experienced because any experience has to be bound to real—and that means concrete—forms of life. From an African perspective, therefore, the relevance of the universal context for human life may be questioned and, as a consequence of this, also the coherence of the Western worldview may be questioned. How to bridge the gap between real human life worlds and the abstract universal context? This question even is raised in the Western world itself, for instance, with regard to the application of some technical developments to the life world. The development of new techniques is based on science and therefore it premises the Western understanding of reality as being one universal context. (I cannot outline the nexus of modern science and the understanding of universality here; the two of them have, however, jointly developed). The techniques are not used, however, in a universal context but only in a concrete life world. In fact, the application of techniques such as some biotechniques to the life world often is discussed quite controversially.

My thesis about the meaning of Ubuntu actually seems to be supported by the mere notion of Ubuntu itself. Although most often translated as meaning "humanness," literally it means something else. *Ntu* is an ending common to many Bantu languages, of which Nguni languages are part. It literally means "vital force"; as such, it is found in the word *muntu*, which means the human being (plural: *bantu*). *Ubu* is a prefix indicating generalization. *Ubuntu* thus refers to something like the generalization of vital force. Vital force, however, must not be understood in the way Tempels (1969) did but has to be seen in the context of experiencing the multidimensionality of human reality through a continuous revival of community at all levels. Thus, the individual members of the community have to realize that their lived experiences are not restricted to their individual lives. The individuals may influence the community, but conversely, their own lives also depend on that of the community. Therefore, in the process of reconstituting (re-viving) the community, they become aware of the multidimensionality of their own being time and time again. In proportion to the well-being of the community, this experience may strengthen or weaken its individuals' well-being.

What Tempels (1969) describes as a force therefore has to be reformulated as meaning the concrete experience of the multidimensionality of human reality. The individual person experiences vital force when she takes part in the process of reconstituting (re-viving) the community. Vital force, however, is neither the essence nor the being of the individual person nor that of any other entity.

Let me go back to the beginning of this chapter and examine what follows from this understanding of Ubuntu in relation to the meaning of traditional African philosophy. In the beginning, I mentioned two factors responsible for the lack of recognition of "philosophical sagacity" as a genuine philosophy by the international community of philosophers. The first reason for that is the oral character of philosophical sagacity. In light of what I have tried to argue for in this chapter, the striving for experiencing the multidimensionality of human reality, the oral character of sagacity actually makes perfect sense. Philosophy in the sense just outlined does not explore the abstract universal world but seeks to realize the multidimensionality of human reality through experience. As a consequence, it does not express any universal truth but gives concrete expression on how to reconstitute (re-vive) yet another dimension of human reality. This already explains its situational character, which is the second element I mentioned as being responsible for the poor recognition philosophical sagacity has in Western philosophy. Finally, there is yet a third aspect; the sayings that make up philosophical sagacity are of communal value rather than of value as universal truth. In the Western understanding, they may therefore be taken to be less valuable, but not in an African perspective. Since the sayings are meant to help in reconstituting (re-viving) the community, they need to have been collected, found, invented, interpreted, selected, and transmitted within the context of the worldview of that community. It is of direct significance to that community that the traditional wisdom is handed down by the fathers and forefathers (or, in some cases, by mothers and grandmothers) of a given community to the next generation. If these sayings were not bound to a community, the wisdom would come from a different source and, therefore, have less authority to the community. Obviously, such wisdom would probably be of less force in the process of reconstituting (re-viving) a given community.

Finally, let me address the issue of the South African Truth and Reconciliation Commission once again and discuss what the understanding of Ubuntu presented in this chapter means for the evaluation of its success. Bishop Tutu as well as President Mandela referred to Ubuntu when setting up the TRC in 1996, as I have pointed out. If Ubuntu simply meant that the community in itself is of greater importance than the individual person in South African society, then reconciliation could never have taken place in the process of the TRC because the community of South African people in fact had been too deeply damaged by all the crimes from the decades before. But because Ubuntu means to strive to experience the multidimensionality of reality, it requires continual renewal of the multiple layers of communal levels. In the process of the TRC, disclosure of truth was thought to help in reconstituting the South African community, and this in turn was meant to allow reconciliation to take place. Thus, the idea was that reconciliation would take place as a result of the reconstitution of community but not the other way around.

I do think that this idea is right and may very well be articulated in reference to Ubuntu. Nevertheless, many South Africans are highly critical of the perceived success of the TRC. The main objection brought forth is that only very little truth has indeed been disclosed during the TRC. In particular, the responsibility of the former government of South Africa has not been scrutinized thoroughly; but also the fact that in many cases offenders have made only incomplete testimonies has caused frustration. But the most important point may yet be something else. The TRC was meant to ensure disclosure of crimes committed by whites and blacks alike, but the concept of Ubuntu is shared by black African peoples only. Thus, many white offenders just bought their way out of responsibility but showed no interest in the process of reconstituting South African community. This is not to say that white South Africans were not interested in a community with all peoples living together in South Africa, but rather that the TRC in their eyes did not bind them to the community but instead discharged them personally of their responsibility for crimes they had committed.

This is not just a problem of black and white cultures. The disclosure of truth may help in the process of reconstituting a community, but it probably does not help to constitute (create) a new community that up to that point never existed. The concept of Ubuntu points to the experience of the multidimensionality of human reality. For a community to be of relevance in this respect, therefore, it has to either be a community that has been part of a person's life in the past already or it has to be a community that is in the process of being created because its members are strengthening their relations in their daily lives. But it cannot be a community that by political logic is required to be part of that person's life in a futuristic sense. That probably also is one of the reasons ethnic groups still play an important role in almost all African societies, including the South African one. At least in the past, ethnic groups have constituted one of the multiple dimensions of human reality. Their relevance cannot be overcome by simply pointing to an abstract national community but only by other forms of communities that have become more and more important in their daily lives. This may at some point also include the national one.

These considerations point to the fact that the concept of Ubuntu may not always be all that harmonious. Since it is about realizing the multidimensionality of human reality as it can be experienced in the various communal levels of a person's life, there may in some cases occur tensions with communities that are not part of that person's life. The idea of a universal community integrating all these different communities, however, is a mere abstract concept. Ubuntu does not refer to an abstract concept like this but to the lived reality. The case of ethnic groups may be a special one, since ethnicity has deliberately been reinforced by colonialism. But Ubuntu, in any case, works only when it can rely on communal experiences realized in daily encounters.

Notes

1. Obviously there are many philosophical traditions in Africa that cannot and must not be reduced to a single understanding of philosophy.

2. For an introduction to this project, see Odera Oruka (1990). Odera Oruka in his lifetime has documented the sayings of at least one sage, Oginga Odinga (Odera Oruka 1992).

3. I have outlined Tempels's analysis of Bantu philosophy, as well as a critique thereon, elsewhere; my reflections on Tempels in this chapter mostly repeat that paper (Weidtmann 1998a).

4. For works that take an approach similar to that of Tempels, see, for example, Kagame (1956, 1976); Griaule (1965); Mbiti (1969); Ruch and Anyanwu (1981).

5. This view was (and still is) shared by many African philosophers since independence of most African countries in 1960. See, for instance, Wiredu (1980); Bodunrin (1984); Masolo (1994).

6. For the following, see Weidtmann (2016).

7. For a critique on Ramose, see Van Binsbergen (2001).

8. For an introduction to the philosophy of Wiredu, see Weidtmann (1998b).

9. For a comparison of African consensus theory with Western dicourse theory, see Ntumba (1989) and Bujo (1993). Graness (1998), in her comparison, particularly refers to Wiredu as well as Apel and Habermas.

10. For the following, I again rely on Weidtmann (1998a).

References

Apel, Karl-Otto. 1988. *Diskurs und Verantwortung. Das Problem des Übergangs zur postkonventionellen Moral*. Frankfurt, Germany: Suhrkamp.

Bodunrin, Peter O. 1984. "The Question of African Philosophy." In *African Philosophy: An Introduction*, 3rd ed., edited by Richard A. Wright, 1–23. Lanham, MD: University Press of America.

Eze, Emmanuel Chukwudi. 1998. "Demokratie oder Konsensus? Eine Antwort an Wiredu." *Polylog* 2:32–42.

Graness, Anke. 1998. "Der Konsensbegriff: Ein Vergleich der Bedeutung des Konsensbegriffs in Wiredus Konsensethik und der Diskursethik von Karl-Otto Apel und Jürgen Habermas." *Polylog* 2:22–31.

Griaule, Marcel. 1965. *Conversations with Ogotemmêli*. London: Oxford University Press.

Gyekye, Kwame. 1997. *Tradition and Modernity: Philosophical Reflections on the African Experience*. Oxford: Oxford University Press.

Habermas, Jürgen. 1987. *Theorie des kommunikativen Handelns*. 4th ed. 2 vols. Frankfurt, Germany: Suhrkamp.

Hountondji, Paulin J. 1983. *African Philosophy: Myth and Reality*. Bloomington: Indiana University Press.

Kagame, Alexis. 1956. *La philosophie bantu-rwandaise de l'être*. Brussels: Académie Royal des sciences coloniales.

———. 1976. *La philosophie bantu comparée*. Paris: Présence Africaine.

Kimmerle, Heinz. 2007. "Ubuntu and Communalism in African Philosophy and Art." In *Prophecies and Protest—Ubuntu in Glocal Management*, edited by Henk van den Heuvel, Mzamo Mangaliso, and Lisa van de Bunt, 79–92. West Lafayette, IN: Purdue University Press.

Masolo, Dismas A. 1994. *African Philosophy in Search of Identity*. Bloomington: Indiana University Press.

Mbiti, John S. 1969. *African Religions and Philosophy*. London: Heinemann.

Ntumba, Marcel Tshiamalenga. 1989. "Afrikanische Weisheit: Das dialektische Primat des *Wir* vor dem *Ich-Du*." In *Philosophie und Weisheit*, edited by Willi Oelmüller, 24–38. Paderborn, Germany: Schöningh.

Odera Oruka, Henry. 1981. "Four Trends in Current African Philosophy." In *Symposium on Philosophy in the Present Situation of Africa*, edited by Alwin Diemer, 1–7. Wiesbaden. Germany: Steiner.

———. 1990. *Sage Philosophy: Indigenous Thinkers and Modern Debate on African Philosophy*. Leiden, The Netherlands: Brill.

———. 1992. *Oginga Odinga: His Philosophy and Beliefs*. Sage Philosophy Series. Vol. 1. Nairobi.

Ramose, Mogobe B. 1999. *African Philosophy through Ubuntu*. Harare, Zimbabwe: Mond Books.

———. 2002. "The Philosophy of *Ubuntu* and *Ubuntu* as a Philosophy." In *Philosophy from Africa: A Text with Readings*, edited by Pieter H. Coetzee und Abraham P. J. Roux, 230–37. Oxford: Oxford University Press.

Ruch, Ernest A., and K. C. Anyanwu. 1981. *African Philosophy: An Introduction to the Main Philosophical Trends in Contemporary Africa*. Rome, Italy: Catholic Book Agency.

Samkange, Stanlake J. T., and Tommie M. Samkange. 1980. *Hunhuism or Ubuntuism: A Zimbabwe Indigenous Political Philosophy*. Salisbury, England: Graham.

Shutte, Augustine. 1990. "Umuntu Ngumuntu Ngabantu." *Philosophy and Theology* 5:39–54.

———. 1993. *Philosophy dor Africa*. Rondebosch, S. Afr.: UCT Press.

Sumner, Claude. 1974. *Ethiopian Philosophy*. Vol. 1, *The Book of the Wise Philosophers*. Addis Ababa, Ethiopia: Commercial Printing Press.

Tempels, Placide. 1969. *Bantu Philosophy*. Translated by Colin King. Paris: Présence Africaine.

Van Binsbergen, Wim M. J. 2001. "Ubuntu and the Globalisation of Southern African Thought and Society." *Quest* 15:53–89.

Wamba-dia-Wamba, Ernest. 1985. "La palabre comme pratique de la critique et de l'autocritique sur le plan de tout la communauté." *Journal of African Marxists* 7:35–50.

———. 1992. "Beyond Elite Politics of Democracy in Africa." *Quest* 6:28–42.

———. 1997. "Democracy *in* Africa and Democracy *for* Africa." In *Philosophy and Democracy in Intercultural Perspective*, edited by Heinz Kimmerle and Franz Martin Wimmer, 129–31. Amsterdam, Netherlands: Rodopi.

Weidtmann, Niels. 1998a. "A Critical Reflection on the Notion of 'Vital Force': African Philosophy in the Intercultural Dialogue." *Athanor Nero* 9 (1): 56–65.

———. 1998b. "Eine Einführung in das Denken von Kwasi Wiredu." *Polylog* 2:6–11.

———. 2016. *Interkulturelle Philosophie: Aufgaben—Dimensionen—Wege*. Tübingen, Germany: UTB.

Wiredu, Kwasi. 1980. *Philosophy and an African Culture*. Cambridge: Cambridge University Press.

———. 1996. "Democracy and Consensus: A Plea for a Non-Party Polity." In *Cultural Universals and Particulars: An African Perspective*, edited by Kwasi Wiredu, 182–90. Bloomington: Indiana University Press.

NIELS WEIDTMANN is Director of the interdisciplinary institute Forum Scientiarum at the University of Tübingen. His research interests are intercultural philosophy, phenomenology, hermeneutics, anthropology, and the philosophy of science. He is author of *Interkulturelle Philosophie: Aufgaben—Dimensionen—Wege* and editor of several book series and has published a wide range of articles. Weidtmann is a board member of the International Society of Intercultural Philosophy and editor of the online journal *Polylog*.

5

RETHINKING UBUNTU

Dirk J. Louw

"I AM BECAUSE WE ARE; AND SINCE WE ARE, therefore, I am"—this is the by now familiar aphorism expressing a traditional African ethic called Ubuntu. Culture-specific versions of this aphorism include *umuntu ngumuntu ngabantu* (Nguni) and *motho ke motho ka batho babang* (Sotho), both of which could be translated as "a person is a person through other persons." To be human means to be through other persons. Any other way of being would be "*in*human" in both senses of the word, that is, "not human" and "disrespectful of or even cruel to others." These, roughly, are the teachings—the descriptions and prescriptions—of Ubuntu (Mkhize 2008, 40).

The Ubuntu ethic has been hailed by many as the antidote for Africa's (and the world's) social ailments, chief of which disparity in the wake of apartheid (or apartheidlike) discrimination and oppression. For example, the interim constitution of the newly democratic Republic of South Africa boldly pointed out that "there is a need for understanding but not for vengeance, a need for reparation but not for retaliation, a need for *ubuntu* but not victimisation" (the interim constitution of the Republic of South Africa as cited by Louw 2006, 161). A winner of the Nobel Peace Prize, Archbishop Desmond Tutu, subsequently credited the "spirit of Ubuntu" for "the healing of breaches, the redressing of imbalances [and] the restoration of broken relationships" (Desmond Tutu as cited by Roche 2003, 27).

However, what seems too good to be true often is. In what follows, I will argue that Ubuntu is attended by controversies that may disqualify it as a vehicle for the successful negotiation of challenges facing Africans today.

Some of these trials exist independently of the Ubuntu ethic, while others are generated by it. I hope to show that a critical and creative revaluation of the Ubuntu ethic may aid Africans in meeting the challenges effectively.

Does Ubuntu Exist?

It stands to reason that my deliberations would make sense only if Ubuntu in fact exists. Differently put, the very existence of Ubuntu has proved to be a bone of contention and, for that reason, is the first challenge for those who wish to muster its resources. *Ubuntu* means "humanity," "humanness" or "humaneness." It articulates an identification with and compassion for others: caring, sharing, warmth, and understanding (Metz 2010, 51–52). These are often not the first activities or attitudes that spring to mind when one reflects on Africa. On the contrary, conflicts still scar the continent and corruption, mismanagement, self-enrichment, disease, and poverty seem ever present. Do Africans in fact adhere to Ubuntu or at least aspire to do so? The question deserves more attention than can be afforded here. The following remarks, however, seem in order.

First, to claim that Ubuntu exists is not necessarily to claim that the identification and compassion that it encapsulates obtains or has obtained always and everywhere in African societies. Of course, it did not and does not. Only some Africans adhere to Ubuntu and they do so only some of the time (Metz 2010, 50). In fact, a confirmation of the existence of Ubuntu often follows only from a willingness to focus on apparently insignificant acts of identification with others and of caring and sharing (see Jansen 2011). Second, though one may doubt the existence of Ubuntu as a fully lived reality, one can hardly deny its existence as a prominent concept, narrative, or myth in Africa and certainly southern Africa. To call the Ubuntu ethic a myth is not to deny its factual truth—though the word *myth* is often used in this sense. The word *myth* as used here depicts that the Ubuntu ethic as an enduring story that—irrespective of its factual truth—inspires morally and reveals the meaning (i.e., value, relevance, or significance) of life to those who participate in it, that is, those who contribute to its telling and retelling (Jordaan 2009). Third (or to put the first and second remarks differently), before one embarks on the denial or affirmation of the existence of something, it would serve one well to engage in relevant conceptual analyses. Exactly what is being denied or affirmed? In this case: exactly what does one mean by *Ubuntu* and *exist*? Fourth, one would do well to speak of Ubuntu primarily as an ethical ideal. Though inspiring instances of compassionate caring already exist, Ubuntu remains something that still needs to be realized (Shutte 2001, 32–33). And, finally, despite my affirmation of the existence of Ubuntu, I concur with Ronald Nicolson (2008a, 6), who warns that "the crises in Africa do mean that we must be careful not to overstate the hold that traditional African ethics have in practice in African society."

Nicolson's warning assumes that the enhancement of traditional African ethics would curb the crises in Africa just alluded to, namely, the moral crises of corruption and self-enrichment (among others), and the growing list of the effects thereof: conflicts, mismanagement, disease, poverty, and other disastrous outcomes. But, as Nicolson concedes, the issue is far more complex. Some may, for instance, argue that these crises obtain precisely because of the hold that traditional African ethics have on Africans. "Are some aspects of traditional African culture—male hegemony, respect for elders and chiefs, the idea that a fortunate individual must share his or her fortune with the wider family in assisting them with jobs—not tantamount to sexism, gerontocracy, authoritarianism, nepotism, and the like?" (Nicolson 2008a, 8). Moreover, could what appears to be immoral or illegal to Western eyes not be valued differently in a traditional African context? Does, for example, "receiving gifts by ruling politicians amount to corruption, or is [it] merely part of African respect for those in authority?" (Nicolson 2008a, 2). The need to critically assess traditional African ethics (including the Ubuntu ethic) clearly exists.

Bipolar Thinking

"Ubuntu and power sharing" has become a favorite conference theme in South Africa, as one would expect from a democracy still finding its feet. In light of the understanding of Ubuntu developed in the foregoing, however, it is strictly speaking misleading to speak of Ubuntu *and* power sharing and more correct to speak of Ubuntu *as* power sharing. Ubuntu *is* power sharing, it constitutes the sharing of power. On this score, the aphorism "a person is a person through other persons" translates as "a person is a person through sharing his or her power (that is, the space that allows the enactment of his or her subjectivity[1]) with other persons." In fact, in a sense, the question "What is Ubuntu?" already constitutes a sharing of—or, more precisely, a struggle for—power. This becomes apparent once the question is understood, as Leonhard Praeg (2008) does, as a political act, and a paradoxical one, at that: "political" because through asking it "the African subject seeksfreedom from a past (and present) represented by [Western] oppression and (neo)colonialism" (371). Paradoxical because an ethic of "*interdependence* is invoked to represent [Africa's] *independence*," that is, "ubuntu is being re-appropriated for political ends radically at odds with what it is taken to mean" (372, emphasis by Praeg). The Dutch political scientist Pieter Boele van Hensbroek (1999, 201) calls this "bipolar think-ing," that is, thinking that sets Africa (the one pole) up against the West (the other pole). As a result, claims Boele van Hensbroek (1999, 201), bipolar thinking blinds its participants to "facts and the diversity of . . . options."

This certainly rings a bell. In a 2009 radio interview, the former presi-dent of South Africa, Thabo Mbeki, described the power-sharing deal struck in Zimbabwe as an "African" solution and as an illustration of why "African" leaders should not listen to "Western" critics but approach mat-ters in an "African" way. Some (see for example Jackson 2009, 14) may argue that this is a classic example of bipolar thinking that blinded its subject to facts (such as that President Mugabe and Zimbabwe African National Union Patriotic Front [Zanu PF] in fact lost the election in March 2008 and that they did so in spite of assaults on Movement for Democratic Change [MDC] supporters) and to alternative options (such as pressurizing pres-ident Mugabe to accept the election results). Whatever the case may be, Boele van Hensbroek (1999) argues for a move away from "the bipolar logic that is inherent in the models of thought that have dominated African po-litical thought in the last 150 years" (200) toward what he calls "discursive conceptions of democracy" (201). "Discursive conceptions of democracy" involve "a problem shift from issues situated between Africa and the West toward issues that are internal to Africa" (200).

Thus understood, bipolar thinking may not only facilitate a stifling vic-tim mentality but also feed the false dichotomies of identity politics, such as the exhausted West (individualistic, cold) versus Africa (communalistic, compassionate) division. These dichotomies ignore the variety of ways in which Africa and the rest of the world (including the West) overlap. They also ignore the internal plurality of these supposedly different ways of being and thinking. Neither "the West" nor "Africa" signifies ahistorical, homo-geneous entities (Van Niekerk 1999, 68).

Still, divorcing oneself from bipolar thinking might be more difficult than Boele van Hensbroek foresees. After all, as Praeg (2008) rightly re-marks, in finding an authentic identity, "we proceed by comparison and negation in a way that is inevitable as it is inadequate" (374). In this sense, so-called internal African issues are never simply internal to Africa.

Consensus or Hegemony?

Ubuntu underscores the importance of agreement. "The communal ethos of African culture," Mogobe Ramose observes, "placed a great value on solidarity, which in turn necessitates the pursuit of unanimity or consensus not only in such important decisions as those taken by the highest political authority of the town or state, but also decisions taken by lower assemblies such as those presided over by the heads of the clan, that is, the councilors" (Mogobe Ramose cited in Eze 2008, 390). Many critics already pointed out, however, that the Ubuntu predilection for agreement is often exploited to *enforce* unanimity, thereby stifling creativity and innovation (see Sono 1994, 7). Which raises the question, Just how attainable is the agreement or consensus at which Ubuntu aims (see Louw 2006, 163)? Does it necessarily involve the oppression of otherness?

The challenge of Ubuntu ethics is in many respects the challenge of applying an ancient or premodern wisdom in a postmodern society. Postmodern society is deeply suspicious of Ubuntu's consensus principle, with its very different notions of solidarity. In a premodern sense, *solidarity* often means being inextricably and exclusively imbedded in or committed to one specific group (note, for example, the importance of initiation rites in traditional African societies—more about these rites later). In a postmodern sense, though, *solidarity* signifies, not permanent and exclusive membership of any particular group, but rather a complex and ever-changing multiplicity of partly overlapping, partly conflicting group memberships (Bouckaert 2001, 2; Eze 2008, 392). Are we witnessing, in Ubuntu as an effort to reach agreement or consensus, the resurfacing of outmoded and suspect cravings for sameness (Van der Merwe, 1996, 12; Ramose 2002a, 105, 106)?

The need to avoid hegemony confronts the proponents of Ubuntu with one of the most important challenges in this regard, namely, the challenge of affirming unity while valuing diversity, of translating "I am because we are" into "we are because I am." As such, it is the challenge of developing an emancipatory understanding of Ubuntu, an understanding that would effectively meet "the essential issue of politics formulated by Hannah Arendt as 'handling plurality'" (Boele van Hensbroek 1999, 201). Such an understanding of Ubuntu is highly reminiscent of Kwasi Wiredu's plea

for a "non-party polity" or "consensual democracy" (1998, 375; also see Ramose 2002a, 113). According to Wiredu, consensual democracy draws on
the strengths of traditional indigenous political institutions and does not,
as such, "place any one group of persons consistently in the position of
a minority" (1998, 375). Instead, it aims to accommodate the preferences
of all participating individual citizens (note: not parties). In this regard,
Wiredu's reference to the importance of a "willingness to compromise" and
to the "voluntary acquiescence of the momentary minority" (1998, 380) is
significant. This allows the community to come to a decision and follow
a particular line of action—an important outcome in a world that often
requires quick decisions to retain control (Nicolson 2008a, 9). Note that
the minority does not simply have to put up with or passively tolerate the
overriding decisions of a majority. Instead, the minority *agrees* to disagree,
which means that its constructive input is still acknowledged or recognized
in communal decisions (Louw 2006, 163–64). The concept of consensus assumed by a consensual democracy therefore both confirms *and* contradicts
the literal meaning of *consensus*," "'general agreement [or] the collective
unanimous opinion of a number of persons'—from the Latin, *consentire*"
(Eze 2008, 391—italics in original). Such an understanding of consensus
takes plurality seriously. It *dis*qualifies Ubuntu as a craving for an oppressive universal sameness or hegemony (see Louw 2001, 21).

What is evidenced by the above is that more work needs to be done in
this regard. Boele van Hensbroek rightly challenges neotraditionalist African theorists to "harness indigenous cultural resources in institutionaliz-
ing democratic practices" (1999, 200). A deliberation on African communal
democracy, or what he also calls "palaver democracy," could, for example,
involve a comparison between the idea of "palaver" and the idea of the
"public sphere" (197). It also may involve the hypothesis that the Ubuntu
ethic dictates that individuals be given as much opportunity as possible to
effect change and decide for themselves how they are governed through, for
example, being allowed, as far as practicable, to elect their public representatives directly. Such issues, Boele van Hensbroek claims (with some justification), are rarely explored in contemporary neotraditionalist discourse.
As he rightly emphasizes, however, such an exploration both requires and
involves the countering of a restrictive culturalism by a emancipating or
liberating understandings of African communalism (192–93, 200).

Dismas A. Masolo's (2004) critical concept of "African communitarianism" comes to mind as an example of counterargument. The concept

includes a reminder that the indigenous sages of Kenya included "*critically-minded individuals* whose *discursive engagements* influenced the content of cultural beliefs" (496—italics mine). Thad Metz's self-consciously revisionist understanding of Ubuntu also qualifies as an example. Metz defines Ubuntu as "friendship," that is, "identifying with others and exhibiting solidarity towards them" but then significantly adds that "thinking of oneself as a 'we' and cooperating are compatible with *a substantial degree of negotiation, bickering, compromise and change*" (2010, 55—italics mine). These outlooks on Ubuntu hardly resonate with an oppressive sameness. Ubuntu does not involve the suppression of otherness, at least not when seen through the eyes of critical commentators like Masolo and Metz.

Community and Exclusivity

In terms of an emancipatory understanding of Ubuntu, so it was claimed above, the Ubuntu ethic takes plurality seriously. It is intended to ensure that all voices are heard. One would expect such an ethic to be inclusive rather than exclusive; to include, not exclude; accommodate, not alienate. But "just how inclusive is the community that Ubuntu both describes and prescribes" (Louw 2006, 164)? Not very inclusive, that is, if one's estimation has to depend on the apparent meaning of initiation rites in traditional African societies. Initiation rites seem to imply that "ubuntu functioned (and still functions) as a binding ethic *exclusively* within the confines of a specific clan" (Louw 2006, 164). The blood that is spilled onto the soil through circumcision and clitoridectomy says that the initiated person "wishes to be tied to the community and people, *among whom he or she has been born as a child* [and] until the individual has gone through the operation, he [or she] is still an *outsider*" (Mbiti, cited in Ramose 2002a, 71—italics added; also Louw 2006, 167). This understanding of the inclusivity (or, rather, exclusivity) of Ubuntu seems a world away from the "universal law of love" that Ubuntu is often made out to be (Keevy 2014, 74–75)!

Generally speaking, "the advocates of the community that is ubuntu emphasize its inclusiveness" (Louw 2006, 165). Some, however, create the impression that, though this community transcends the confines of a specific clan, it includes only those whose origins lie in Africa. Ramose (2002a), for example, speaks of an African "family atmosphere," that is, "a kind of philosophical affinity and kinship among and between the different *indigenous people* of Africa" (81—italics added). While this remark "under-scores the fact that Ubuntu does not exclusively apply within specific clans" (Louw 2006, 165), it nevertheless seems to imply that the community that is Ubuntu does not include—as Van Binsbergen puts it—"beings who so-matically and historically clearly stand out as *not* autochthonous" (2001, 55, cited in Louw 2006, 165).[2] Such an exclusion would contradict Johann Broodryk's (2002) explanation of the Ubuntu concept of extended family. Broodryk points out that the community that is Ubuntu "has the potential or seems to be capable of extension even beyond those related by blood, kin-ship or marriage to include strangers" (98). For some, though, the African concept of community, in its fullest sense, even transcends the society of the living. Ramose (2002a), for example, refers in this regard to the "con-stant communication between the living and the living-dead ('ancestors')," as well as to "the triad of the living, the living-dead and the yet-to-be born," which "forms an unbroken and infinite chain of relations" (94). "In the last resort," surmises Augustine Shutte, "humanity itself is conceived of as a family, a family that one joins at birth, but does not leave by dying. Because of this, no one is a stranger" (2008, 28; see also Shutte 2001, 29).

That no one should be a stranger within the assumed scope of the com-munity that embodies Ubuntu seems important for at least two reasons. First, Ubuntu's potential to derail into a totalitarian communalism could also be understood as its tendency to exclude rather than include, as one would expect from an ethic of caring and sharing. As an excluding ethic, a derailed Ubuntu represents the fortification and preservation of a specific group identity through limitation and segregation. According to such an ethic, the slogan *simunye* ("we are one") ironically signals class, cultural, or ethnic purity; racism and xenophobia—a phenomenon with which (South) Africans are all too familiar. (See "SA Still Plagued by Xenophobia" 2009.) Second, as a traditional ethic, Ubuntu functioned (and still functions) in the relatively small communities of the "indigenous people" (to use Ra-mose's [2002a, 81] term) of sub-Saharan Africa. The plural *communities* is appropriate here, since, as a rough demographic analysis would reveal, these people constitute anything but one monolithic society. Moreover, the population of sub-Saharan Africa (and especially southern Africa) also in-cludes those whose ancestral origins lie in other parts of the world (among whom are those whose colonial or recent ancestors have lived in Africa for several generations) and those with mixed ethnic ancestry. Which raises the question, Can Ubuntu work beyond the confines of a small indigenous community and be applied when the community in question comprises a heterogeneous plurality of ethnicities, cultures, and faiths (see also Nicolson 2008a, 8)? Addressing Africa's colonial scars effectively may require a focus on the affairs or interests of her "indigenous communities"—even of a specific "indigenous community" (compare Nicolson 2008a, 7–8). In this regard, the ethnic or cultural undertone of Ubuntu as a traditional ethic may have an important heuristic value. Be that as it may, the ethic of Ubuntu can hardly "handle plurality" (Arendt; see Boele van Hensbroek 1999, 201) if it involves the exclusion of cultures, ethnicities, or identities.

Religion

Ubuntu's understanding of consensus and solidarity may not be the only controversial aspect of its ancient wisdom in postmodern African polities. Its deeply religious roots may seemingly also allow attitudes and practices unbefitting constitutional democracies such as South Africa (whose constitution, one is proud to acknowledge, includes a progressive bill of rights).[3] In his explanation of the religious worldview underlying the Ubuntu ethic, Mkhize (2008) notes that "ancestors act as guardians of morality. While they generally remain interested in the well-being of their offspring, they punish bad conduct by withdrawing their interest in family matters. When this happens, having been disconnected from God, the source of life, the family is thrown into a state of imbalance or disequilibrium. . . . Such a state of affairs requires the family to engage in acts of libation in order to restore the state of equilibrium and hence connection with God" (37). But, one may now rightly ask, what *exactly* would, in this context, count as instances of "bad conduct," the throwing of the family "into a state of imbalance or disequilibrium," disconnection from God, punishment, the withdrawal of the ancestors' interest, "acts of libation," or the restoration of "the state of equilibrium and hence connection with God"? Mkhize (2008, 41) answers this question in terms of a list of (apparently) noble acts or attitudes, all of which are "geared toward reconstructing, preserving and enhancing the community." The list, among other things, includes respect toward oneself, others, and the cosmos; the maintenance of justice; empathy; and having a conscience. The absence of these acts or attitudes would, Mkhize seems to argue, constitute "bad conduct." The withdrawal of the ancestors and resultant "disequilibrium" or disconnection from God would then serve as punishment, while engaging in or displaying such acts or attitudes would qualify as "acts of libation."

But, in spite of his emphasis on the "lived experiences of the people in question" (Mkhize 2008, 35), Mkhize fails to provide concrete examples (i.e., examples from everyday life) of these acts or attitudes. His list sounds laudable until one realizes that, within the context of Ubuntu as an ancient ethic, these acts and attitudes may have harbored (and may still harbor, in traditional African communities) "hegemonic or oppressive masculinities" (Chitando 2008, 57; see also Keevy 2014, 70–72), or may have included (and certainly, in the hinterlands of South Africa, still include) witchcraft, including dehumanizing beliefs such as the belief "that childless women are witches" (Manda 2008, 133; see also 131), or the burning of women and men (and often also their families) for being witches (Mnisi and Sithole 2007; Keevy 2014, 73). Cast in this light, traditional African society is hardly an ideal to hold in high regard (Richardson 2008, 79–80), which necessitates critical and creative rereadings of the ancient Ubuntu narrative. This is what Mkhize seems to aim at, though his failure to mention these atrocities may create the impression that he is "merely appropriating [Ubuntu's] bright side" (Van Binsbergen, cited by Richardson 2008, 80). Nevertheless, Mkhize's rendition of the Ubuntu narrative thoroughly acknowledges what is still an important driving force for many, though not all Africans (Chitando 2008, 48–49), namely, religious beliefs.

For those who are willing to rearticulate it critically and imaginatively, the ancient wisdom that is Ubuntu has a lot to offer for addressing the many challenges that contemporary society confronts us with. Its communal emphasis may, for example, counter unbridled capitalism (thought by many to be the cause of the current global economic meltdown) (Mafunisa 2008, 113–17; Murove 2008, 90–96, 103–8). Its holistic view of healing may supplement the predominantly physical and mechanistic approach of Western medicine (Manda 2008, 136–38). And, finally, its (little-known) appreciation for retribution may offer critical assessments of the work of the Truth and Reconciliation Commission in South Africa, thought by some as having administered cheap or superficial justice (Richardson 2008, 73–78). In spite of all that has already been said about the traditional ethic of Ubuntu's capacity to inspire forgiveness (Richardson 2008, 67), it would nevertheless be wrong to assume that a restorative, harmonious settlement of criminal cases have *always* been reached in traditional African indigenous communities. Moreover, when such settlements failed or when settlements were dishonored, restorative practices often made way for retributive measures. "As a legal category," Van Binsbergen claims, Ubuntu "is not infinitely accommodating, not without boundaries" (2001, 55).

Plurality and Individuality

The notions of "accommodation" and "boundaries" reintroduce the challenge raised at the outset of our assessment of Ubuntu, namely, the challenge of celebrating both diversity in unity and unity in diversity. Can Ubuntu "handle plurality"?

I believe it can. Or, at least, its principle of agreeing to disagree constitutes an important first step in this direction. This principle can handle plurality insofar as it inspires us to expose ourselves to others, to encounter the difference of others' humanness so as to inform and enrich our own (Louw 2001, 23). Thus understood, "being a person through other persons" translates as "To be human is to affirm one's humanity by recognizing the humanity of others in its infinite variety of content and form" (Van der Merwe 1996, 1) or "A human being is a human being through (*the otherness of*) other human beings" (Van der Merwe 1996, 1, italics added). This respect for or acknowledgment of otherness is vital for the survival of post-apartheid South Africa.

As such, the principle of agreeing to disagree underscores Ubuntu's respect for individuality. Though, as has often been noted, within the context of the Ubuntu ethic, personal identity does not primarily reside in individualistic properties, but in relationships (Du Toit 2004, 33). "Ubuntu *defines* the individual in terms of his/her relationship with others" (Louw 2006, 168). Individuals exist *in* their relationships with others, or, to borrow from Christian de Quincey, "we don't form relationships, *they form us*" (cited in Forster 2007, 275, italics in original). This is not to say that one's identity is being dictated by others. Rather, as Dion Forster points out, within the context of the community that is Ubuntu, personal identity resides in *reciprocal interconnection*: though "the community enriches, builds up, maintains and develops the individual, . . . it is the individual who enriches, builds up, maintains and develops the community" (273). True Ubuntu therefore does not constitute an oppressive communalism, but rather suggests that an individual, as Forster puts it, "grows more fully human, more true in [his/her] identity, through engagement with other persons" (274). This understanding of Ubuntu's respect for individuality resonates widely. Ndaba (1994), for example, stresses that, instead of enveloping the African subject, Ubuntu allows the person to grow and prosper "in a relational setting provided by ongoing contact and interaction with others" (14). And, in 1997, the South African government noted, through its White Paper for Social Welfare, that, according to Ubuntu, "each individual's humanity is ideally expressed through his or her relationship with others and theirs in turn through a recognition of the individual's humanity" (Department of Welfare 1997, 12).

Through his concept of interconnection, Forster (2007) comes close to translating the well-known Ubuntu maxim "I am because we are" into "we are because I am." Such a translation, I argued above (perhaps too hastily), would constitute an emancipatory understanding of Ubuntu. Yet neither Forster nor—insofar as it could be established—any other proponent of the Ubuntu ethic uses this translation. Why is this so? Though I do not wish to speak on behalf of others, one may hypothesize that the exponents of Ubuntu avoid the translation in question because it creates the impression that the community (i.e., "we") *depends on the individual.* This may be true insofar as "we" signifies the sum total of other individuals. In the final analysis, however, the word *we*, as used in classic Ubuntu aphorisms, does not refer to the sum total of individuals, but to the community as a *system* or, if you like, a living organism, that is, a dynamic whole that is always and already more than the sum total of its parts. As is the case with all living organisms, one "vital" (pun intended) quality disallows the quantification of the community that is Ubuntu—life. It is the life of this community, that is, the *inter*actions of its members (and not the action of any specific member), that determines identity as an ongoing process. Others therefore do not dictate the individual's identity, nor does the individual dictate the identities of others. Rather, to put it in Ubuntu's religious parlance, as human beings, we participate in a *common* identity that resides in *seriti*—the power, life force, or creative energy that emanates from God and in which each individual exists as a unique or distinct focus (Shutte 2008, 29). This is perhaps what Ifeanyi Menkiti had in mind when he pointed out that African thought "asserts an *ontological independence* to human society, and moves from society to individuals" (cited in Shutte 2008, 27, italics added); not the other way round, as in much European thought. It also seems to resonate with Leopold Senghor's concept of "a community-based society, communal, not collectivist." For Senghor (cited in Shutte 2008, 27–28), African community does not refer to a mere collection of individuals, but to "people conspiring together, *con-spiring* in the basic Latin sense, united among themselves even to the very centre of their being." Through this understanding of community, Ubuntu philosophy exposes the I/others dichotomy as false, thereby giving a distinctly African meaning to the concept of power sharing, as discussed earlier."

Concluding Remarks

In terms of the conception of Ubuntu developed in this chapter, the community that is Ubuntu constitutes an *open* society insofar as it celebrates the universal *and* the particular, sameness *and* difference, agreement *and* disagreement, tradition *and* innovation, continuity *and* change, religious belief *and* discursive rationality. A society, in short, that avoids the totalitarianism that Sono (1994, 7) rightly warns us against. This understanding of Ubuntu is admittedly a rearticulation of an ancient ethic, inspired by what is perceived to be its best attributes. Its aim is not to serve as a smokescreen for the anomalies or atrocities of traditional African societies. On the contrary, the conception of Ubuntu developed herein was also cautioned by what may be the worst attributes of these societies (compare Richardson 2008, 82). Nor is it meant as a call to return to the value orientations and practices of precolonial (southern) African villages. It is, in any event, impossible to restore the so-called original version of *Ubuntu*. Our accounts of *Ubuntu* can at best be innovative reconstructions (as I have written before), inevitably colored by our postmodern values, beliefs, and biases. In this sense, any attempt to answer the question "What is Ubuntu?" (read: "How was it first formulated?") would be misguided. Though a reflection on Ubuntu can hardly ignore inherited notions thereof, surely the more important question has to be "How *should* Ubuntu be understood and utilized for the common good of *all* Africans, and of the world at large?" These and related questions generated and are generating a variety of emancipatory rereadings of the Ubuntu narrative,[4] showing that "instances in which precolonial sub-Saharan societies exhibited ubuntu" can be "refurbished for a modern [South African] context" (Metz 2014, 212). Whether we conceive of the African way forward as a renaissance or, with Mogobe Ramose (2002b, 607–8), as the "*Mokoko-Hungwe* period (i.e. 'the age of restitution and reparation to Africa')," both call for "critical rereadings of existing narratives of reconciliation and reintegration, including the Ubuntu narrative. It does *not* call for the romanticization of an indigenous past" (Louw 2006, 171). Such is the challenge of Ubuntu ethics.

Notes

I wish to acknowledge that parts of this chapter have appeared in the following publications: Cornel W. Du Toit, ed., *Power Sharing and African Democracy* (Pretoria: Research Institute for Theology and Religion, 2010); *Tijdschrift voor Filosofie* 77 (1): 7–26; and D. Sullivan and L. Tifft, eds., *Handbook of Restorative Justice: A Global Perspective* (London: Routledge, 2006). I am grateful to the editors of the publications for granting us permission to reproduce aspects of the essay here.

An Afrikaans version of this chapter appeared as Louw (2015). It partially overlaps with Louw (2010) and feeds on Louw (1999, 2001, 2006).

1. *Subjectivity* here signifies the capacity to originate thought and action (compare Shutte 2008, 27).

2. This may not be what Ramose had in mind here. His emphasis on the indigenous character of Ubuntu may also be understood, not as an exhaustive demarcation of its scope, but merely as an explanation of the sense in which Ubuntu may serve as the basis of African law (Ramose 2002a, 81). Moreover, thinking of the community that is Ubuntu in exclusivist terms seemingly does not resonate with his reflections on "ecology through Ubuntu," in terms of which this community includes not only human beings but also "physical or objective nature" (Ramose 2009, 309).

3. That is, "progressive" in terms of the Universal Declaration of Human Rights. Africans may not, however, unconditionally endorse the declaration's emphasis on individual rights (compare Nicolson 2008a, 9–10; Mkhize 2008, 39–40, 42).

4. Compare Nicolson (2008b), Murove (2009), Eze (2010), Praeg and Magadla (2014), Praeg (2014), and Metz (2016), to name but a few examples of what Siphokazi Magadla and Ezra Chitando (2014) would call the "reinvention of Ubuntu," resulting in an ethic "that does not somehow 'belong' to traditional elders and the living-dead" but rather constitutes a "contemporary, revolutionary" ethic—Ubuntu as a 'living tradition'" (188; see also Cornell 2014, 167–75).

References

Boele van Hensbroek, Pieter. 1999. *Political Discourses in African Thought: 1860 to the Present.* Westport, CT: Praeger.

Bouckaert, Luk. 2001. "Ubuntu: African Reciprocity in a Multi-cultural Context." Paper presented at a Covenant-Symposium of the Departments of Philosophy of the Universities of Leuven and Nijmegen, Leuven, Belgium, May 22–23.

Broodryk, Johann. 2002. *Ubuntu: Life Lessons from Africa*. Pretoria: Ubuntu School of Philosophy.

Chitando, Ezra. 2008. "Religious Ethics, HIV and AIDS and Masculinities in Southern Africa." In Nicolson 2008b, 45–63. Scottsville, S. Afr.: University of KwaZulu-Natal Press.

Coetzee, Pieter H., and Abraham P. J. Roux, eds. 2003. *The African Philosophy Reader.* New York: Routledge.

Cornell, Drucilla. 2014. "Ubuntu and Subaltern Legality." In Praeg and Magadla 2014, 167–75. Scottsville, S. Afr.: University of KwaZulu-Natal Press.

Department of Welfare, South Africa. 1997. *White Paper for Social Welfare*. Accessed November 10, 2014. https://www.gov.za/sites/default/files/White_Paper_on_Social _Welfare_0.pdf.

Du Toit, Cornel W. 2004. "Technoscience and the Integrity of Personhood in Africa and the West: Facing Our Technoscientific Environment." In *The Integrity of the Human Person in an African Context: Perspectives from Science and Religion*, edited by Cornel W. Du Toit, 1–46. Pretoria: Research Institute for Theology and Religion, University of South Africa.

Eze, Michael O. 2008. "What Is African Communitarianism? Against Consensus as a Regulative Ideal." *South African Journal of Philosophy* 27: 386–99.

———. 2010. *Intellectual History in Contemporary South Africa*. New York: Palgrave Macmillan.

Forster, Dion. 2007. "Identity in Relationship: The Ethics of Ubuntu as an Answer to the Impasse of Individual Consciousness." In *The Impact of Knowledge Systems on Human Development in Africa*, edited by Cornel W. Du Toit, 245–89. Pretoria: Research Institute for Theology and Religion, University of South Africa.

Jackson, Neels. 2009. "Mbeki maak dit bitter moeilik." *Beeld*, February 18, p. 14.

Jansen, Jonathan. 2011. *My South Africa*. Accessed November 10, 2014. http://sagoodnews.co .za/this-is-my-south-africa-is-it-yours/.

Jordaan, Wilhelm. 2009. "Sonder mites kan mens nie lewe." *Beeld*, March 4, p. 13.

Keevy, Ilze. 2014. "Ubuntu versus the Core Values of the South African Constitution." In Praeg and Magadla 2014, 54–95. Scottsville, South Africa: University of KwaZulu-Natal Press.

Louw, Dirk J. 1999. "Ubuntu: An African Assessment of the Religious Other." *Paideia: Philosophical Research Online*. Accessed November 10, 2014. http://www.bu.edu/wcp /Papers/Afri/AfriLouw.htm.

———. 2001. "Ubuntu and the Challenges of Multiculturalism in Post-apartheid South Africa," *Quest* 15, nos. 1–2:15–36.

———. 2006. The African Concept of Ubuntu and Restorative Justice. In *Handbook of Restorative Justice: A Global Perspective*, edited by Dennis Sullivan and Larry Tifft, 161–73. New York: Routledge.

———. 2010. "Power Sharing and the Challenge of Ubuntu Ethics." In *Power Sharing and African Democracy*, edited by Cornel W. Du Toit, 121–37. Proceedings of the Forum for Religious Dialogue Symposium of the Research Institute for Theology and Religion held at the University of South Africa, Pretoria, on March 26–27, 2009. Pretoria: RITR, UNISA.

———. 2015. "Ubuntu heroorweeg." *Tijdschrift voor Filosofie* 77:7–26.

Mafunisa, John M. 2008. "Ethics, African Social Values and the Workplace." In Nicolson 2008b, 111–24. Scottsville, S. Afr.: University of KwaZulu-Natal Press.

Magadla, Siphokazi, and Ezra Chitando. 2014. "The Self Become God. Ubuntu and the 'Scandal of Manhood.'" In Praeg and Magadla 2014, 176–92. Scottsville, S. Afr.: University of KwaZulu-Natal Press.

Manda, Lucinda D. 2008. "Africa's Healing Wisdom: Spiritual and Ethical Values of Traditional African Healthcare Practices." In Nicolson 2008b, 125–39. Scottsville, S. Afr.: University of KwaZulu-Natal Press.

Masolo, Dismas A. 2004. "Western and African Communitarianism: A Comparison." In *A Companion to African Philosophy*, edited by Kwasi Wiredu, 483–98. Oxford, UK: Blackwell.

Metz, Thaddeus. 2010. "African and Western Moral Theories in a Bioethical Context." *Developing World Bioethics* 10:49–58.

———. 2014. "In Search of Ubuntu: A Political Philosopher's View of Democratic South Africa." In *Liberation Diaries: Reflections on 20 years of Democracy*, edited by Busani Ngcawen, 205–14. Johannesburg: Jacana Media.

———. 2016. *Relational Ethics: An African Moral Theory*. Cape Town: Oxford University Press Southern Africa.

Mkhize, Nhlanhla. 2008. "Ubuntu and Harmony: An African Approach to Morality and Ethics." In Nicolson 2008b, 35–44. Scottsville, S. Afr.: University of KwaZulu-Natal Press.

Mnisi, Oris, and Zinkie Sithole. 2007. "Witchcraft Act Being Finalised." *News24.com*. Accessed March 24, 2009. http://wwwnews24.com/southafrica/news/witchcraft-act -being-finalised-20070507.

Murove, Munyaradzi F. 2008. "On African Ethics and the Appropriation of Western Capitalism: Cultural and Moral Constraints to the Evolution of Capitalism in Post-Colonial Africa." In Nicolson 2008b, 85–110.

———. 2009. *African Ethics: An Anthology of Comparative and Applied Ethics*. Scottsville, S. Afr.: University of KwaZulu-Natal Press.

Ndaba, W. J. 1994. *Ubuntu in Comparison to Western Philosophies*. Pretoria: Ubuntu School of Philosophy.

Nicolson, Ronald. 2008a. "Introduction." In Nicholson 2008b, 1–13. Scotsvillle, S. Afr.: University of KwaZulu-Natal Press.

———. 2008b. *Persons in Community: African Ethics in a Global Culture*. Scottsville, S. Afr.: University of KwaZulu-Natal Press.

Praeg, Leonhard. 2008. "An Answer to the Question: What Is [Ubuntu]?" *South African Journal of Philosophy* 27:367–85.

———. 2014. *A Report on Ubuntu*. Scottsville, S. Afr.: University of KwaZulu-Natal Press.

Praeg, Leonhard, and Siphokazi Magadla, eds. 2014. *Ubuntu: Curating the Archive*. Scottsville, S. Afr.: University of KwaZulu-Natal Press.

Ramose, Mogobe B. 2002a. *African Philosophy through Ubuntu*. Rev. ed. Harare, Zimb.: Mond.

———. 2002b. "'African Renaissance': A Northbound Gaze." In Coetzee and Roux 2003, 600–610. Cape Town: Oxford University Press Southern Africa.

———. 2009. Ecology through Ubuntu. In *African Ethics: An Anthology of Comparative and Applied Ethics*, edited by M. F. Murove, 308–14. Scottsville, S. Afr.: University of KwaZulu-Natal Press.

Richardson, R. Neville. 2008. "Reflections on Reconciliation and Ubuntu." In Nicolson 2008b, 65–83. Scottsville, S. Afr.: University of KwaZulu-Natal Press.

Roche, Declan. 2003. *Accountability in Restorative Justice*. Oxford: Oxford University Press.

"SA Still Plagued by Xenophobia." 2009. *News24.com*. Accessed May 12, 2009. http://www .news24.com/News24/South_Africa/News/0,,2-7-1442_2514746,00.html.

Shutte, Augustine. 2001. *Ubuntu: An Ethic for a New South Africa*. Pietermaritzburg, S. Afr.: Cluster.

———. 2008. "African Ethics in a Globalising World." In Nicolson 2008b, 15–34. Scottsville, S. Afr.: University of KwaZulu-Natal Press.

Sono, Themba. 1994. *Dilemmas of African Intellectuals in South Africa*. Pretoria: UNISA Press.

Van Binsbergen, Wim. 2001. "Ubuntu and the Globalisation of Southern African Thought and Society." *Quest* 15:53–89Van der Merwe, Willie L. 1996. "Philosophy and the Multicultural Context of (Post)apartheid South Africa." *Ethical Perspectives* 3: 1–15.

Van Niekerk, Anton A. 1999. "The African Renaissance: Lessons from a Predecessor." *Critical Arts* 13: 66–80.

Wiredu, Kwasi. 1998. "Democracy and Consensus in African Traditional Politics: A Plea for a Non-party Polity." Coetzee and Roux 2003, 374–82.

DIRK J. LOUW teaches African philosophy, applied ethics, and philosophical counseling in the Department of Philosophy of Stellenbosch University (South Africa). He is also a clinical psychologist and former editor of the *South African Journal of Philosophy*.

6

UBUNTU AND ORUKA'S
HUMANITARIAN VIEW OF PUNISHMENT

Oriare Nyarwath

THIS CHAPTER SEEKS TO CONNECT THE CONCEPT OF Ubuntu and the worldview it encapsulates to Kenyan philosopher H. Oruka's argument on punishment (Oruka 1985). Ubuntu presents the wholeness of the universe and how an individual is inextricably linked to other human beings, a view candidly expressed by Okot p'Bitek (1986) in his argument on the sociality of the human self. Ubuntu therefore represents a form of social organization often described as communitarian that generates its own human conception and moral discourse about the individual as a socially embedded self. A look at Oruka's argument on punishment reveals a background that views individual identity, moral responsibility, and consequently punishment in a radically different way from backgrounds that generate a conception of the individual as an unembedded self. Oruka's argument on punishment falls under a humanitarian conception that views moral responsibility as primarily social and not private. This position apportions criminal responsibility to both individual and society. It is neither a retributive nor a utilitarian view of punishment.

Oruka considers any proposed punishment legal terrorism if it is based solely on the criminal responsibility of the offender without considering social forces that make it possible for the offender to commit the crime or any alleged punishment that far exceeds the offense (Oruka 1985, 19, 103–4). Oruka argues that, in the long run, punishment should be abolished and replaced by institutions of treatment for both society and the individual criminal (Oruka 1985, 78–79). Such treatment should aim at rehabilitating the offender and returning him or her into society. He argues that criminals are not born but bred by society, which implies that society has a greater role in determining whether one becomes a criminal. This means that when one becomes a criminal, it is society that bears the greater contribution to that criminality than the individual criminal himself or herself. One of the implications of this position is that in apportioning criminal responsibility, society must have its share of that responsibility. Failure to apportion to society its share of responsibility for crime leads wrongly, unjustifiably, and unfairly to solely blame and punish the individual offender.

The other implication of this view of responsibility for crime and punishment is that the individual is conceived as being inextricably tied to society. This inextricable interconnectedness between an individual and society expresses one of the essential aspects of Ubuntu.

In this chapter, I attempt to demonstrate that the values that form the foundation of Oruka's view of punishment reflect the very worldview represented by the concept of Ubuntu, which, despite being a Bantu term, expresses a universal reality and typifies a communitarian view of society. The conclusion of this chapter is that Oruka's view of punishment is consistent with the Ubuntu metaphysics of the human person in which punishment should aim at rehabilitating or restoring social order and should not be retributive.

It may appear inconsistent and problematic to talk, as Oruka does, about a conception of punishment—in this case, a humanitarian conception of punishment—and argue at the same time for the abolition of the very idea and practice of punishment (Oruka 1985, 54, 78–86). Oruka considers the abolition of punishment a mere ideal for now but one that is worthy of our focus and effort. He believes that punishment is still going to be with us for a long time. And so long as it is still practiced, we should try to make it as humane as possible.

Oruka's View of Punishment

H. Oruka (1944–1995) was a Kenyan philosopher who is considered one of founding fathers of contemporary African philosophy, or one of the key figures in the discourse about the existence, nature, and role of philosophy in contemporary Africa. Oruka took his bachelor's degree in the sciences and his postgraduate degree in philosophy at Uppsala University in Sweden.

He also got his master's degree in philosophy from Wayne State University in the United States. While at Uppsala, he developed great interest in philosophy through the influence of a renowned professor of practical philosophy Ingemar Hedenius. This influence led him to abandon the study of the sciences for philosophy. Practical philosophy is an aspect of philosophy that focuses on the application of philosophical reflections to the analysis and understanding of various spheres of human life, such as politics, law, economics, religion, culture, and the environment. Oruka came to philosophy from that practical orientation.

Fully aware of the great many problems Africans faced that resulted from the colonial experience, Oruka realized that practical philosophy would be the most appropriate disciplinary approach not only for the liberation of Africa from colonialism but also for the development of awareness of various myths related to colonialism. It is from this practical orientation to philosophy that many of Oruka's philosophical works, such as *Punishment and Terrorism in Africa* (1976), *The Philosophy of Liberty* (1991), *Trends in Contemporary African Philosophy* (1990), *Sage Philosophy: Indigenous Thinkers and Modern Debate on African Philosophy* (1990), and *Practical Philosophy in Search of an Ethical Minimum* (1997), are best understood (Oruka 1997, 212–17, 281–87).

Oruka's *Punishment & Terrorism in Africa* (1985), the major work in which he discusses punishment, brings out justice and injustice as the main issues that span Oruka's philosophical career. In this work, he focuses on his argument that punishment should be abolished either because it is difficult to justify morally or, as it is commonly practiced in Africa, because it tends to become a form of legal terrorism (Oruka 1985, 55–74, 102–13). Legal terrorism is defined as using law to punish an innocent person or to punish him or her beyond a reasonable maximum. His argument is that because commensurability between an offense and punishment is one of the principles by which justified punishment is determined, to punish beyond a reasonable maximum is tantamount to acting against one of the basic principles of punishment (Oruka 1985, 104).

This reading of Oruka's view on punishment can be categorized under a forward-looking view (Oruka 1985, 52–54) classified as humanitarian. The humanitarian view of punishment holds the position that crimes and criminals are products of society and that factors that drive persons into crime are external to them. The societal factors of crime are the primary causes of crime, not the individual person's, as it is often assumed. In most cases, so-called criminals cannot successfully withstand these social factors or forces without endangering their health or sanity. Criminals then are seen as simply secondary factors. Being secondary factors, they cannot reasonably be held responsible, let alone solely responsible, for their crimes. It is the primary forces that inhere in society outside the individual that should be held to be primarily responsible for crimes. Therefore, according to this position, to punish the so-called criminal because he or she is believed to be solely responsible is immoral and morally impermissible. Such a view of criminal factors seems to give primacy to community (social structure) over individual autonomy, which is problematic in itself.

Under the forward-looking view of punishment also falls utilitarianism as a contending philosophical justification of punishment. The utilitarian position states that crimes should be punished only if the punishment promises a greater good than evil to either the offender or society. A utilitarian does not view punishment as an end in itself but as a means to reaping maximum utility. This position holds that punishment in itself is morally wrong. But it permits punishment if and only if it will, or is intended to bring about, a greater balance of good over evil than any available alternative. Therefore, utilitarianism accepts punishment if it is intended to reform and rehabilitate an offender, to deter others from committing similar crimes, or to protect society from offenders (Porter 1995, 50–51). The utilitarian theory of punishment may be criticized on several grounds, such as for ignoring the principle of desert—that punishment should be meted out because it is deserved and not for any other reason. It allows for nonpunishment of an offender if there is no good or utility to be reaped; that respect for human dignity demands that a human being should be treated as an end and not as a means to some goals for other persons. It is also criticized on the grounds that it perverts justice by ignoring the principle of commensuration between punishment and offense by being concerned only with the amount of punishment that promises greater good (Kant 1997 38–39; Oruka 1985, 25–26). One can be given heavier punishment that is not commensurate to the offense if that is deemed necessary to bring about greater good than lesser punishment that would be proportional to the offense.

At the other extreme is the backward-looking view of punishment underpinned by the theory of retribution. According to this view, an offender who is assumed to be responsible for an offense deserves punishment. Whoever breaks the law merits punishment, and only when such a person is punished can justice be seen to have been served. Therefore, the backward-looking view necessarily links punishment to an already committed offense and does not focus on the consequences of punishment.

The retributivist position is that through punishment the offender is made to return a good for the good taken from his victim, or evil for the evil visited on the victim. This happens either by restitution or compensation. Punishment is therefore seen as a redress of the wrong committed by an offender. The retributivist position is that the offender has a right to punishment. He wills or invites it by violating other people's rights. By violating others' rights, offenders concede that it is all right for others to violate their own rights as well by punishing them. Therefore, whoever inhibits another's freedom wills the inhibition of his own freedom; otherwise, one should not do to others what one would not want done to oneself (Bierman 1980, 495–499). Critics often point out, however, that a retributivist theory of punishment uncritically ignores the social conditions that breed criminality or the root causes of crime (Bierman 1980, 499; Oruka 1985, 24–26).

Although humanitarian, utilitarian, and retributive justifications of punishment may seem to be conceptually unrelated, in practice, they are not mutually exclusive. Any penal institution designs modes of punishment that would aim at a combination of the respective goals of those justifications; rehabilitation, deterrence, and justice (desert).

Punishment is often understood and justified on the principle of intentional violation of the law, which implies that one is a sane adult and has prior full knowledge of the law and the consequences of violating it. A person is therefore assumed to have violated the law out of free will (Oruka 1985, 7–10). But Oruka argues that free will is necessary but not sufficient for criminal responsibility (Oruka 1985, 11). In other words, free will alone cannot be used to determine criminal responsibility. Free will is not an independent factor for a person whose acts are mostly determined by other, primary, factors external to him—such as hereditary, sociopsychological, economic, and environmental factors over which one has very little or no control at all (Oruka 1985, 17–18). Adverse factors of these kinds affecting a person—as, for instance, the case of irresponsible parenting, extreme poverty, discrimination and suppression, and bad education—are likely to produce a criminal person.

Oruka therefore believes that in defining criminal responsibility, these external primary causal factors should be taken into account. He proposes that criminal responsibility should be defined as intentionally committing or allowing a crime that is humanly avoidable (Oruka 1985, 11). An action is humanly avoidable if one can refrain from it without endangering one's life or well-being or the well-being of one's community (Oruka 1985, 11–14). There are several intentional crimes that are therefore humanly unavoidable and for which one should not be held responsible or be punished (Oruka 1985, 18–19). One may, for instance, intentionally steal to avoid starvation either by oneself or by one's family, intentionally commit assault to avenge one's own or one's family members' humiliation, or intentionally allow the commission of a crime to save one's family. The point here is that the motivation or disposition to intentionally commit a crime emanates from outside a person. They are a result of values or attitudes that one has acquired from the very nature of the society in which one is brought up. In other words, a criminal character is a product of socialization. This position should not be seen to undermine individual free will and choice, but rather that the exercise of free will and choice is itself determined by societal forces.

The underlying point in Oruka's argument is that a person and her or his actions cannot be easily isolated from one's society. Therefore, punishment that ignores the individual's social embedment and is not directed to the primary causes of crime cannot achieve its intended aim. Both retributive and utilitarian views of punishment do not address the primary causes of crime. Instead, they focus on the criminal who in most cases is just a secondary factor (Oruka 1985, 79–82).

The humanitarian view of punishment in particular and communitarianism in general raise the issue of the nature of the relationship between the individual and society. Some people tend to look at the issue in terms of which of the two, the individual or the community, has primacy over the other. Masolo identifies some pioneers of political and cultural independence in Africa in the 1960s as holding such a view (Masolo 2010, 230). Taking a position can be problematic because emphasizing one over the other would entail relegating one to a secondary status. But the issue is not necessarily a matter of emphasizing one or the other. It is possible to give equal weight to both and to see the balance between the two as fundamental to the full development of personhood. This is the position favored by people like Masolo (2010, see esp. 249–50) and Kwame Gyekye (1997, see esp. 35–76).

When, however, Oruka emphasizes the primacy of causes of crime that he identifies as external to the offender over the secondary cause, which is the individual free will and choice, he seems to be giving primacy to the community and social forces over individual autonomy, and he therefore appears to advocate what Gyekye calls radical or unrestricted communitarianism with the attendant implication of making the individual's whole life dependent on the values and needs of the community (Gyekye 1997, 36–41). This assertion, if true, would have serious adverse ontological and moral implications for the person. Although the implication of radical communitarianism seems to be a serious legitimate weakness of Oruka's (1985) argument on punishment, it should not be taken to reflect his general philosophical view on the relationship between the individual and community because in his other works, such as the one on sage philosophy (1991) and liberty (1996), Oruka recognizes the value and significance of individual autonomy. For instance, Oruka contends that a sage is a member of a community who is capable not only of isolating his or her thoughts from the cultural beliefs and practices of his or her community but also of offering a critique or even recommending the abandonment of some beliefs and practices of that community. A sage therefore is not a person who is necessarily subservient to values, beliefs, and practices of their community (Oruka 1991, 34–36). Despite the problematic nature of the relationship between individual and community in Oruka's position, the important point that we need to underscore in his argument on criminal responsibility and punishment is the need to give due consideration to both the social conditions that breed crime and the individual offender's exercise of free will.

According to Oruka, we need to have an enlightened and rational view of society if we are to have social harmony, without which there can never be a lasting social security. Such a view of society should aim at eliminating or reducing crime by addressing the criminal forces that induce people to crime (Oruka 1985, 28–30). Without making changes to society to address the criminal forces at play in society, criminals would continue to be generated by those forces (Oruka 1985, 83–84). An enlightened and rational society strives toward objective or pure justice for all. Such a society would be concerned with creating humane conditions for all:

> A society's enlightenment and rationality depends on the degree to which such a society practices pure justice. In pure justice good and evil cease to be relative—my good is my neighbour's good; and my misfortune or suffering is as much the misfortune of my neighbour, and vice-versa. If my neighbor is a criminal I cannot blame him and praise myself, for I am also a criminal; if certain individuals in a society are criminals the rest of the society is as much criminal. The reason why it may not be obvious that the rest of the society is

criminal is because its crimes are implicit and do not appear to contravene the Law that be. (Oruka 1985, 84–85)

It can be seen that Oruka looks at society as a whole in which individual lives are inescapably connected such that goods and evils are equally shared. That implies that in order to improve society, an individual must be improved, and vice versa. For Oruka, the amount of punishment in a society is proportional to the amount of crime and consequently to injustice in that society. The more the punishment, the more the injustice brought about by both those who have committed the crimes and those who inflict punishment on the offenders (Oruka 1985, 55).

It is instructive to remember that, having assumed that a person is inextricably bound up with others, the punishment of a person adversely affects other people who seem to have nothing directly to do with the crime and therefore are innocent. The offender still has rights and duties in relation to others that are curtailed by punishing her or him (Oruka 1985, 102–3). This observation underscores the fact that the practice of punishment cannot avoid adversely affecting apparently innocent people related to individual offenders. This is one more reason that Oruka would advocate abolishing the practice of punishment.

Oruka goes on to argue that a society that strives for pure justice has to look at itself as a whole. This means that the practice of punishment that is based on individual responsibility without addressing the whole society as the source of criminal forces should be abolished and replaced with treatment. In treatment, crime is seen as a sickness that emanates from society rather than from the patient. So, in order to eliminate crime, treatment has to be directed at both the individual and the society (Oruka 1985, 85). Oruka therefore hypothetically recommends the creation of a treatment board to serve that function.

On the treatment board should sit experts from various disciplines who would diagnose what kinds of ailments afflict the individual and society. After the diagnosis, the board would recommend the best treatment for both the individual and the society. Treatment is different from punishment in the sense that, unlike punishment, it aims at curing the so-called criminal and rehabilitating him or her back into society. Oruka's proposal to replace punishment with treatment with the aim of rehabilitating and reintegrating the so-called offenders into society may be seen to be consistent with an Ubuntu worldview.

From the perspective of Ubuntu, the greatest good is social harmony, and crime disrupts social harmony; it is an affront to this greatest good. Therefore, in an Ubuntu response to crime, society places the highest premium on the restoration of social harmony. It is from this perspective that some people view Ubuntu as engendering restorative instead of retributive justice (Okello 2012, 55). That is why it is most important that the wholeness of life be restored and both the victim and the perpetrator of crime be healed and rehabilitated into the wholeness of life. Crime injures and diminishes the dignity and humanness not only of the victim but also of the perpetrator. The so-termed criminal must himself be undignified and dehumanized in order to abuse the dignity and humanness of his victim. This is the point underscored by Desmond Tutu when, in reference to the apartheid regime, he says

> *Ubuntu* means that in a real sense even the supporters of apartheid were victims of the vicious system which they implemented and which they supported so enthusiastically. Our humanity was intertwined. The humanity of the perpetrator of apartheid's atrocities was caught up and bound up in that of his victim whether he liked it or not. In the process of dehumanizing another, in inflicting untold harm and suffering, the perpetrator was inexorably being dehumanized as well. I used to say that the oppressor was dehumanized as much as, if not more than, the oppressed and many in the white community believed that this was another provocative hate mongering slogan by that irresponsible ogre, Tutu, whom most whites at the time loved to hate. (Tutu 1999, 35)

A society like the apartheid South Africa that created separation and inequality between its citizens and consequently enacted subjective laws, which were never applied objectively and equally, often ended up with greater social tensions and hatred among the citizens. Such societies have little or no social harmony. Discriminatory application of law may bring about an illusion of social security in such societies, but it is unlikely to bring about social harmony, which is contingent on the eradication or reduction of social inequalities and tensions and, by extension, criminality (Oruka 1985, 29–30).

The fact that Oruka believes that the primary forces that drive people into crimes emanate from the social conditions implies that any attempt to eradicate or reduce crime must direct itself to the very structure of society which is the real source of crime. A change in the structure of society making it more humane would greatly reduce crime if not completely remove it. Much attention should be given to the values and economic conditions of society. Educational, cultural, and religious systems should be directed toward nurturing values for the respect of human life and dignity, compassion, and care. Achieving those values to a great extent would bring about social harmony in society. Beliefs and habits such as cultural, racial, ethnic, and religious fanaticism should be discouraged, as well as the culture of elevating material wealth above the value of human life. This would check the rampant abuse of human life and rights in the pursuit of material gain.

Another aspect of social structure that calls for closer scrutiny and improvement is the economic conditions, since most crimes are economically driven and generally motivated by the desire to fulfill real economic needs. Toward this goal, Oruka (1985, 117–18) advocates the recognition and adoption of the right to a minimum standard of living, which mostly belongs to the category of economic rights. This right is variously referred to as the right to a human minimum or moral minimum. Before we look at the concept of the right to a human minimum, let us examine the concept of Ubuntu and how it relates to the sociality of the human self.

Ubuntu and the Sociality of the Human Self

Whenever we state, as we often do, that a human being is a social animal, we are simply saying that sociality is an essential attribute of a human being. When Rousseau asserts that "man is born free, and everywhere he is in chains" (Rousseau 1998, 5), he was partly stating the inescapable sociality of human beings. Once in society, a human being has to find how best to live within the social conventions. Okot p'Bitek clearly and forcefully explains the universal sociality of the human self when he states that "man is not born free. He cannot be free. He is incapable of being free. For only by being in *chains* can he be and remain 'human'" (p'Bitek 1986, 19). By disagreeing with Rousseau's claim that man is born free, p'Bitek asserts that the very process by which a human being comes into existence necessarily involves other human beings. While in the mother's womb, the unborn depends on the mother for survival and at birth that dependency is transferred to other human beings—the society—for the continuation of care for survival. But while in society, a human being has duties, rights, and privileges in relation to other human beings that dictate her behavior and actions. It is the duties, rights, and privileges that constitute the chains by which she is connected to other human beings and from which she cannot break if she is to remain human, because it is the chains that define her as a human being. p'Bitek adds, "In African belief, even death does not free him" (p'Bitek 1986, 19) from the chains. This may not be the case only for African belief, but it seems to be simply universally human. A human being who seems to be free from the chains becomes less "human" or loses humanness completely in the social sense of the term *human* as exemplified by the case of a mad person.

The concept of Ubuntu expresses the inescapable sociality of the human self. This calls for the recognition of the unity and wholeness of humanity. An individual's dignity and well-being are necessarily tied to the dignity and well-being of other human beings. This is what Archbishop Desmond Tutu and Mpho Tutu mean when they say that God invites us to a life of wholeness: "God's invitation to wholeness always includes more than ourselves. God's invitation to wholeness is *ubuntu*" (Tutu and Tutu 2010, 47). Their statement should not be taken to mean that there is mingling of a Christian worldview and Ubuntu, but that there is an aspect that is common to both. Ubuntu refers both to the fact that to be human is to recognize the humanity of others and to the fact that our humanity is inextricably intertwined with the humanity of others. As a result, an individual cannot truly flourish at the expense of others. One's dignity and well-being are equally bound up to the dignity and well-being of others. Ubuntu therefore calls for behavior and relating to fellow human beings and the environment in ways that would promote the well-being of all. Ubuntu also entails the nurturing of certain human qualities that would enhance the good of all. Let me again refer to Archbishop Desmond Tutu: "When we want give high praise to someone we say '*Yu, u nobuntu*'; 'Hey, he or she has Ubuntu.' This means that they are generous, hospitable, friendly, caring and compassionate" (Tutu 1999, 34). It is these qualities that bring out the moral character of a human being and that essentially define our humanness.

We have to care for both fellow human beings and our environment. It is for our good and the good of all. Caring for the environment benefits not only the present but also future generations. We should be prudent in the use of the resources within our environment. Advanced technology has intensified interaction among human beings as well as exploitation of natural resources to the extent that the impact of any abuse of environment is felt far and wide. We have to strive to avoid the pursuit of selfish and narrow interests in the use of natural resources (Tutu and Tutu 2010, 47–48). Therefore, by referring to the life of wholeness as Ubuntu, Archbishop Desmond Tutu and Mpho Tutu remind us that we should relate to both fellow human beings and the environment in ways that would ensure that our flourishing enhances the flourishing of other human beings and not to their destruction (Tutu and Tutu 2010, 47). Ubuntu, therefore, is not only the code for interhuman relations but also that which regulates the relationship between humans and nature. The concept of sharing natural resources is built around the respect that people have for nature, which is effectively the mother of them all. They live and die at the behest of Mother Nature (Okello 2012, 59). From the perspective of Ubuntu, social harmony is the greatest good (Tutu 1999, 35) because it enhances humanness. Social harmony is a life of peaceful coexistence among people, on the one hand, and between people and nature, on the other. It emanates from recognition and emphasis of social complementariness, which brings about tolerance, equality, a sense of justice, cooperation, and greater cohesion. It creates a feeling of connectedness and oneness. We increase our humanness and become more humane by belonging, participating, and sharing in the community. When we enhance other people's well-being, we enhance our well-being too. When we dehumanize others, we dehumanize ourselves also (Tutu 1999, 35). It is by positively participating in the lives of other human beings—the community—that we become human (Masolo 2010, 240–41).

It is from this standpoint of the sociality of self that p'Bitek finds it terrifying to ask questions such as "Who am I? What is the purpose of life? What is happiness?" They are terrifying because they can be asked only by a person who has taken a flight into a temporary solitary life. Such questions cannot meaningfully be answered in isolation from one's social networks and terms like *wife, husband, son, daughter, uncle, aunt, chief,* and *ancestor,* since a person's identity and value are necessarily determined by a web of relations (p'Bitek 1986, 19–22; Kirwen 1987, 71–72). These different relationships represent different kinds of personal identity. Society has already given answers to these questions. What constitutes happiness or purpose of one's life has already been prescribed by the society in which one lives through its values and norms. A human being therefore derives meaning and purpose of his existence from the society and in turn gives meaning and purpose to society. It is instructive, at this point, to clarify that human society or community is not limited to the family, relatives, or political entity, but to the whole of humanity. So an individual and society are inextricably bound together in terms of meaning and purpose. This perspective allows us to understand the famous statement "a person is a person through other persons" or "I am because we are; and since we are, therefore

I am" (Mbiti 1969, 108; Okello 2012, 49). The corporate nature of human existence lends credence to the claim that human life is a gift received through others—not only from the perspective of individual survival and growth, but also in the acquisition and development of those qualities that define a human being and that make community life possible (Shutte 2001, 24–25; Kirwen 1987, 71–12).The qualities of care, compassion, and generosity entail sharing not only in individual joys and successes but also in hardships and disappointments. The sharing in life involves offering support and comfort to one another, which makes community life possible (Tutu and Tutu 2010, 44–45). This is what the Tutus mean by the life of wholeness; conducting ourselves in such a way that gives meaning and sustains life and hence creates social harmony (Tutu and Tutu 2010, 44–52). The life of wholeness is a life of community and not a solitary life. It is not living a life whose concern is with I, me, and my, but with we, us, and ours. It is a life of flourishing together and for the pursuit of collective good. This is what Tutus mean by a life of beauty; of creating beauty in one's life and in the lives of others (Tutu and Tutu 2010, 48–52).

But the awareness of our shared humanity and the interconnectedness of our lives and the implications of that awareness on how we should conduct our lives and relate to fellow human beings is not given to everybody, and so that awareness needs to be developed.

Developing Consciousness of Ubuntu

Consciousness of the meaning and implications of Ubuntu is not always present in our lives; otherwise, our lives would always be characterized by social harmony. Which obviously is not the case. It is therefore inaccurate to take it for granted or claim as some people would, for instance, that

> the African person easily understands this word *humanism* "Ubuntu" even on the day to day basis. Africa is the unique continent that historically was applauded for her human values of solidarity and hospitality without limit. It was not until Africans were provoked that they had to fall back on thinking on means of self defense. Africans are a people that predominantly embrace peace and cherish one another's equality. Africans embody the essence and spirit of Ubuntu in their work, family, and community. Africanness encourages and inspires the use of inherent abilities to the fullest in talking, sharing, solidarity, working and even in the rites of passage. (Njue 2012, 25)

Njue's passage definitely romanticizes the ordinary life of Africans. The consciousness of Ubuntu and its implications are not commonplace in the life of ordinary Africans. As Masolo aptly observes, it is taught and nurtured (Masolo 2010, 249). And only few people seem to have acquired the consciousness. There is still need of awakening the consciousness in the majority of people; "it is not true that Ubuntu is all the time in evidence and its impact felt. It remains a strong virtue that needs reawakening and celebration" (Okello 2012, 50). Casting our eyes not only across Africa but the whole world, we see several instances of dehumanization resulting from, among other causes, wars, poverty, disease, and environmental degradation, which do not manifest extensive awareness and practice of Ubuntu (Biney 2014). Therefore, we would easily agree when Biney observes that "For the ordinary people of Africa, both the colonial and post-independent experiences have been replete with brutalities that fly in the face of the philosophy and practice of African humanism/Ubuntu" (Biney 2014, 40).

The practice of Ubuntu is problematized by the fact that both humanization and dehumanization often coexist (Biney 2014, 40; Tutu 1999, 36). Both in society and in a person's life there are moments when Ubuntu and lack of it are manifested in how we relate to one another. This remains an issue. We need to increase the awareness and practice of Ubuntu so that we may reduce the contrary behavior in society. How best that can be done needs further reflection. Probably, more effort should be expended toward making Ubuntu an integral part of general socialization, the school curriculum, and legal systems. South Africa seems to have a head start in this respect for having incorporated Ubuntu in its legal practice (Furman 2014).

Human Minimum as a Principle of Global Justice

Oruka's recommendation to replace punishment with treatment of the so-called offenders is an attempt to create an enlightened, rational, and humane society that inches toward pure justice or greater social justice. It is assumed that in such a society, the humanity of every member is recognized and respected so that every member enjoys a human minimum or a moral minimum. The human minimum defines the minimum standard of life worthy of a human being, the minimum that a human being requires in order to live and exercise rationality in society. The human minimum constitutes the rights to subsistence, health, and physical security (Oruka 1997, 85–90; Shue 1980, 19–20). These three constitute the inviolable right to life, which is a fundamental right of everybody.

The right to life is the minimum that any human being who is unable to secure it by his or her own effort can reasonably demand from fellow human beings. It is also the minimum that any human being can reasonably owe a fellow human being who lacks it (Masolo 2010, 248). The human minimum is owed as a right, not as an act of supererogation. Therefore, to provide it is not an act of charity. It is the minimum a human being needs to live as a dignified moral being without being reduced to a life of desperation in which one would be forced to do anything, however immoral or illegal, to remain alive or avoid injury to one's health or sanity. A situation of desperation and loss of personal dignity makes it impossible for a person to recognize and respect the rights and dignity of other persons.

Being fundamental, this right is therefore universal and absolute. It is universal because it is a basic right for every human person. And it is absolute because no other right or consideration can rationally override it. It is both a right for those who lack it and a duty for those who have the means to provide it for those who cannot enjoy it by their own effort. Being a moral right and duty, it cannot be limited by any boundary, since no consideration of greater moral significance could be possible. As a universal right, it has a corresponding universal duty and hence obligates anybody who has the means regardless of one's race, ethnic group, gender, religion, or national sovereignty to assist those who are unable to provide it for themselves by their own means. The imperative of the right to a human minimum therefore extends the frontiers of our moral duty to the whole of the human community.

In his article "Parental Earth Ethics," first published in the journal *Quest* (Oruka 1993) and later as a book chapter (Oruka 1997, 146–51), Oruka attempts to morally ground the right to a human minimum. He argues that human beings share in the common humanity and planet Earth and are therefore historically and materially interconnected. This fact has various implications. First, the security of an individual person or of a section of humanity depends on the security of others, since people are bound by the same existential conditions. The poor conditions of existence of our neighbors definitely affect adversely on our own security. They might result from wars, famine, poverty, disease, floods, or displacement caused by migration. The threat from terrorism, diseases such as Ebola and HIV, migrations caused by poverty and wars are a few examples. Second, being human means that one would be emotionally and psychologically affected by the suffering of fellow human beings. Some people tend to emphasize either the rational or the sentimental aspects as integral to the definition of being human, but I am of the view that both are integral to it. Paradoxically, whenever we claim that a person is inhuman, we imply that the person seems to lack the very sentiments that characterize a human person, and not that the person lacks rationality. So, a well-nurtured person cannot afford to be callous to the suffering of a fellow human being without having a feeling of shame. Third, one's misfortune or fortune is inherent in the history and development of humanity so that one alone is not fully responsible for one's poverty or affluence, and therefore the poor have a right to demand assistance from the rich and the rich should recognize their duty to assist the poor.

There is a sense in which this right is connected to the concept of Ubuntu. The human minimum sets the lower benchmark for the recognition of the universality of humanness and the universal responsibility that goes with that recognition. It is the minimum that a person owes a fellow human being and the minimum that a person can morally and reasonably demand from a fellow human being as a right. It is also the economic minimum that defines a human being, since its enjoyment enables one to live and function as a decent and dignified rational person without being forced into desperate instinctual animal behavior. A rational being must have the capacity to exercise rational choice, which is possible only when one's human minimum is already met.

When it comes to the practice of punishment, the right to human minimum is significant in at least two ways. It is the minimum necessary for the exercise of choice and hence the determination of criminal intentionality. It is or should be a commonsense principle in moral and criminal responsibility that one cannot be held responsible unless one intentionally committed a humanly avoidable prohibited act. As Oruka argues, a humanly avoidable act is one from which one can refrain or avoid without endangering one's life or health (Oruka 1985, 9–13). But those people who lack the human minimum already have their lives under threat because they lack the basic needs necessary to support a decent and dignified life. For instance, if one refrains from stealing food when one is at the brink of starving to death, that would be morally recklessness because compliance with moral principles is primarily to preserve or enrich human life. It is not good moral sense to expect a person to observe moral rules even if that would lead to one's own death. Some people may find this assertion controversial, but I believe that a moral requirement exists to give primacy to preserving and enriching human life.

The other way in which the human minimum is significant is that if one freely commits a crime, especially crimes related to economics, when one's human minimum has already been met, it may be rational to hold such a person criminally responsible. We are assuming that some other factors such as poor or irresponsible parenting, upbringing, bad education, social discrimination and oppression, and mental instability are not overwhelmingly still affecting the person. But even if they are still at play, in general, the crime rate would still be remarkably reduced if we accept the fact that most crimes are economic crimes (Oruka 1985, 18).

Oruka proposes the human minimum as a basic principle of social and global justice. The recognition and enjoyment of the human minimum would not only enhance social security by reducing many economic crimes but also improve the moral quality of human life in society. The suffering of the poor should make the rich ashamed, because such sufferings diminish the humanity of the rich as well (Oruka 1996, 1997).

Conclusion

The recognition of the universality and inextricability of the interconnectedness and wholeness of human life puts us on a secure ground for the pursuit of social and global justice. Ubuntu reminds us of how best we should relate not only to fellow human beings but also to our environment for the promotion of the well-being of all—both in the present and future times. The legal practice of punishment is extremely limited when it comes to the issue of justice in society. It only coerces but cannot bring about long-lasting social security and social harmony. Ubuntu should be the basis of global justice in which society cares for its most unfortunate members if humanity is to establish a sound basis for a humane world. The Ubuntu ethic demands not only the recognition and the affirmation of our common humanity but also the safeguarding and flourishing of life of every human being.

The improvement of the economic conditions also requires, to some extent, the narrowing of the gap in wealth that necessarily creates differences in access to social services and facilities such as schools, health, residence, clubs, and acquisition of social goods, which in turn encourages separateness in lifestyle, a situation that makes it impossible to attain social harmony.

Therefore, talk about the need to inculcate the spirit and practice of Ubuntu without critically addressing and improving economic conditions in society would not achieve much either in terms of reduction of crime or safeguarding the primacy of human life and dignity.

References

Bierman, Arthur K. 1980. *Life and Morals: An Introduction to Ethics*. New York: Harcourt Brace Jovanovich.

Biney, Ama. 2014. "The Historical Discourse on African Humanism: Interrogating the Paradoxes." In Praeg and Magadla 2014, 27–53. Pietermaritzburg, S. Afr.: University of KwaZulu-Natal Press.

Furman, Katherine. 2014. "Ubuntu and the Law: Some Lessons for the Practical Application of Ubuntu." In Praeg and Magadla 2014, 150–66. Pietermaritzburg, S. Afr.: University of KwaZulu-Natal Press.

Gyekye, Kwame. 1997. *Tradition and Modernity: Philosophical Reflections on the African Experience*. Oxford: Oxford University Press.

Kant, Immanuel. 1997. *Critique of Practical Reason and Other Works on the Theory of Ethics*. 6th ed. Translated by Thomas Kingsmill Abbott. Delhi, India: Surjeet.

Kirwen, Michael C. 1987. *The Missionary and the Diviner*. New York: Orbis.

Masolo, D. A. 2010. *Self and Community in a Changing World*. Bloomington: Indiana University Press.

Mbiti, John S. 1969. *Africans Religions and Philosophy*. Nairobi: Heinemann Kenya.

Njue, John. 2012. "African Humanism Ubuntu: The Spiritual Lung for the Future of Humanity." In Trevisiol 2012, 23–48. Rome: Urbaniana University Press.

Okello, Stephen. 2012. "Western Humanism in Dialogue with African Ubuntu for the Greater Good." In Trevisiol 2012, 49–60. Rome: Urbaniana University Press.

Oruka, H. Odera. 1985. *Punishment and Terrorism in Africa*. Nairobi: Kenya Literature Bureau.

———, ed. 1991. *Sage Philosophy: Indigenous Thinkers and Modern Debate on African Philosophy*. Nairobi: African Centre for Technology Studies.

———. 1993. "Parental Earth Ethics." *Quest* 7 (1): 21–28.

———. 1996. *The Philosophy of Liberty*. 2nd ed. Nairobi: Standard.

———. 1997. *Practical Philosophy in Search of Human Minimum*. Nairobi: East African Educational.

p'Bitek, Okot. 1986. *Artist the Ruler*. Nairobi: Heinemann Kenya.

Porter, Burton F. 1995. *The Good Life: Alternatives in Ethics*. New York: Ardsley House.

Praeg, Leonhard, and Siphokazi Magadla, eds. 2014. *Ubuntu: Curating the Archive*. Pietermaritzburg, S. Afr.: University of KwaZulu-Natal Press.

Rousseau, Jean-Jacques. 1998. *The Social Contract*. Translated by H. J. Tozer. Ware, UK: Wordsworth.

Shue, Henry. 1980. *Basic Rights*. Princeton, NJ: Princeton University Press.

Shutte, Augustine. 2001. *Ubuntu: An Ethic for a New South Africa*. Dorpspruit, S. Afr.: Cluster.

Trevisiol, Alberto, ed. 2012. *In ascolto dell'Africa: contesti, attese, potenzialita*. Rome: Urbaniana University Press.

Tutu, Desmond. 1999. *No Future without Forgiveness*. London: Rider.
Tutu, Desmond, and Mpho Tutu. 2010. *Made for Goodness*. London: Rider.

ORIARE NYARWATH is Senior Lecturer of Philosophy in the Department of Philosophy and Religious Studies, University of Nairobi, Kenya. He is author of *Traditional Logic: An Introduction*.

7

UBUNTU AND *BUEN VIVIR*

A Comparative Approach

Anke Graness

T HIS CHAPTER WILL COMPARE TWO CONCEPTS FROM DIFFERENT parts of
the world, the South African concept of Ubuntu and the Latin American concept of *buen vivir*. Despite obvious similarities between the two concepts, *buen vivir* has rarely been considered in the intense current debate on
Ubuntu. Using relevant texts from the latest academic literature, the chapter starts with a short description of both concepts, followed by a discussion
of the similarities between them—especially the objectives and sociopolitical functions associated with each concept. After discussing some pitfalls
in dealing with indigenous knowledge systems, the chapter explores the
potentials of indigenous concepts as moral and political alternatives. The
chapter concludes that both concepts are valuable contributions to a new
global ethics for the twenty-first century, which can be established only in
an open, equal intercultural polylogue between the various traditions and
schools of thought in all regions of the world.

Ubuntu

Ubuntu, currently one of the most popular African indigenous concepts,[1]
has benefited from increasing discussion and awareness, even outside the
African continent, since the 1990s. In South Africa, it is a central concept
not only in current academic discourse but in the public sphere as well,
where it is widely used by politicians, by marketing and business people,
and even as the name of a security company,[2] offering armed security

guards to their clients, which—as we will see—is a strong contradiction of the core values of the Ubuntu concept.

But what exactly is Ubuntu? This question is not easy to answer because of the growing body of literature on the topic and the multifaceted nature of the academic discourse on it, which encompasses such diverse disciplines as theology, philosophy, economics, education, jurisprudence, sociology, migration research (see Hankela 2014), and literature and art. Christian Gade shows that the number of publications dealing with Ubuntu has virtually exploded since the end of apartheid. There were 57 publications on Ubuntu in 1992; in 2009, there were 12,600 (Gade 2011, 319), reflecting a complex debate about a great variety of definitions and interpretations of Ubuntu.[3]

It is now widely known that the term *Ubuntu* belongs to the Nguni language family in South Africa and has equivalents in many other African languages, like *utu* in Swahili or *botho* in Sesotho and Setswana. The South African philosopher Mogobe B. Ramose (1999) explains Ubuntu as follows:

> Ubuntu is actually two words in one. It consists of the prefix *ubu-* and the stem *ntu*. Ubu evokes the idea of be-ing in general. It is unfolded be-ing before it manifests itself in the concrete form or mode of ex-istence of a particular entity. . . . *Ubu-* and *-ntu* . . . are mutually founding in the sense that they are two aspects of be-ing as a one-ness and an indivisible whole-ness. . . . *Ubu-* as the generalized understanding of be-ing may be said to be distinctly ontological. Whereas *-ntu* as the nodal point at which be-ing assumes concrete form or a mode of being in the process of continual unfoldment may be said to be the distinctly epistemological. (36)

There is no consensus, however, on what Ubuntu actually means, and the precise content of the concept is still contested. The translations range from "humanity" and "charity" to "common sense" and "generosity." A brief overview of the fairly broad literature on Ubuntu makes it clear that the term is used in at least two ways. On the one hand, Ubuntu is seen as a concept enshrined in a traditional philosophy of life, although one needs to further differentiate between Ubuntu as a moral quality of a person, as a way of living[4] (Broodryk 2008), a worldview, a philosophy (Ramose 1999), or an ethical framework (Shutte 2001). On the other hand, since the 1990s, Ubuntu has become a key abstract term in the process of transition from an apartheid regime to a new "rainbow nation" and for an African renaissance, and functions here as a kind of vision or utopia for a new South Africa.[5] The first approach seems to be concerned with the reconstruction of historical indigenous knowledge; the second is clearly future-oriented.

The core meaning of the concept Ubuntu is frequently expressed using the Zulu-Xhosa aphorism "umuntu ngumuntu ngabantu"—"A human being is a human being through other people,"[6] meaning that every human being needs other people in order to be human; every person is part of a whole, integrated into a comprehensive network of mutual dependencies. The aphorism expresses "the African idea of persons: persons exist only in relation to other persons. The human self . . . only exists in relationship to its surroundings; these relationships are what it is. And the most important of these are the relationships we have with other persons" (Shutte 2001, 23). Thus, the aphorism refers to the deep relational character of Ubuntu and underlines at the same time that human beings (*umuntu*) are a "being becoming" (Ramose 1999, 36–37) in an already existing community. The human being is seen as an organic part of a community and the community as the necessary precondition for any human being. Two interrelated central aspects of Ubuntu, which are widely accepted by many authors, are expressed here—namely, the nonstatic and evolving nature of human beings and the importance of the community.

Moreover, the aphorism emphasizes the existence of a universal bond that connects all people to each other and all other types of existence in the universe. Interdependence and interconnectedness are considered the main features of this conception of the world. As the Ethiopian philosopher Workineh Kelbessa describes it, "Traditional African worldviews also recognize the interconnection between the natural and supernatural, physical and metaphysical, visible and invisible dimensions of the world. Currently living human and nonhuman beings, ancestors, the yet unborn, and the natural world are interconnected" (2011, 569–70). Because of these three interrelated dimensions of Ubuntu (the living, the departed, the yet-to-be-born), Mogobe B. Ramose calls the Ubuntu understanding of be-ing an "onto-triadic structure of be-ing" (1999, 46; 2003b, 236).

On a moral level, Ubuntu is a basic attitude of mutual respect and recognition of the rights of others in order to promote human dignity and harmonious, peaceful coexistence. Michael O. Eze (2010) interprets Ubuntu as follows:

> "A person is a person through other people" strikes an affirmation of one's humanity through recognition of an "other" in his or her uniqueness and difference. It is a demand for a creative intersubjective formation in which the "other" becomes a mirror (but only a mirror) for my subjectivity. This idealism suggests to us that humanity is not embedded in my person solely as an

individual; my humanity is co-substantively bestowed upon the other and me. Humanity is a quality we owe to each other. We create each other and need to sustain this otherness creation. And if we belong to each other, we participate in our creations: we are because you are, and since you are, definitely I am. The "I am" is not a rigid subject, but a dynamic self-constitution dependent on this otherness creation of relation and distance. (190–91)

A widespread general view considers Ubuntu as a uniquely African world-view or ethic. In that view, scholars usually describe Ubuntu as an ethics or a philosophical concept rooted in the precolonial knowledge systems of Africa, a concept that belongs to the "essence" of a specific African mode of being, which, in contrast to the individualistic worldview of "the West,"[7] they describe as being more community oriented. The South African philosophers Augustine Shutte and Mogobe B. Ramose explicitly refer to an Ubuntu ethics[8] (Shutte 2001; Ramose 2003a). Characteristic features of Ubuntu ethics are compassion toward others, respect for the rights of minorities, conduct that aims at consensus and understanding, a spirit of mutual support and cooperation, hospitality, generosity, and selflessness.

Ramose attributes these standards to linguistic peculiarities and the epistemological structures of the Bantu language. In accordance with the approach of Placide Tempels (Tempels 1945) and Alexis Kagame (Kagame 1956, 1976), neither of whom explored the concept of Ubuntu deeply in his analysis,[9] Ramose describes the Bantu terms *muntu* (human), *kintu* (thing), *hantu* (space and time), and *kuntu* (modality) as the four basic categories of African philosophy. He adds a fifth: Ubuntu. For him, Ubuntu is a normative ethical category that defines the relationship between the other four categories. Moreover, it is the fundamental ontological and epistemological category in the "African thought of the Bantu-speaking people," which expresses the indivisible unity and totality of ontology and epistemology (Ramose 2003a, 324–25). Thus, he calls Ubuntu "the root of African philosophy. The be-ing of an African in the universe is inseparably anchored upon *ubuntu*" (2003b, 230).

And yet Ubuntu refers not only to the relationship between people but also to the relationship between human beings and the entire universe. The relationship is made clear by the prefix *ubu*, which defines being as embedded, and the root *ntu* signifies the unfolding of being by means of a continuous manifestation through certain forms and modes of being (Ramose 1999, 36). As Ramose emphasizes, this concept implies that individual human beings are inseparable from an all-encompassing universe

(Ramose 1999, 65). In the understanding of most Africans, Ramose argues, the earth is a source of life that deserves respect (Ramose 2004, 2009). This sounds very much like a (potential) environmental ethic, an idea that is indeed explored by such authors as Workineh Kelbessa (2011) and Mark O. Ikeke (2011). Ikeke points out that the principle "*ndubuisi*" (life is the highest good), a classic part of the Ubuntu thesis, refers to the life of all animate and inanimate beings. Anchored in the African philosophy of Ubuntu are the ideas of communal humanity and social consciousness, which search for the good within others and within the community. According to these authors, the Ubuntu approach could play a major role in shaping ecological restoration and sustainability practices,[10] as well as advance the contemporary idea of the social responsibility of multinational oil companies and other corporations (Ikeke 2011, 111).

The concept started to have political influence during the 1990s. After decades of apartheid and the successful transition from a racist undemocratic society to a democracy, South Africa's process of reconciliation became associated with Ubuntu, which served as the moral basis of the Truth and Reconciliation Commission (TRC) of 1996–98 appointed by President Nelson Mandela under the authority of the Promotion of the National Unity and Reconciliation Act to investigate crimes against humanity. Ubuntu found its way into the transitional constitution of South Africa of 1993.[11] The term cannot be found in the current legal constitution of 1996, however, a fact that is rightly criticized by Ramose (2014): "The placement of Ubuntu as an 'endnote' in the interim Constitution of 1993 and its subsequent exclusion from the 1996 Constitution amounts to the exclusion of certain peoples . . . and their Ubuntu philosophy from substantive political and economic engagement and consequently violates their right to life" (122).

In particular with reference to the work of the TRC, a further way to interpret Ubuntu became influential, namely the Christian interpretation of Ubuntu as advocated by Desmond Tutu, certainly one of the best known representatives of the concept of Ubuntu worldwide. Tutu, former archbishop of Cape Town, winner of the Nobel Peace Prize (1984), leading figure of black liberation theology (often referred to as Ubuntu theology), and former chairman of the TRC, describes Ubuntu as follows: "When we want to give high praise to someone we say, '*Yu, u nobuntu*'; 'Hey, so-and-so has *ubuntu*.' Then you are generous, you are hospitable, you are friendly and caring and compassionate. You share what you have. It is to say, 'My humanity is caught up, is inextricably bound up in yours'" (Tutu 1999, 31).

Or "Harmony, friendliness, community are great goods. Social harmony is for us the *summum bonum*—the greatest good. Anything that subverts or undermines this sought-after good is to be avoided like the plague. Anger, resentment, lust for revenge, even success through aggressive competitiveness, are corrosive of this good" (Tutu 1999, 35).

For Tutu, the central Christian concepts of reconciliation and forgiveness are also main characteristics of Ubuntu. In Christian theology, reconciliation is a basic concept that aims at overcoming the separation and alienation between God and man. The destroyed relationship is to be restored by an act of repentance, an approach that is also reflected in the concept of the South African TRC, where truth-telling and confessing to crimes committed was the requirement for an amnesty and the individual act of forgiveness by the victims or their relatives. Reconciliation and forgiveness are, according to Tutu, at the same time central components of restorative justice, which was characteristic of traditional African jurisprudence. "Here the central concern is not retribution or punishment. In the spirit of Ubuntu, the central concern is the healing of breaches, the redressing of imbalances, the restoration of broken relationships, a seeking to rehabilitate both the victim and the perpetrator, who should be given the opportunity to be reintegrated into the community he has injured by his offense" (Tutu 1999, 54–55). Thus, for him Ubuntu—here taken as social or communal harmony—offers an approach to justice, anchored in traditional African society and value systems and Christian belief, to start the long process of healing and transformation after the traumatic experience of colonialism and apartheid.

Calling for an African renaissance, the former South African president Thabo Mbeki demanded in the late 1990s that all Africans become aware of their own values, their own strength and power, their own creativity. Africa, he insisted, must face up to its responsibility and take its fate into its own hands; slavery and colonialism can no longer be an excuse for inaction. Corruption, war, and economic hardship, Mbeki argued, are not problems that can be solved from outside but ones that need to be overcome by the Africans' own efforts. The African renaissance, he asserted, must be based on the material, the spiritual, and the cultural development of Africa (Mbeki 1996). In this context, Ubuntu became a kind of utopian blueprint for peaceful coexistence in a modern, multicultural society. Here the concept acts as a vision of a future peaceful, harmonious coexistence, as a guiding political principle for overcoming today's social conflicts on a national and a global scale (Van Binsbergen 2001; Louw 2001). In this context, Ubuntu is concerned with building a modern Africa, in which various traditions encounter each other and have to be reconciled. It's a means to achieve emancipation, antiracism, humanism, and social justice. It is a tool for forming a new moral community as a precondition for a new national political order and identity. To take Ubuntu as a (political) imaginary, and to ask what Ubuntu can do for the solution of today's problems, is also Eze's approach. He argues for an understanding of Ubuntu as an open and dialogical historical process (Eze 2010, 161) and an "emerging tradition within a particular historical context" (186).

Buen Vivir / Sumak Kawsay

A similarly popular concept is the Latin American idea of *buen vivir* or *sumak kawsay*, which plays a central role in academic and sociopolitical debates in Latin America. Moreover, social movements such as Attac or Occupy refer to this concept and draw inspiration from it. The number of publications on the concept has increased significantly in the last decade.[12]

Buen vivir is the Spanish translation of the Quechua phrase *sumak kawsay*, which means "good life" or "living well." Josef Estermann (1999, 2010) translates the term as "good life" and emphasizes its difference from concepts of "good life" in the European tradition.

The concept of *buen vivir/sumak kawsay* builds on the indigenous knowledge systems of Latin America's Andean population. The historical origins of the concept are difficult to trace; it is presently understood as an indigenous Andean worldview and ancestral knowledge based on four main principles: a relationality that underlines the interconnection between all elements of the world; the idea that all elements correspond harmoniously; a reciprocal relationship between human beings and nature; the idea that opposites can be complementary.

Buen vivir/sumak kawsay concerns harmony among human beings and between human beings and nature. The concept, which includes a dimension of human spirituality, aims to foster human coexistence according to ecological and social standards. *Buen vivir/sumak kawsay* involves recognition of the right of all individuals to a good or wholesome life that satisfies basic human needs and a communal life in harmony with the environment. In this concept nature, too, is understood as an entity that can have rights, for example, the right to preservation. Such an approach changes the relationship between nature and humans to a more bio-pluralistic view that eliminates the separation between nature and society. The recognition of nature's rights constitutes an important change of perspective, not only in the context of dominant neoliberal concepts of society, but also in the context of dominant concepts of anthropocentric ethics that consider nature only a resource for the satisfaction of human interests. The concept of *buen vivir / sumak kawsay* offers a new paradigm that may offer alternative modes of development.

In contrast to Western approaches, *buen vivir / sumak kawsay* encompasses everything that exists. The whole of nature, not merely humankind, is the center of this concept. Furthermore, the cornerstone is not the individual, but the community. For this reason, the concept is often epitomized by the image of Pachamama, the all-embracing Mother Earth.

In his description of the Andean Pachasophy[13] condensed in the metaphor of *buen vivir,* Josef Estermann (2013) summarizes the following main principles: Everything has life; nothing is mere dead matter. The universe is a living organism in which all parts are connected to each other. The basic principle of any development, therefore, must be life as a whole, the entire *Pacha.* Nature is not meant to be dominated and exploited in the service of humankind (as the theories of Kant, Marx, and Max Weber, for instance, insist) but exists rather as a unity of life. Nature is not considered in terms of a contrast between nature and mankind. In consequence, natural resources are not simply viewed as resources that are available to human beings but as organs in the great cosmic organism, which cannot be privatized. They serve to preserve and to further life in general. To avoid violating the cosmic balance, natural resources must be used sustainably and restored for future generations and nonhuman life. This requires not only a ban on the privatization of energy resources but also a guarantee of free access to water, one of the most fiercely contested issues of our time.

The good life is considered a mode of existence in balance with all other elements of the *Pacha.* Therefore, development is not understood as an anthropocentric accumulation of goods and money but as an organic maturation of every being according to its needs and abilities and in accordance with the overall ecological balance. Man is not the measure of all things; the rights of Mother Earth take precedence. Furthermore, development is neither linear nor irreversible, and the good life is not only ahead of us but also in a past that needs to be rehabilitated. Even the economy is not thought of in terms of growth but in terms of a rational dealing with the collective house. And progress is not measured according to quantitative indicators, but in terms of quality of life. The point of life is not to accumulate wealth, but to achieve a state of balance (Estermann 2013, 32–34).

The idea of *buen vivir / sumak kawsay* is not simply an alternative philosophical and ethical concept. On the contrary, it has gained political significance since the 1990s as a general critique of capitalism and its colonial and neocolonial implications. It has also provided an alternative embedded in Latin American indigenous knowledge systems to "Western" (neoliberal) models of development and policy. As such, it has been taken up in social and political discourse. For example, the concept of *sumak kawsay* is one of the four main pillars of the Council for Development of the Nationalities and People in Ecuador (CODENPE), along with multinationality, interculturality, and the rights of the nature. CODENPE considers *sumak kawsay* an alternative for the deep transformation processes in societies, in opposition to the capitalist logic of economic growth and profit accumulation.

Sumak kawsay was introduced during the Ecuadorian national crisis (1995–2006) as a key concept for a new political project that questioned dominant white, liberal, and neoliberal social values (Cortez and Wagner 2010; Fatheuer 2011). The concept gained constitutional status in Ecuador (2008) and Bolivia (2009).[14] In a conscious turn toward Andean indigenous knowledge, Pachamama has been recognized in the Ecuadorian and Bolivian constitutions as a philosophical and legal category (Gudynas 2012, 8–11.). Politically speaking, this is a big step, not least because the demographic structure and the cultural and intellectual heritage of the various peoples of both countries are now for the first time reflected more adequately in their constitutions: Fifty-five percent of Bolivia's population are indigenous peoples; thirty-five percent of Ecuador's people are indigenous. Some interesting issues can be raised, however, about the reconstruction of indigenous knowledge systems and their relevance for contemporary problems.

Relevance of Indigenous Concepts—Some Critical Remarks

Both Ubuntu and *buen vivir / sumak kawsay* are linked to indigenous, mainly orally transmitted, knowledge systems.[15] Both reflect attempts to reconstruct these knowledge systems and to make them fruitful for the interpretation and solution of today's problems. It is interesting that the two concepts have some obvious similarities: emphasis on the community over the individual; stress on the interdependence of all beings, including humans, and the associated nonanthropocentric focus; prioritization of harmony; clear differentiation from Western concepts of development and morality.

Moreover, the fact that both concepts entered into widespread discourse in the 1990s is quite interesting. Currently, both concepts are not only reviewed and discussed on a theoretical level (in their relevance to philosophy, theology, ethics, and so forth) but also introduced into political and developmental discourses. The ecological side effects of the predominant neoliberal models of global social and economic formation are devastating, and neoliberalism's effect on a sustainable improvement of the living conditions in so-called underdeveloped countries has been constantly put into question. Alternative developmental models are urgently needed, and Ubuntu and *buen vivir / sumak kawsay* enter into the discussion as guiding principles.

Both concepts are used in very different theoretical and social contexts, as for example in political and ideological discourse, in developmental discourse, in the discourse of environmental ethics, in legal discourse (in terms of preservation of "traditional" legal systems for indigenous groups), and also in philosophy, in theology (especially Ubuntu), and in historical discourse. The next section will discuss some of the difficulties associated with the application of indigenous concepts in political contexts.

Ubuntu and *Buen Vivir*—A Construct?

Ubuntu and *buen vivir* are described as indigenous knowledge and value systems rooted deep in the culture and history of certain peoples in South Africa and the Andes. But colonization, liberation struggles, and the post-colonial periods have led to profound social changes in these regions that inevitably had an impact on the knowledge systems, morals, beliefs, and cultural and political institutions of the formerly colonized peoples. For this reason, the reconstruction of indigenous knowledge systems is not an easy task. One has to be aware of the following questions while reconstructing orally transmitted indigenous knowledge: To what extent have the concepts undergone changes or transformations? Who was or is responsible for the preservation and reconstruction of that knowledge? What are the goals of the reconstruction, and what terminology has been (should be) used? Who exactly are the bearers of the respective knowledge or values today?

To what extent can these concepts still be considered living knowledge or values? Who are the protagonists and players in the reconstruction of these concepts today, and what are their goals and their concerns? Are these concepts still rooted in the consciousness of the people?[16] And finally, what are the overlapping points with the ways of life, worldviews, and normative systems in contemporary Africa or Latin America?

Consequently, when dealing with concepts such as Ubuntu or *buen vivir* today, one has to be aware that these concepts do not build on indigenous ideas alone; they have been reconceptualized from today's point of view, according to today's standards, in light of today's problems. Thus, both concepts should be seen as open concepts evolving and changing in a constant dialogic or polylogical historical process, and as "emerging tradition within a particular historical context" (Eze 2010, 186). As we confront the revival of Ubuntu and *buen vivir*, we must be conscious that it is a revival at a certain point in history and recognize the circumstances that made the revival possible or necessary. So why, under certain circumstances, is there a tendency to have recourse to certain indigenous concepts, and what answers and solutions are thereby sought? One must inquire into the politico-ideological a priori implicit in the revival of such concepts. Thus, in the case of Ubuntu and *buen vivir*, the historical circumstances in Latin America, South Africa, and the rest of the world during the 1990s must be examined to understand the reasons recourse to indigenous knowledge seemed fruitful and necessary at that point in time.

The research of Christian Gade is particularly insightful about transformation and functionalization of indigenous concepts in contemporary discourse. From his painstaking research into the written discourse about the term *Ubuntu* stretching back to 1846 (Gade 2011, 2012) he draws the interesting conclusion that, even though the term *Ubuntu* occurs repeatedly in texts from 1846 onward, the usage of the term changed considerably around the year 1980. Until then, Ubuntu was described as the moral quality of a person (Gade 2011, 308). It was only after 1980 that it was increasingly defined as a kind of concept, an African humanism, a philosophy, an ethical framework, or a worldview. Now it is commonly used in this sense. The connection to an environmental ethics is even more recent; here, too, the amount of literature has steadily increased in recent years. According to Gade's research, only between 1993 and 1995 did it become common to define Ubuntu on the basis of the aphorism "umuntu ngumuntu ngabantu." By now this particular connection to Ubuntu is assumed to be a foregone conclusion in many texts (Gade 2011, 313). It is clear in Gade's reconstruction of the use and content of the term *Ubuntu* that an intellectual construction of worldviews has taken place, a kind of academization of indigenous knowledge, as well as a political exploitation. Gade's analysis of texts and documents shows that Ubuntu, as the concept is described today, has been deliberately constructed and politically instrumentalized in the process of transition from a white minority government to a black majority government in Zimbabwe[17] and South Africa—although undoubtedly following indigenous thought patterns in postcolonial times (Gade 2011, 303, 320).

Van Binsbergen pronounces that he sees Ubuntu

> in the first place as a contemporary academic construct, called forth by the same forces of oppression, economic exploitation, and cultural alienation that have shaped Southern African society over the past two centuries. With Ramose I subsume these forces under the term of globalisation. However, on the basis of an extensive discussion of format I deny the identity between the academic evocation in the form of ubuntu philosophy, and the actual value orientation informing precolonial Southern African villages. Therefore, although ubuntu philosophy may be able to curb some (certainly not all) of the contemporary traumatic effects of globalisation/conquest, it is a new thing in a globalised format, not a perennial village thing in an authentic format. (Van Binsbergen 2001, 62)

In Bolivia there is quite a heated debate about the indigenous origin of the concept of *buen vivir* and its rootedness and persistence in the popular mindset. For example, Uzeda Vasquez (2009) explicitly uses the term *visiones indígenas* (indigenous visions, which may be comparable to the term *imaginaire* as used by Leonhard Praeg [2014]) and raises the question whether the *suma qamaña*[18] can be viewed as a legitimate, genuine indigenous concept at all.[19]

In addition, we have to be aware of the linguistic rupture and its consequences. The systematic description and analysis of these orally transmitted concepts has taken place only recently in order to provide a written basis for their formulation and interpretation. For the most part, this goes hand in hand with a linguistic rupture; Ubuntu is described and construed mostly in English, *buen vivir/sumak kawsay* in Spanish—that is, in translations. The respective discourses do not take place in the original languages of the concepts, for instance, in the Nguni language of the Xhosa or in Quechua. Thus, it can be assumed that the reconstruction of the concepts is already accompanied by conceptual and epistemological changes.

To what degree concepts are rooted in people's minds and a living praxis is a crucial factor when it comes to their political implementation. It is important to question whether Ubuntu and *buen vivir* in their various interpretations are visions of an ideal of human coexistence (an *imaginaire*) rather than lived moral and political values and norms.

Dichotomies

The use of the concepts of Ubuntu or *buen vivir* often takes the form of a dichotomy between monolithic concepts, as, for example, the self versus the other, Africa or Latin America versus the West, tradition versus modernity. The quest for an ethical framework adequate for the South African or Latin American context or as an alternative to dominant neoliberal social theories is set against Western Judeo-Christian tradition or Western morality, or more often, the Cartesian "Cogito ergo sum." Various Western schools of thought are not explicitly discussed (e.g., in a comparative analysis of related concepts); instead, a certain unified image of the West is constructed. For example Estermann (2013, 39–40) juxtaposes two models of civilization and development in a table (the dominant Western modernity versus the Amerindian civilization, or capitalist development versus the indigenous good life). Trying to boil "dominant Western modernity" down to its essence using only thirteen categories—including terms such as mechanicity, anthropocentrism, and individualism—is quite an ambitious undertaking. Since freedom, autonomy, and human dignity are categories that remain unmentioned, the choice of characteristics of the Western model seems quite selective. Overlooking the various alternative approaches in the Western tradition is an inadmissible reduction that does not do justice to the internal pluralism of the West.

It seems to me equally questionable whether the Amerindian civilization can be described exhaustively with thirteen categories. Moreover, all terms used to describe the Amerindian civilization oppose concepts of Western modernity (organicity instead of mechanicity; biocentrism and cosmocentrism instead of anthropocentrism, etc.). With this approach, it is interesting to note, Estermann follows an "excluding dualism," which is actually a method he places in the "prevailing occidental modernity" section of his table, presumably to be criticized. His descriptions of indigenous worldviews thus remain defined by a Western model, an approach that has been a legitimate point of contention in nineteenth- and twentieth-century ethnology: describing others by contrasting them to opposing Eurocentric values (e.g., nature/culture, rationality/emotionality).

An approach like Estermann's, which is quite widely used in dealing with indigenous knowledge—Négritude and ethnophilosophy in Africa are based on the same kind of approach—is the root of essentialism, which assumes the existence of "pure cultures" and reduces cultures and societies to a few relevant features that can never do justice to the inner plurality and even the contradictory nature of societies and knowledge systems. Looking at the precolonial African and Latin American societies in an essentialist and romanticized way leads to a revival of the Africa-West dichotomy and the production of stereotypes that need to be overcome. Especially as regards the search for solutions to problems on a global scale, such as environmental protection and the eradication of poverty, fruitful points of contact have to be sought, not contrasts. A dialogue of traditions is necessary, in which traditions of thought and value systems of the various regions of the world are recognized in their inner plurality.

It is very important to determine whether there are alternative values and concepts that can be mobilized today to counter the negative effects of the ones spread through modernization and colonization from the West to the rest. One must recognize, however, the inner plurality of every culture, every knowledge system. In principle, such alternative values may come from Alpine mountain farmers, too, though this kind of indigenous knowledge system is not a major focus at present. Along with models from other regions of the world, discussions and dialogues must consider European or North American concepts and political or social movements that try to offer alternatives to the dominant neoliberal socioeconomic model. Europeans and North Americans, too, are greatly aware of the limits and destructive traits of modernity, and they also question and seek alternatives to the current compulsive growth paradigm. This is demonstrated by people, especially the younger population, who are turning toward movements that value ecologically sustainable economies and seek to exit the spiral of consumption. Such initiatives try to limit consumption by sharing and exchanging rather than making new purchases of cars and other goods. Guerrilla gardening and self-catering neighborhood fruit and vegetable gardens represent attempts to lessen the environmental destruction caused by commercial agriculture. Such people are also joining civil-society movements, including Attac, Occupy, and Unconditional Basic Income. Much work has been done in the theoretical field in recent years. Environmental philosophy and ethics are now key issues in Euro-American philosophy and are increasingly institutionalized.[20] Furthermore, today's research focuses on principles of global justice and strategies of conflict resolution. A one-sided critique of the West wrongfully ignores such subversive movements and concepts.

On the other hand, so-called non-Western academics' and social activists' critiques of environmental and civil-society movements as well as European and North American academia are quite justified, since the necessary openness and readiness for a dialogue with non-Western concepts and models is still lacking for the most part. The prevailing ignorance of non-Western concepts and widespread belief in the universality of Western values and theoretical concepts are serious obstacles for an intercultural dialogue. A dialogue that includes various approaches and concepts is crucial, because ultimately the target is not a Latin American, European, or African solution, but a global definition of the relationships between humanity and nature and between the various social, cultural, and religious groups in this world and, finally, a global solution to the distribution of the goods of this world. Alternatives to the paradigm of progress and growth can be sought only in the context of global challenges. In that search, one must avoid dichotomies and include concepts from all regions of the world.

A Critical Approach to Indigenous Concepts

Indigenous African and Latin American knowledge systems are possible tools for developing a new humanistic and environmentally responsible model of development. This approach marks an attempt to apply local (historical) concepts to global (contemporary) problems, such as environmental protection or global justice. Here, we have to center on the question suggested by Leonhard Praeg: When we translate a historical praxis into a contemporary context, which elements of the praxis are to be included in that translation and which are not? (Praeg 2014, 141). And what are the reasons behind the choice?

Referring to the concept of *buen vivir / sumak kawsay*, David Cortez and Heike Wagner (2010) note that although present-day political and social discourse draws on the ethical content of indigenous concepts, the discourse itself is modern. The changes that go hand in hand with such use of historical and local concepts in a contemporary globalized context are usually not explicated. Cortez and Wagner deem the blanket comparison of a

Western tradition with a concept of *sumak kawsay,* which may already have experienced Western and non-Western revisions, problematic. The Congolese philosopher Valentin Y. Mudimbe (1997) calls processes of the transformation of historical, local discourses into modern, global languages and discourses "retrodiction":

> retrodiction seems to be the main technique that establishes both the new right to speech (and the power of spatializing indigenous localities) and the intellectual efficiency of its interpretation. Retrodiction—from Latin retro (on the back side, behind, in time back) and dicere (to speak)—denotes the idea of speaking (and thus synthesizing) from an illusory, invented moment back in time. In the process, the present invests its values in the past with its questions and hypotheses, and rediscovers in the invented, reorganised spaces, laws, paradigms, or the truth of its suppositions. Indeed, the new creation is often in contradiction with the colonial adapted Enlightenment paradigms and its library. (95)

The unease encountered here about the tension between historical indigenous concepts (of course, not all indigenous or local concepts are historical) and their application to contemporary discourses points to an important issue: The handling or use of indigenous concepts (historical and contemporary ones) must be accompanied by continual critique of its conditions, its terminology, its function, and its objectives.

Cortez and Wagner (2010) offer such a critique of the *buen vivir / sumak kawsay* approach, asking

- What are the political-theoretical preconditions that led to the original construction of the holistic concept *sumak kawsay* frequently applied nowadays?
- What differences can be established in comparison to "Western" traditions of the "good life"?
- What are the current theoretical adaptations of the concept and what changes must it undergo in order to maintain its theoretical and political legitimacy?
  What is the critical content of *sumak kawsay* in terms of an engagement with modernity?

The same questions can be raised about Ubuntu or other indigenous concepts in their various interpretations.

Workineh Kelbessa (2005), who outlined an environmental ethics on the basis of indigenous concepts and lived practices of the Oromo (the largest ethnic group in Ethiopia), underlines the need to deal with indigenous concepts thoughtfully and critically. He emphasizes that a romanticized attitude toward indigenous practices and knowledge is not helpful in solving our current problems, for not all indigenous knowledge is valuable and environmentally friendly. On the contrary, there are practices that have adverse effects on the environment. Admittedly, an excessive dependence on indigenous beliefs could hinder the identification and objective assessment of the real causes of shortcomings. He also points out that many indigenous technologies and practices are not universally applicable; they have been adapted to local conditions and are therefore often only locally applicable. As a result of such localization, indigenous knowledge systems often lack the intellectual resources to help them deal with issues raised by global capitalism. Kelbessa's critique draws attention to a third important point: the exclusion and oppression of women, as, for example, in Oromo society, where men and women do not enjoy equal status. Women are excluded from political and legal processes, as well as managerial functions. Kelbessa argues that this inequality has implications for the treatment of nature as well. He emphasizes "that the uncritical romanticization of indigenous environmental knowledge does not help either the people or the natural environment; and that indigenous knowledge needs to be complemented by modern knowledge in order to be more efficient" (Kelbessa 2005, 27).

In his investigations, Kelbessa draws a number of conclusions, which he formulates as recommendations to protect the indigenous intellectual property rights of marginalized peoples and to create incentives that encourage a rediscovery and development of indigenous knowledge. Furthermore, he recommends that this knowledge be integrated into dialogues and debates dealing with global development policies (Kelbessa 2005, 39). His recommendation is tied to the view that negative tendencies in indigenous worldviews such as resistance to the distribution and free use of knowledge and the marginalization of women must be overcome.[21] Similarly, one needs to resist the tendency to idealize indigenous knowledge and the indigenous way of life (Kelbessa 2005, 40).

In his book *A Report on Ubuntu*, Leonhard Praeg (2014) goes one step further in his analyses of Ubuntu discourse: he describes the Ubuntu discourse as part of an identity politics taking place on personal, social, and cultural levels. Praeg notes that "every attempt to speak about Ubuntu is an exercise in power, a primordial attempt to get the fact and meaning of blackness, black values, traditions and concepts recognized as of equal value to the people for whom they matter" (14). In speaking about Ubuntu, "we need to make a point about being black in a white world and African in a Western-dominated world" (14). The point of the discussion is to eliminate the oppression of black people in the world and to confirm the right to be recognized as African. This kind of linkage between the ethical and the political dimensions of Ubuntu has to be analyzed and made obvious. Consequently, Praeg's criticism focuses on the political instrumentalization of Ubuntu in the process of nation building in postapartheid South Africa, where a set opposition between the old and new South Africa, apartheid and democracy, Eurocentrism and Afrocentrism, leads to a problematic identity politics that sets up a dichotomy between Europe and Africa (as we know already from European ethnology) and seeks to provide a homogeneous picture of Africa that excludes those forms of individualism and stratification that might complicate the picture. This leads to a repetition of the myth of primitive unanimity. Further, the assumption of African unanimity (if applied today) easily excludes all opposing ideas as un-African, a process Praeg terms "conceptual violence" (154). To avoid such pitfalls, Ubuntu has to be repeatedly and critically rethought. It can serve as a kind of critical horizon for critical humanism. According to Praeg, critical humanism must avoid becoming an ideology; its task is to recall the injustices the new order is meant to eliminate and the prevailing power structures that shape every discourse from the beginning. In this sense, Ubuntu might play an important role in the formation of South African society.

Indigenous Concepts as Moral and Political Alternatives

Discourses on Ubuntu and *buen vivir/sumak kawsay* first and foremost do have significance and value as modes of being and agency independent from and external to the dominant discourse of a universalized model of modernity and as part of the context of identity discourses in their respective communities. But the current international popularity and relevance of Ubuntu and *buen vivir* in the context of developmental debates, as part of environmental ethics, or in the search for a new ethics for the twenty-first century, can be explained by a growing consciousness about the dark side of Western modernity and the disastrous effects of the capitalist economic and social model on nature and social cohesion. Environmental destruction and poverty are directly related—a circumstance that becomes particularly obvious in countries on the so-called periphery. Representing alternative concepts based on indigenous knowledge, both Ubuntu and *buen vivir* are considered possible solutions to crises facing national and international society.

To acquire social significance, however, indigenous ideas need theorists like Alberto Acosta and Eduardo Gudynas, leaders like Archbishop Desmond Tutu, or philosophers like Mogobe B. Ramose and Augustine Shutte to create a theoretical concept based on indigenous knowledge that might serve as an alternative to prevailing theoretical concepts and developmental models. In this respect, one has to agree with Eduardo Gudynas, who identifies *buen vivir* as a concept currently in the making that is not a unified idea but rather a pluralistic one used in different contexts (Gudynas 2011, 1; 2012, 5).[22] This fact is reflected in political and social movements that also act as carriers of such ideas. The collective power of such political groups as civil movements, political parties, nongovernmental organizations, and churches and other religious associations is necessary to establish *buen vivir* or Ubuntu as a moral and political alternative with policymaking power. But even within these groups, as well as in various organizations of indigenous people in Latin America, such concepts are understood quite differently.[23]

The emphasis on the pluralistic nature of approaches such as *buen vivir* and Ubuntu is very important, because both concepts are often presented as a kind of general solution to present-day national and global crises. Today, scholars, as well as ecological and anticapitalist movements, in the West like to refer to both concepts as a kind of general solution for the problems of the world. This assertion overlooks the fact that there is no original concept of *buen vivir* or Ubuntu; in the way they are retrodicted through contemporary discourses, both represent reconstructions whose interpretations are vigorously contested. Thus, *buen vivir* or Ubuntu are concepts still in the making. Or, as Acosta emphasizes, the inestimable contribution of *buen vivir* is the opportunities for new dialogues about "good lifes" offered by this approach (Acosta 2015, 196). Acosta underlines here not only the plurality of ideas of "good life" but also the procedural character of the concept of *buen vivir*, a process of reappropriation of useful indigenous concepts to contemporary conditions and needs, in form of an intensive academic and social dialogue. The same applies to Ubuntu.

National and international society as a whole need to discuss various concepts and approaches to find solutions to the social problems of our time. At this point, the issue of which concept is the closest in the description of a precolonial reality may not be decisive or even relevant. In order to find solutions to our contemporary problems, it is not advisable to return to historical forms of society—a return to the social, environmental, and spatial environment of the village community that is certainly envisaged by some representatives of the two approaches.[24] In any case, this is not the objective of most representatives of *buen vivir* or Ubuntu. Augustine Shutte, for example, envisages Ubuntu as "an ethic for a new South Africa" (2001). Alberto Acosta calls *buen vivir* an "indigenous utopia" (and not a return to a Golden Age; Acosta 2015, 69), and Eduardo Gudynas holds that the features of *buen vivir* are neither backward nor representative of a return to the past; rather, they are, in Mudimbe's terminology, a kind of retrodicted alternative to conventional development prognoses. The various forms of expression, whether old or new, original or hybrid, open up the possibility of exploring other strategies (Gudynas 2012, 14). The goal is to start a process of fundamentally rethinking our relationships with nature and with other human beings, a process that looks for solutions that attempt to harmonize our very different notions of a good life with the task of preserving nature and social peace. This can only be negotiated in an intercultural dialogue.[25] A more intense dialogue between Latin American concepts of *buen vivir* / *sumak kawsay* and African concepts of Ubuntu will surely enrich the debate.

Conclusion

Ubuntu and *buen vivir* / *sumak kawsay* are two concepts from different parts of the world that seem to have many similarities, both in content and in terms of their function in social transformation processes. Furthermore, the handling of both concepts highlights such similarities as the danger of romanticizing or essentializing the concepts as well as the problems inherent in functionalizing the concepts in political processes of structural change.

In the search for self-determined alternatives to the current crisis of the dominant capitalist model of society and its paradigm of development as economic growth, thoughtful, critical recourse to indigenous approaches, which have been neglected and marginalized for centuries, can certainly contribute to fruitful, lively social discourses. Such a critical analysis surpasses a simplistic notion of a return to the roots and confronts the complexity of today's world. The effort must be centered on a metareflexive critical approach to intellectual traditions and value systems that fathoms the possibilities and limits these concepts hold for reshaping our world, rather than a romanticized view or the construction of an ideal harmonious past. Only in this way does it become possible to find realistically viable alternatives to the dominant model of society and development. A critical, intercultural approach that avoids idealizations, ideological abuse, and identitarian dichotomies and engages in a dialogue about other ideas makes it possible for indigenous concepts to unfold their emancipatory potential, contribute to the process of a "conceptual decolonization,"[26] or a "decolonization of knowledge" (Gudynas 2012, 25), and aid in the search for solutions to the burning issues of today's world.

Notes

1. I use the phrase *indigenous concepts* here to refer to local knowledge systems deeply rooted in the history of a certain society, which form the information base of this particular society and render agency and decision-making possible. In the cases of *buen vivir* and Ubuntu, the term also refers to the presumed rootedness of both concepts in precolonial times. But an opposition between the pre- and the postcolonial is as problematic as that between tradition and modernity, indigenous knowledge systems and international knowledge systems, myth and logos, and the like. Such binary oppositions obscure the inner and historical ties between historical epochs and concepts and veil the fact that modernity comprises elements of tradition, just as tradition already contains elements of modernity; that myth contains elements of the logos as the logos comprises elements of myth; that international knowledge systems are always based on local knowledge (even though there is almost no awareness about it); and that local knowledge arises in engagement with other traditions of thought and, especially today, in response to global developments. Thus, in using the phrase *indigenous concepts*, I want to refer to the locality of these concepts and explicitly avoid describing them as traditional knowledge, which would open up the tradition–modernity dichotomy.

2. See Ubuntu Security http://ubuntusecurity.co.za/ (accessed April 2017). "In view of such inappropriate use several authors lament the overuse of the concept in South Africa. See Munyaka and Motlhabi (2009, 64) and Shutte (2001, 14).

3. Leonhard Praeg (2014) identifies five "conceptual personae" in the discourse on Ubuntu: the archivist and the cosmopolitan, who condemn Ubuntu as anachronistic nationalism; the conformist and the prophet, who take Ubuntu as salvation of the African self; and the savior, who understands Ubuntu as a critique of the destructive individualism of the West. Also see the various views and approaches in Murove (2009), Praeg and Magadla (2014), and Gade (2012).

4. Ramose (1999, 3–4) and Mungwini (2011, 779) argue that referring to Ubuntu as merely a way of life is degrading it—and moreover perpetuates the myth that only the white man is a "rational animal" and has philosophy.

5. Leonhard Praeg (2014, 11) introduces the useful distinction between *ubuntu* (a traditional world view and way of life) and *Ubuntu* (a postcolonial concept).

6. Gade (2011, 313) points out that it first became common between 1993 and 1995 to define Ubuntu on the basis of the aforementioned aphorism and that it was Augustine Shutte who introduced the link between this aphorism and a definition of the concept of Ubuntu.

7. The opposition between Africa and "the West," which is a common feature of various discourses, is usually used to highlight a presupposed (cultural) difference. But the concept of the West is very problematic because it denotes not even a geographical entity, but only a compass direction. Usually the concept of the West is used to refer geographically to Europe and North America and to associate these geographical entities with a certain enlightened, secular, and idealized "scientific" mode of thought. Furthermore, it is presupposed that individual freedom is the central ethical idea of the West in opposition to the key ethical idea of Africa, communitarianism. The inner plurality of these geographical entities (Africa, Europe, and North America) in culture, religion, worldviews, historical developments, philosophical schools, and so on, is totally neglected in such an approach.

8. Thaddeus Metz (2007) and Metz and Gaie (2010) uses features of Ubuntu ethics to work out an African moral theory worth taking seriously as a rival to dominant Western ethical conceptions. For a recent attempt in this direction, see Chuwa (2014).

9. Gade (2012, 488) writes, "To my knowledge, Alexis Kagame, a Rwandese historian, philosopher, and Catholic priest from the Tutsi group, was the first African to publish a text containing the term '*ubuntu*.' In this text, entitled *La philosophie bantu-rwandaise de l'être* . . . '*Ubuntu*' is translated as '*libéralité.*'"

10. See also Mawere (2014).

11. Chapter 15, the Article on National Unity and Reconciliation, states, "These can now be addressed on the basis that there is a need for understanding but not for vengeance, a need for reparation but not for retaliation, a need for ubuntu but not for victimisation" (Constitution of the Republic of South Africa, Act 200 of 1993, accessed December 21, 2018, https://www.gov.za/documents/constitution/constitution-republic-south-africa-act-200 -1993).

12. In the German-speaking region alone there are a number of examples; for example, Fatheuer (2011); Acosta (2009, 2015); Gudynas (2009); Estermann (1999, 2010, 2013).

13. Estermann (2013) argues for replacing the Western term *philosophy* with the Quechua-Aymara-Greek term *Pachasophy* to indicate the wisdom (*sophia*) of Pacha, a complex, fundamental concept of Andean thought. Pacha means the "ordered universe," "time-space," "everything that exists and has life" (31n24).

14. The 2008 constitution of Ecuador, for example, refers to *sumak kawsay* in its preamble and in Article 14: "The right of the population to live in a healthy and ecologically balanced environment that guarantees sustainability and the good way of living (sumak kawsay), is recognized." It is also mentioned in articles 250, 275, and 387. Furthermore, the constitution affirms rights of nature (e.g., in articles 71, 73) and a basic right to clean water (http://pdba .georgetown.edu/Constitutions/Ecuador/english08.html, accessed April 27, 2017).

15. In the case of Latin America, there are a few written sources like the *Popol Vuh* (Book of Counsel) a corpus of mytho-historical narratives of the K'iche kingdom in Guatemala.

16. In the case of South Africa, events like xenophobic mob attacks on African immigrants in 2008 or the Marikana miner's strike, which ended in a massacre by South African security forces in 2012, give reason to doubt the rootedness of the concept in the

population, or at least in a certain section of the population. Even though one might argue that Marikana was an isolated incident from which no generalization can be made about the degree of adherence to cultural values (which is, in my opinion, too narrow a view, since Marikana is just a spike in the violence against poor people fighting for their rights), one can still ask the question, Where was the spirit of Ubuntu there?

17. For Zimbabwe, see Samkange and Samkange (1980), in which Ubuntu is introduced as a political philosophy.

18. The translation of *buen vivir/sumak kaway* in Aymara, language of the Aymara people in Bolivia.

19. Estermann (2013, 42n49) mentions this point, too, and draws on Spedding Pallet (2010) and Medina (2006). Unfortunately, Estermann does not discuss further this interesting point about the academization of colloquial terms or academic inventions of indigenous concepts but remains confined to a footnote.

20. A list of references on this topic would go beyond the constraints of this chapter, but let me point to Stone (1972), Hargrove (1989), Hösle (1991), and Jonas (1979). Also note the growing literature on plant and animal ethics and the theory of deep ecology devised by the Norwegian philosopher Arne Næss. See Glasser, Drengson, and Næss (2005) and Næss (1986). Acosta justifiably refers to deep ecology in his works.

21. African feminists also argue for that. They criticize juridical practices that postulate an opposition between the individual rights of women and the protection of cultural rights, which is ultimately used to restrict the rights of women using the protection of traditional values as justification. Moreover, some raise questions about the extent to which contemporary notions of African tradition and culture represent constructs based on data supplied by European anthropologists. To what extent are African societies described through a Christian-patriarchal lens, which completely ignores or misinterprets institutions and traditions of women in precolonial societies because they do not fit into Christian-patriarchal social norms? See, for example, Nzegwu (2006), Oyěwùmí (1997), and Keevy (2014). Gathogo (2008, 49) makes the criticism that Ubuntu has failed to address the concerns of African women because of the patriarchal nature of the traditional society.

22. Gudynas (2012) emphasizes the need for a dialogue that includes other alternative concepts, such as deep ecology, for example.

23. Almut Schilling-Vacaflor (2008), for example, draws attention to the diversity of indigenous points of view and organizations. She points out that the indigenous organizations in Bolivia are not a monolithic entity but represent extremely heterogeneous notions of cultural identity and necessary state transformations.

24. An African example of this is the failed Ujamaa project by Julius Nyerere in Tanzania.

25. Knowledge has to be decolonized in order to end the superiority of the West, argues Gudynas (2012, 18–21, esp. 21). At the same time, the diversity of cultures must be respected, without being hierarchized. This target can be approached by an intercultural dialogue (intercultural philosophy) that aims to dismantle the foundations upon which the superiority of a subject or a culture over another can be justified.

26. This term is, for instance, used by the Ghanaian philosopher Kwasi Wiredu (1996), who employs it to demand a fundamental critique of the colonialism and neocolonialism uncritically presumed by Western languages, values, institutions, and so on. He also demands investigation of whether indigenous languages, values, and institutions can be used to shape today's world, or whether they may even offer more adequate solutions.

References

Acosta, Alberto. 2009. "Das 'Buen Vivir': Die Schaffung einer Utopie." *Juridicum* 4:209–13.
———. 2015. *Buen vivir: Vom Recht auf ein gutes Leben*. Munich: Oekom.
Broodryk, Johann. 2008. *Understanding South Africa: The Ubuntu Way of Living*. Pretoria: Ubuntu School of Philosophy.
Chuwa, Leonard. 2014. *African Indigenous Ethics in Global Bioethics: Interpreting Ubuntu*. Dordrecht, Neth.: Springer.
Constitution of the Republic of South Africa, Act 200 of 1993. Accessed April 27, 2017. http://www.gov.za/documents/constitution/constitution-republic-south-africa-act-200-1993.
Coetzee, Pieter H., and Abraham P. J. Roux, eds. 2003. *The African Philosophy Reader*. New York: Routledge.
Cortez, David, and Heike Wagner. 2010. "Zur Genealogie des indigenen "guten Lebens" ("sumak kawsay") in Ecuador." In *Lateinamerikas Demokratien im Umbruch*, edited by Leo Gabriel and Herbert Berger, 167–200. Vienna: Mandelbaum.
Estermann, Josef. 1999. *Andine Philosophie: eine interkulturelle Studie zur autochthonen andinen Weisheit*. Frankfurt: IKO.
——— 2010. "'Gut Leben' als politische Utopie: Die andine Konzeption des 'guten Lebens' (suma qamaña/alli kawsay) und dessen Umsetzung im demokratischen Sozialismus Boliviens." In *Gutes Leben als humanisiertes Leben: Vorstellungen von Guten Leben in den Kulturen und ihre Bedeutung für Politik und Gesellschaft heute: Dokumentation des VIII. Internationalen Kongresses für interkulturelle Philosophie*, edited by Raul Fornet-Betancourt, 261–88. Mainz, Ger.: Wissenschafts.
———. 2013. "Zivilisationskrise und das gute Leben: eine philosophische Kritik des kapitalistischen Modells aufgrund des andinen *allin kawsay/suma qamaña*." *Concordia* 63:19–48.
Eze, Michael. O. 2010. *Intellectual History in Contemporary South Africa*. New York: Palgrave Macmillan.
Fatheuer, Thomas. 2011. *Buen vivir—recht auf gutes Leben*. Berlin: Heinrich-Böll-Stiftung.
Gade, Christian B. N. 2011. "The Historical Development of the Written Discourses on *Ubuntu*." *South African Journal of Philosophy* 30:303–29.
———. 2012. "What Is Ubuntu? Different Interpretations among South Africans of African Descent." *South African Journal of Philosophy* 31 (3): 484–503.
Gathogo, Julius. 2008. "African Philosophy as Expressed in the Concepts of Hospitality and Ubuntu." *Journal of Theology for Southern Africa* 130:39–53.
Glasser, Harold, Alan Drengson, and Arne Næss, eds. 2005. *The Selected Works of Arne Næss*. Vol. 10, *Deep Ecology of Wisdom: Explorations in Unities of Nature and Cultures: Selected Papers*. Dordrecht, Neth.: Springer.
Gudynas, Eduardo. 2011. "Buen vivir: germinando alternativas al desarrollo." *América latina en movimiento* 462:1–20.
———. 2012. *Buen vivir: das gute Leben jenseits von Entwicklung und Wachstum*. Berlin: Rosa Luxemburg Stiftung Reihe Analysen.
Hankela, Elina. 2014. *Ubuntu, Migration and Ministry: Being Human in a Johannesburg Church*. Leiden, Neth.: Brill.
Hargrove, Eugene C. 1989. *Foundations of Environmental Ethics*. Englewood Cliffs, NJ: Prentice Hall.

Hösle, Vittorio. 1991. *Philosophie der ökologischen Krise.* Munich: Beck.

Ikeke, Mark O. 2011. "The Value of Ubuntu in Restoration and Sustainability of Nigeria's Niger Delta." *Journal of African Environmental Ethics and Values* 1:97–115.

Jonas, Hans. 1979. *Das Prinzip Verantwortung: Versuch einer Ethik für die technologische Zivilisation.* Frankfurt: Suhrkamp.

Kagame, Alexis. 1956. *La philosophie bantu-rwandaise de l'être.* Brussels: ARSC.

———. 1976. *La philosophie bantu comparée.* Paris: Présence africaine.

Keevy, Ilze. 2014. "Ubuntu versus the Core Values of the South African Constitution." In Praeg and Magadla 2014, 54–95.

Kelbessa, Workineh. 2005. "The Utility of Ethical Dialogue for Marginalized Voices in Africa." Discussion paper. Institute for Environment and Development. Addis Ababa University. http://pubs.iied.org/13508IIED/.

———. 2011. "Indigenous Environmental Philosophy." In *The Oxford Handbook of World Philosophy,* edited by Jay L. Garfield and William Edelglass, 569–70. Oxford: Oxford University Press.

Louw, Dirk. 2001. "Ubuntu and the Challenges of Multiculturalism in Post-apartheid South Africa." *African Renaissance and Ubuntu Philosophy.* Special issue, *Quest* 15 (1–2): 15–36.

Mawere, Munyaradzi. 2014. *Environmental Conservation through Ubuntu and Other Emerging Perspectives.* Mankon, Cameroon: Langaa RPCIG.

Mbeki, Thabo. 1996. "I Am an African." Accessed April 27, 2017. http://www.anc.org.za /content/i-am-african-thabo-mbekis-speech-adoption-republic-south-africa -constitution-bill.

Medina, Javier. 2006. *Suma qamaña: por una convivialidad postindustrial.* La Paz, Bolivia: Garza Azul.

Metz, Thaddeus. 2007. "Towards an African Moral Theory." *Journal of Political Philosophy* 15:321–41.

Metz, Thaddeus, and Joseph B. R. Gaie. 2010. "The African Ethic of Ubuntu/Botho: Implications for Research on Morality." *Journal of Moral Education* 39 (3): 273–90.

Mudimbe, Valentine-Yves. 1997. *Tales of Faith: Religion as Political Performance in Central Africa.* London: Athlone.

Mungwini, Pascah. 2011. "The Challenges of Revitalizing an Indigenous and Afrocentric Moral Theory in Postcolonial Education in Zimbabwe." *Educational Philosophy and Theory* 43 (7): 773–87.

Munyaka, Mluleki, and Motlhabi Mokgethi. 2009. "Ubuntu and Its Socio-Moral Significance." In Murove 2009, 63–84.

Murove, Munyaradzi F., ed. 2009. *African Ethics: An Anthology of Comparative and Applied Ethics.* Pietermaritzburg, S. Afr.: University of KwaZulu-Natal Press.

Næss, Arne. 1986. "The Deep Ecological Movement: Some Philosophical Aspects." *Philosophical Inquiry* 8 (1–2): 10–31.

Nzegwu, Nkiru. 2006. *Family Matters: Feminist Concepts in African Philosophy of Culture.* Albany: State University of New York Press.

Oyěwùmí, Oyèrónkẹ́. 1997. *The Invention of Women: Making an African Sense of Western Gender Discourses.* Minneapolis: University of Minnesota Press.

Praeg, Leonhard. 2014. *A Report on Ubuntu.* Pietermaritzburg, S. Afr.: University of KwaZulu-Natal Press.

Praeg, Leonhard, and Siphokazi Magadla, eds. 2014. *Ubuntu: Curating the Archive*. Thinking Africa Series. Pietermaritzburg, S. Afr.: University of KwaZulu-Natal Press.

Ramose, Mogobe B. 1999. *African Philosophy through Ubuntu*. Harare, Zimb.: Mond.

———. 2003a. "The Ethics of Ubuntu." In *Philosophy from Africa*, 2nd ed., edited by Pieter H. Coetzee and Abraham P. J. Roux, 2003, 324–30. Cape Town: Oxford University Press Southern Africa.

———. 2003b. "The Philosophy of *Ubuntu* and *Ubuntu* as a Philosophy." In *Philosophy from Africa*. 2nd ed., edited by Pieter H. Coetzee and Abraham P. J. Roux, 230–38. Cape Town: Oxford University Press Southern Africa.

———. 2004. "The Earth 'Mother' Metaphor: An African Perspective." In *Visions of Nature: Studies on the Theory of Gaia and Culture in Ancient and Modern Times*, edited by Fons Elders, 203–6. Brussels: VUB Brussels.

———. 2009. "Ecology through Ubuntu." In Murove 2009, 308–14.

———. 2014. "Affirming a Right and Seeking Remedies in South Africa." In Praeg and Magadla 2014, 121–26. Scottsville, S. Afr.: University of KwaZulu-Natal Press.

Samkange, Stanlake, and Tommie M. Samkange. 1980. *Hunhuism or Ubuntuism: A Zimbabwe Indigenous Political Philosophy*. Salisbury, Zimbabwe: Graham.

Schilling-Vacaflor, Almut. 2008. "Indigene Identitäten und politisch-rechtliche Forderungen im bolivianischen Verfassungsänderungsprozess." *Journal für Entwicklungspolitik* 24:122–45.

Shutte, Augustine. 2001. *Ubuntu: An Ethic for a New South Africa*. Pietermaritzburg, S. Afr.: Cluster.

Spedding Pallet, Alison. 2010. "Suma qamaña" ¿kamsañ muni? (¿Qué quiere decir 'vivir bien'?)." *Fey Pueblo* 17:4–39.

Stone, Christopher D. 1972. "Should Trees Have Standing? Toward Legal Rights for Natural Objects." *Southern California Law Review* 45:450–87.

Tempels, Placide. 1945. *La philosophie bantoue*. Elisabethville, Congo: Lovania.

Tutu, Desmond. 1999. *No Future without Forgiveness*. New York: Random House.

Uzeda Vasquez, Andrés. 2009. "Suma qamaña: visiones indígenas y desarrollo." *Traspatios* 1:33–51.

Van Binsbergen, Wim. 2001. "Ubuntu and the Globalisation of Southern African Thought and Society." *African Renaissance and Ubuntu Philosophy*. Special issue, *Quest* 15 (1–2): 53–89.

Wiredu, Kwasi. 1996. *Cultural Universals and Particulars: An African Perspective*. Bloomington: Indiana University Press.

ANKE GRANESS is Elise Richter Fellow in the Department of Philosophy at the University of Vienna (Austria), and Project Leader of a Fonds zur Förderung der wissenschaftlichen Forschung (FWF)-funded research project on the history of philosophy in Africa at the University of Vienna. She is author of *Das menschliche Minimum: Globale Gerechtigkeit aus afrikanischer Sicht; Henry Odera Oruka*. She is editor (with Kai Kresse) of *Sagacious Reasoning: H. Odera Oruka in Memoriam*, and editor (with Franz Gmainer-Pranzl) of *Perspektiven interkulturellen Philosophierens: Beiträge zur Geschichte und Methodik von Polylogen*.

8

UBUNTU AND CHRISTIANITY

Augustine Shutte

A LTHOUGH UBUNTU IS A CONCEPT ROOTED IN THE traditional culture of Africa, the human value it identifies is, so I believe, true and therefore universal. This is, of course, the case with all moral values that are not simply relative to a particular culture, group, or individual. In South Africa, however, during apartheid, African moral values were contrasted with European ones and seen as inferior; hence, in no way universal. At the same time, Christianity was seen as a European religion with universal values that everyone, including people with an African cultural background, should recognize. In this article, I want to provide a corrective to these two mistaken attitudes. I will argue that the ethic of Ubuntu, though very different and apparently opposed, is in fact complementary to the classical ethical tradition of Europe. I also maintain that both these ethical traditions are consonant with, indeed support, two central elements of Christian faith and thus provide a conceptual foundation for a genuine enculturation of Christianity in Africa. Doing so is especially necessary in South Africa, probably the most developed country in Africa, where the dominant culture of the ruling white minority is European in its present materialist and consumerist form but where the culture of the majority of South Africans is that of Africa.

Christianity refers, in the first place, not to a system of ideas or even to an insight or revelation, but to the interaction between Jesus and the first followers of his. It began when they first came into contact with him and did not come to an end with his death.

Because this interaction was an intersubjective relationship between persons, it included an understanding of what was going on, an understanding of Jesus and of themselves and of what was happening to them. It was this understanding that came to be expressed in such terms as *savior, redemption, eternal life*, and *apostle*.[1]

This interpersonal relationship with Jesus involved more than just a change of outlook. It was a change that affected all the dimensions of their lives: their feelings, attitudes, commitments, and behavior, as well as their ideas. They called this a change of heart (*metanoia*).

Christians believe that what happened between Jesus and his disciples is something of unique and universal importance. And, moreover, that it is something that can still happen to anyone. Whenever it does happen, however, it is still a personal interaction between a person and the person of Jesus.

The insights of the first Christians into what had happened in the interaction between them and Jesus were acquired and expressed in the Jewish language and culture. But as the Christian movement penetrated Greek and Roman society, the church leaders and the authors of the New Testament used new concepts drawn from Greek and Roman culture for the same purpose. The enculturation of Christianity had begun.[2]

Christianity, as I have defined it, is not a worldview but an intersubjective relationship between persons and Jesus. But it always takes place in a specific cultural context, and every culture has its own worldview or set of worldviews. And because the Christian interaction is a personal one, it includes an understanding of what is taking place.

This understanding is inevitably particular and exclusive of others. Thus, it excludes certain worldviews, is not compatible with all. And because this understanding must be expressed in the language of a particular culture, it is never complete and final such that a particular form of words embodies it perfectly for all times and places. Every attempt to express the meaning of the interaction with Jesus, including the first, was an experiment. And it was an experiment that each person had to do alone, Greek or Roman or Jew.[3]

When Christianity entered Europe, cultures and worldviews were already in place. The Christian interaction had to be defined in terms of them. And, in turn, its own nature and dynamism modified the culture, introducing new ideas, new expressions. So powerful was the influence of Christianity on the cultures of Europe that it was easy to make the mistake of identifying them.

The history of colonialism eventually put a stop to that. We see, now that European culture is colonizing the world, that it is not the privileged vehicle of the Christian experience. Because of what Christianity claims for itself, no single culture could be wholly adequate to embody it. Every culture has its own weaknesses, wounds, and blind spots. And, in its contact with the other cultures of the world, European culture has had its own selection of them mercilessly exposed.

Christian interest in South Africa, where European and African cultures meet, is twofold. We want to enculturate Christianity in Africa so that it finds expression in an African way. We also want to overcome the cultural separation produced by apartheid so that African and European cultures can engage with each other and even, perhaps, marry and be fruitful. Then South Africa will be truly a product of what Leopold Senghor (1963, 11) liked to call "cultural miscegenation." And Christianity will face a new challenge of enculturation!

It is my view that European culture has something that is an authentic insight into one aspect of the Christian interaction. And so has the traditional culture of Africa. They are different insights—indeed, to all appearances, contradictory. Nevertheless, I judge them to be both true in themselves and a true reflection of two complementary aspects of Christianity. So, if we can reconcile them, we will have gone some way toward uniting Europe and Africa in a common worldview. We will also have provided a new and appropriate conceptual instrument for the enculturation of Christianity in the new South Africa.[4]

The European insight I am thinking of is the discovery of individual freedom, both as a fact about human nature and as a value for human life. This discovery culminated in the modern period of European philosophy, initiated by the development of natural science, by the Reformation, by the breakup of the Holy Roman Empire, and by the renaissance in art and literature. This flowering of the idea of freedom in the modern period is, however, only the end product of a long process of growth, a process that has its roots in Greek and biblical thought. Ultimately, however, it is the development of science and secularization that creates the climate in which the idea flowers into fruition. This climate is beautifully expressed by Giovanni Pico della Mirandola in his *Oration on the Dignity of Man*. God is speaking to Adam:

> Neither a fixed abode nor a form that is yours alone nor any function peculiar to yourself have we given you Adam, to the end that according to your longing and according to your judgement you may have and possess what abode, what form, what functions you yourself shall desire. The nature of all other beings is

limited and constrained within the bounds of laws prescribed by Us. You, constrained by no limits, in accordance with your own free will, in whose hand We have placed you, shall ordain for yourself the limits of your nature. We have set you at the world's centre that you may from there more easily observe whatever is in the world. We have made you neither of heaven nor of earth, neither mortal nor immortal, so that with freedom of choice and with honour, as though the maker and moulder of yourself, you may fashion yourself in whatever shape you shall prefer. (qtd. in Taylor 1989, 199–200)

Pico is writing at the very beginning of the modern period. By the time of Kant, this idea of freedom as self-determination is understood as a transcendence of the whole realm of nature and the laws that the natural sciences have discovered. Unfortunately, because of the way in which these laws were understood at the time, such transcendence seemed inseparable from dualism. Nevertheless, the notion that no conceivable scientific account could be sufficient to explain the nature of human persons and their acts was a new and authentic insight into the nature of human freedom. It is only with existential philosophy in the twentieth century that this insight became wrenched free from dualism and one is given a positive (and not merely a negative) account of human freedom and transcendence as a capacity for genuine self-realization.

It is impossible to exaggerate the centrality of this idea in European culture and thought. But what is it in the distinctive Christian interaction that it answers to? What is there in the relationship between Jesus and his disciples that finds its expression in the European idea of freedom? The answer stares one in the face from the heart of the Christian phenomenon. But one has become so accustomed to it that it is easy not to see it.

It is the conviction that the transcendent itself is present in Jesus and his disciples, in Jesus first and foremost but also in them. This is the conviction captured in the doctrines of the incarnation of God's Word and the descent of his Holy Spirit. The first Christians came to believe that a genuinely transcendent power was present and showed itself in Jesus and also in their lives because of their relationship with him. It showed itself especially in what one could call an inner state or disposition, in the personal attitudes (intellectual, emotional, and volitional) of faith, hope, and self-giving love.

As I have said, the idea that God is present in human life and persons is so common in European thought and culture that one is often unaware of its consequences. But they are there all the same and have had a huge influence on European history. The idea of the absolute value of the individual, of inalienable human rights, of conscience, of the transcendence of death, of spirituality and the inner life—all these and other common themes emerge from it. In the course of history, some of these ideas have found their fullest expression in the secularized society that has replaced the sacral world in which they first developed. But we are now in a position to see, I think, that the secularization of society is itself partly a result of Christianity and its revelation of the transcendent within human lives and history.

The presence and revelation of transcendent power in the interaction between Jesus and his disciples is reflected in the growth and flourishing of the idea of human freedom in the history of Europe. Freedom as self-determination, as transcendence over all forms of worldly causality, natural and social, is the mirror image of the transcendent life experienced in the Christian interaction.

Let us now consider the African insight that I feel also emphasizes, in a way typical of it, an essential element of the Christian interaction. It is the insight that is the conceptual foundation of the ethical notion of Ubuntu, an insight into the nature of persons and personal relations expressed in the saying *umuntu ngumuntu ngabantu*, a human being becomes human through relationships with others.

I have provided a philosophical analysis of this conception of community and the concept of a person that it contains, as well as the ethic of Ubuntu that flows from it, in other places. Here I will just highlight the aspect of it that is relevant to our present interest.[5]

The key idea is that a human person exists and develops as a person only in relation to other persons. The human self is not to be seen as something already formed and present in each human individual at birth. It is still to be formed in the course of living. And it can come into existence only through the gift and influence of others. It is thus in no way material, something inside the body of the individual, for instance, as a mind-brain identity theorist might surmise. Insofar as it exists in a place, it exists outside the body, in relationships with other persons and the whole material environment. It is truer to the African idea, however, to see self and other as coexisting, each in the other in the sense of being identified with each other. It is not just a cultural reality either, but something natural. The fundamental human reality must be seen as a unified field of personal energy in which each individual emerges as a distinct pole or focus. This field of life is the same in each; in each it is their humanity. All persons form a single person, not as parts form a whole, but as friends draw life and character from the spirit of a common friend. They have a common identity.

It is a difficult idea to define precisely. Biblical scholars should, however, be familiar with something very similar in the thought of St. Paul. He uses the metaphor of a human body to describe the community of Christians with Jesus. This is not just a matter of parts making a whole but of the way in which the spirit, or the head, is present in each of the other parts. He wants to give an idea of how each is in Christ and Christ is in each. There is a kind of identity implied. "We are to grow up in every way into him who is the head, into Christ," he says, "until we all attain . . . to mature manhood, to the measure of the stature of the fullness of Christ" (Eph. 4:13–15).

The African conception of persons and community is quite different from both modern European individualist and collectivist conceptions. Both of these are fundamentally materialist. It is not dualist either, but something else, for which our dominant culture (and philosophy) has no name.

It is, however, this idea of the self's dependence on others for its very existence as a human self that is at the heart of traditional African thought and the foundation of the ethical notion of Ubuntu and that is, to my mind, an apt vehicle for expressing an essential aspect of the Christian interaction.

Once again, I am thinking of something so central to Christianity and so taken for granted that it is scarcely noticed. This is the fact that the disciples experience Jesus as their savior. Whatever else this celebrated term connotes, it entails that Jesus did something for them that they could not do for themselves. Although it was their faith that saved them and it was their hearts that were changed, it was all due to the influence Jesus had over them. It was his spirit that forgave their sins and set them free.

It is easy to overlook the absoluteness of the dependence of the disciples on Jesus for the change he wrought in them. But for those present at the time, it was clear. We can see this best by reconsidering the idea that Jesus forgave people, especially his disciples, their sins. If we think of forgiveness in merely legal terms, then we will not truly understand the transaction between Jesus and his disciples or the reaction to his claim on the part of those present. They did not see his forgiving sins as a merely legal matter. They saw it as actually destroying sinfulness, removing it, changing the heart of the sinner. And because of what sin was, this was something that only God could do. And Jesus was claiming to do it! So they objected, and he had to demonstrate he had the power by performing a miracle of healing.

We have here the quintessential New Testament example of salvation: salvation from sin. And it is an example of the same interpersonal causality we have remarked in the African conception of community. The disciple is wholly dependent on Jesus for salvation. The sin-destroying change of heart is due wholly to Jesus's influence. Yet it is at the same time the most deeply inward act of the disciple. It is a paradox, but it perfectly prefigures the African idea. The more I come under a certain kind of influence of the other, the more the act is my own. It is this influence of the other that creates, and in this case re-creates, me.[6]

In fact, we can look at the interpersonal transaction that is the heart of Christianity as one mutual act that can be seen from two sides. From Jesus's side it is forgiveness and grace; from the disciple's, repentance and faith. But the forgiveness and grace are logically, though not necessarily temporally, prior to the repentance and faith. Strictly speaking, we must say that the forgiveness is the cause of the repentance, the grace is the cause of the faith.

The traditional African idea of persons and community is thus, on my understanding of it, an apt vehicle for this central aspect of Christianity. There remains the apparent contradiction between the European idea of individual freedom and the African idea of our dependence on others for all that we are and do. The contradiction is, or so I believe, merely apparent.

The clue to the complementarity of the two insights lies in the capacity of both to articulate the central datum of Christianity, the interaction between Jesus and his disciples. In the case of freedom, it was the way it echoed the transcendent presence in the incarnation. Is there anything of the same in the dependence of the disciples on Jesus for salvation? Surely there is. The fact that the disciples' hearts are changed by Jesus's influence indicates a kind of causality that no finite being could achieve. Certainly this is what those present believed. But we can see that it must be so. His act on them is also their most inward act. There is an incommensurability of influence and activity here that reveals the presence of a transcendent power. If the power that Jesus exerted over the disciples were finite in any way, they would have become subject to him through its exercise, enslaved by him rather than set free. Instead, the more they come under his influence, the freer they are.

The deepest manifestation of sin, as St. Paul tells us, is an inner slavery, an inability to exercise one's capacity for freedom. The wound is so deep that our freedom is destroyed. And just as only a transcendent power can create beings like us with the capacity for self-determination, so only a transcendent power can enable that capacity to develop or revive it when destroyed.

Thus, both our capacity for self-determination and our dependence on other persons to develop as persons reveal something transcendent in human nature. In the case of self-determination, it is our transcendence of the causal systems of nature and the conditioning of society. In the case of our dependence on other persons, it is a self-transcendence toward others that is able to assimilate all that they are and do, including them in our lives and making their inmost activity our own. These two manifestations of transcendence answer to the two aspects of an image. An image is both like what it is an image of and wholly dependent on it. We are like the transcendent creator, and this likeness is revealed in our freedom. We are also wholly dependent on him, and dependent for this very likeness: the more dependent, the more like. And this dependence is revealed in our dependence on others for being the person that we are.

I have argued at great length and as rigorously as I know how in several publications (particularly in two articles in *Modern Theology*, October 1984 and January 1987) for the truth that the exercise, development, and fulfilment of our capacity for self-determination depends on a certain kind of influence from other persons. Here I have simply asserted this truth. If truth it be then it provides a conceptual connection between the best and most central insights of European and African thought. The connection, in turn, could provide the foundation for creative cultural miscegenation in South Africa. And as far as Christianity is concerned, if I am right in identifying these elements in the Christian interaction, this new South African culture will provide an even more adequate language for the enculturation of the faith.

Notes

1. I am indebted to Sebastian Moore for this idea of deriving the meaning of Christian doctrines from an analysis of the relationship between Jesus and his disciples. Moore does this in a masterly series of publications from *No Exit* in 1968 to *Let This Mind Be in You* in 1985.

2. The best work I know on the concept of enculturation is Aylward Shorter (1989).

3. For an exhaustive analysis of what is involved in contemporary interpretation of the New Testament writings, see Schillebeeckx (1980).

4. I attempt the integration of central ethical insights from the European and African philosophical traditions in Shutte (2001).

5. See Shutte (2001), chapter 2.
6. For a contemporary elaboration of this idea, see Shutte (1993).

References

Moore, Sebastian. 1968. *No Exit*. London: Darton, Longman and Todd.

———. 1985. *Let This Mind Be in You*. London: Darton, Longman and Todd.

Schillebeeckx, Edward. 1980. *Christ: The Christian Experience in the Modern World*. London: Student Christian Movement Press.

Senghor, Leopold. 1963. *Negritude and African Socialism*. St Anthony's Papers no. 15, edited by K. Kirkwood, 9–22. London: Oxford University Press.

Shorter, Aylward. 1989. *Toward a Theology of Inculturation*. Maryknoll, NY: Orbis.

Shutte, Augustine. 1984. "What Makes Us Persons?" *Modern Theology* 1:79.

———. 1987. "A New Argument for the Existence of God" in *Modern Theology* 3:157–77.

———. 1993. *The Mystery of Humanity*. Cape Town: Snailpress.

———. 2001. *Ubuntu: An Ethic for a New South Africa*. Pietermaritzburg, S. Afr.: Cluster.

Taylor, Charles. 1989. *Sources of the Self*. Cambridge, MA: Harvard University Press.

AUGUSTINE SHUTTE was Honorary Research Associate in the Philosophy Department of the University of Cape Town. He wrote *Ubuntu: An Ethics for a New South Africa*. Dr. Shutte passed on in 2016.

9

UBUNTU, RECONCILIATION IN RWANDA, AND RETURNING TO PERSONHOOD THROUGH COLLECTIVE NARRATIVE

Anna-Marie de Beer

THIS CHAPTER EXPLORES THE RELATIONSHIP BETWEEN UBUNTU—AS a concept that advocates shared humanity—and possibilities of reconciliation in postconflict societies such as postgenocide Rwanda. Furthermore, it makes the link between Ubuntu's appeal to communal and interdependent relationships and the role that can be played by the "creation of a shared history" in contexts of violent conflict (Staub 2006, 867). The chapter underlines the duty of society to provide appropriate listening to those marked by collective forms of trauma such as genocide, where human dignity has been undermined. Finally, it explores how certain aspects of Ubuntu (or similar value systems) are embodied in literary narratives that represent the trauma of postconflict societies by looking specifically at Véronique Tadjo's (2000a, 2002) travel account, *The Shadow of Imana: Travels in the Heart of Rwanda*.

In spite of having assumed a variety of forms at various times in the history of southern Africa, the concept of Ubuntu, sometimes referred to as "Afro-communitarianism" (Metz and Gaie 2010, 273), or "interconnectedness-towards-wholeness" (Krog 2008, 355), is widely considered to be an indigenous African perspective. It is popularly associated with the affirmation of human dignity and personhood, the favoring of "interpersonal bonds," interconnectedness, interdependence and solidarity, and a communal rather than an individualist organization of a society (Gade 2012, 486; Gaylard 2004, 270–71). It is the potential of this concept and its advocacy of shared humanity for reconciliation in postconflict societies such as postgenocide Rwanda and postapartheid South Africa that interests me.

To explore its potential, I will first consider theories of reconciliation as set out by Ervin Staub (2006) and observations by Jennie Burnet (2012) on practices of reconciliation in Rwanda and in particular the experiences of ordinary people at a grassroots level. I hope to make the link between Ubuntu's appeal to communal and interdependent relationships and the role that can be played by the "creation of a shared history" in contexts of violent conflict between groups who typically possess what Staub (2006, 867) has called "contradictory histories." To do this, I will investigate the restorative potential of a collective, plural narrative that insists on including traditionally marginalized voices.

A brief exploration of how the concept of a shared humanity provides possibilities of reconciliation in postconflict societies will allow us to set the scene. I base this discussion on the following assumptions about Ubuntu in order to move on rapidly to the notion of reconciliation. My premise is that the present readership is fairly familiar with the concept of Ubuntu and its various definitions, the values attached to it, the role that is ascribed to it in the Truth and Reconciliation Commission (TRC),[1] and its possible uses and abuses that various scholars have pointed out. I subscribe to Thaddeus Metz's (2011, 534–35) "normative-theoretical" description of Ubuntu, which takes into account its indigenous roots and its application beyond the borders of South Africa, which includes a contemporary understanding of this worldview, instead of limiting the concept to how indigenous southern African societies understood it in the past.

During a recent conference at the University of Pretoria, one of the participants described the notion of Ubuntu as a "battlefield."[2] If Ubuntu has something to say about reconciliation and restoration in the face of depersonalization and dehumanization, it grapples with issues such as dignity and broken relationships, and this is indeed a battlefield. It is the role of literature in this battle that personally interests me. This chapter therefore explores how certain aspects of Ubuntu (or similar value systems) are embodied in a collection of literary narratives that represent the genocide in Rwanda.

The texts that frame this discussion are those that constitute the joint writing project, *Rwanda: écrire par devoir de mémoire* (Rwanda: writing as a duty to memory), initiated in 1998 by nine Francophone African intellectuals in response to the genocide against the Tutsis in Rwanda. Thus, four years after the genocide, they embarked on an extended journey to Rwanda in order to meet its inhabitants and visit orphanages, genocide sites, and prisons. This collective effort led to the publication, between 2000 and 2002, of four novels, two travel narratives, and one collection of poetry, all by non-Rwandans. Added to this body of work by writers from diverse African countries is a Tutsi survivor's testimony and an essay by a Tutsi who was in exile during the genocide. Although the majority of them were established writers in their own contexts, most of the participants had never been to Rwanda before, and of the two Rwandans, only one had personally experienced the 1994 genocide.[3]

Trauma, Reconciliation, and Return to Personhood

The genocide in Rwanda is one of the ultimate examples of human-rights violations and of the destruction of the "capacity to exhibit" the "traits of identity and solidarity" toward the other (Metz 2011, 548). Apartheid has equally been described as a *"break down* in interconnectedness" (Krog 2008, 359; emphasis in original).When trauma is intentionally inflicted by one human being on another, it may lead to what Susan Brison has called the "undoing of the self" (1999, 40, 44). Ervin Staub (2006, 876) posits that trauma "creates insecurity, mistrust, and disconnection from people." Judith Herman (1992, 53) notes that a traumatic event can destroy "the belief that *one can be oneself* in relation to others" and Brison (1999, 41) adds that "without this belief one can no longer be oneself even to oneself, since the self exists fundamentally in relation to others" (41). Thus, trauma "severs the sustaining connection between the self and the rest of humanity" (Brison 1999, 40). These descriptions of the effects of trauma inflicted by the other, whether provided in an African and collective context (Metz 2011; Krog 2008) or in a personal context (Herman 1992; Brison 1999), all allude to a breakdown in trust and relationships that have been severely damaged. Trauma can thus be seen as a form of disintegration of personhood, of the self, and of the self's relation to others (Brison 1999, 41, 48).

My concern is in the potential for healing and reintegration in the aftermath of such a breakdown, and my focus here is Rwanda. The psychological effects of genocide on survivors include a sense of vulnerability, devaluation, abandonment, and betrayal, as well as a need for security and control and for the reestablishment of a positive identity and positive connections to others (Staub 2006, 871). Staub's definition of reconciliation as the restoration of damaged relationships makes it clear why reconciliation would be a major concern for those who uphold the values of human dignity and personhood or who seek to counter the psychological effects of trauma: "The essence of reconciliation is a changed psychological orientation toward the other. Reconciliation means that victims and perpetrators, or members of hostile groups, do not see the past as defining the future, as simply a continuum of the past. It means that they come to *see the humanity of one another*, accept each other, and see the possibility of a constructive relationship" (Staub 2006, 868, my emphasis).

Clearly, what interests Staub is the psychological recovery that needs to take place in order to again "see the humanity of the other," not only in the victim, but in the perpetrator as well, who also has been damaged by the violence. Staub demonstrates that perpetrators and passive observers of mass violence also undergo trauma, caused by their own devaluing of the victims, diminishment of their empathy, and tacit justification of the atrocities that they committed or allowed. He asserts that, because they minimize trauma caused by such actions, the "profound changes in identity, values, views of themselves and views of the victims, and probably of human beings in general makes it extremely difficult for perpetrators of and bystanders to mass violence to acknowledge, presumably to themselves as well as others, that their actions were wrong" (872). This inability to acknowledge their role "interferes not only with reconciliation, but also with being reincluded in the moral community" (872–73). Healing would thus need to include changes in the attitudes of perpetrators toward their own actions, victims, and "people in general" (873).

Because trauma leads to a disconnection from people and "victimization creates mistrust and fear of other people, especially those outside the group," Staub (2006, 874) describes the value of engaging with painful experiences and reconnecting with people. He warns that if these issues are not addressed, victims can in turn become perpetrators when a new threat or conflict arises (871). In this regard, Krog (2008) suggests the term "interconnectedness-towards-wholeness" in her discussion of the postapartheid context.[4] She demonstrates through examples from the TRC how an "interconnected" perspective views forgiveness as part of a process that "includes both victim and perpetrator" in its aim toward achieving fuller personhood and rehumanizing those involved or, in her words, "to allow people back into humanity" (356, 362). The process implies an expectation of change on the side of the perpetrator because, as Krog aptly concludes, "interconnected forgiveness says: I forgive you so that you can change/heal here on earth, then I can start on my interconnected path towards healing" (357).

Shared Stories and Collective Histories

It is commonly accepted that establishing the truth is essential in the process of reconciliation and transitional justice (Staub 2006, 880–81; Wolfe 2014, 66). Equally important to acknowledge, however, is that truth, and the memory of the truth, is more often than not multiple and plural, not to mention contradictory (Burnet 2012, 9; Dauge-Roth 2010, 173; Hinton and O'Neill 2009, 5), and can take on dimensions as widely diverse as the "factual," the "personal and narrative," the "social," and the "restorative" truth (Sanders 2007, 3).

Ideally, the process of truth-telling would include acknowledgment of the trauma that was experienced (Staub 2006, 874), enabling a victim to reestablish a relationship with the other through narrative and thus facilitate a "return to personhood" (Brison 1999, 41, 45). Brison advances the consideration that "how (and even whether) traumatic events are remembered depends on not only how they are initially experienced, but also how (whether) they are perceived by others, directly or indirectly, and the extent to which others are able to listen empathetically to the survivor's testimony" (42). Alexandre Dauge-Roth (2009, 167) describes giving and listening to testimony as a "dialogic space" where survivors attempt to "redefine the present meaning derived from their experience and its haunting resonance." Thus, they seek to "re-envision and re-assert themselves" (167–68) and, by doing so, to move from a position of being a subject of violence to a position of agency and the "possibility of crafting the meaning of who they are" (168).[5]

Staub (2006) suggests that, in that the genocide in Rwanda was a collective crime affecting the whole community, and in that the society is collectivist and community-oriented, healing would ideally entail a collective approach. A further key step to healing is to acknowledge that the "perpetrator group was not monolithic" and, therefore, come up with a more "complex and differentiated" way of perceiving the group, for example, by acknowledging the role of those who opposed genocide or attempted to save Tutsi victims (877).

In establishing a shared history and a collective meaning for a community where competing and often contradictory narratives exist, it would be important to acknowledge trauma experienced by all parties involved and encourage the inclusion of everyone's account (Alcoff 1991, 20), in spite of the reality that injuries suffered may be "substantially unequal" (Staub 2006, 881). Such a collective narrative would require a "reexamination and reinterpreting of history, involving a process of negotiation" and a shared consideration of the origins of violence (882).

Unity and Reconciliation

Staub (2006, 880) suggests that reconciliation efforts should ideally take place on psychological, political, institutional, and cultural levels. He cautions that reworking the past and dealing with differing views of history is a difficult and long road that involves various societal processes, many of which Rwanda has already engaged in.[6] In spite of his concern over the fact that the society is expected to abandon the use of the terms *Hutu* and *Tutsi*, Staub commends the government initiative of creating a policy of unity and reconciliation, which is a "rare, intentional, societal process" (870).

In her text based on more than a decade of fieldwork among Rwandan women, anthropologist Jennie Burnet (2012) offers some useful insights about postgenocide Rwanda and the process of reconciliation and national unity.[7] She highlights the dangers of imposing simplistic understandings of Rwandan history, together with a "dyadic Hutu perpetrator/Tutsi victim logic" (110–11, 166). Burnet notes that "when remembering becomes a collective process, the structuring effect of hegemonic discourses overpowers the diversity of individual experience, erasing difference or disguising it in such a manner as to preserve the broad categories of social delineation, whether based on nationality, ethnicity, gender, or class" (8).

Burnet, whose text was published six years after Staub's, underlines the importance of including a diversity of individual voices and demonstrates how a hegemonic discourse can alienate, exclude, and silence certain voices in the society (111, 112). Bhekizizwe Peterson (2014) echoes this caution in his work on the South African context, which has identified certain "silences and contradictions" (214) that have arisen but are often repressed in South Africa in an attempt to promote unity, forgiveness, nation building, and reconciliation. Peterson problematizes the notion of "leaving the past behind" (217) and thus subscribing to a form of amnesia, rather than attempting to work through it. He contrasts initiatives offered by the state with the life-affirming endeavors of ordinary people to overcome trauma through African ontological notions of "personhood, sociality and ancestral veneration" (215).

Burnet (2012) also makes observations about the use of Rwandan cultural traditions pertaining to reconciliation and revenge.[8] She demonstrates how both reconciliation and its reverse, revenge, are promoted by cultural traditions. On the one hand, according to certain Rwandan proverbs that are seen as a form of traditional wisdom, not seeking revenge is considered a sign of weakness. On the other hand, traditional punishments that were normally used in cases of "social rupture emphasized the reintegration of the errant individual into good social standing" (153). Burnet thus advances the proposition that "justice could be conciliatory, according to Rwandan custom. The 'delinquent should correct himself,' and then the community should 'pardon him for his actions and live in harmony again'" (153). This custom seems to be in line with what is commonly accepted as an objective of restorative justice within the Ubuntu worldview, namely the restoring of harmony, relations, and humanity of those involved.

Another invaluable observation that emerged from Burnet's fieldwork is on how reconciliation increasingly was a grassroots process. Reconciliation seemed often to have started off as simple cohabitation, which was a matter of necessity in postgenocide Rwanda because the inhabitants lived in proximity due to the dense population of the country. This initially involved merely learning to exist together without too much hostility and establishing basic types of interaction and exchange (169). The conditions that determined whether individuals could advance from an initial phase in order to arrive at some form of reconciliation included being free from fear of immediate violence, a minimal amount of economic independence, a desire to reconcile, the long-standing relationships they had with each other before the genocide, and a safe social space in which to express themselves (170–71).

Even then, reconciliation often took place only when both parties from different social categories were able to share their narratives of suffering, while acknowledging their individual responsibilities, recognizing certain common experiences, and mutually and empathetically exchanging their stories of suffering (172–73, 193). Often people's stories did not fit with the univocal narratives and the collective identity that they were expected to adhere to, which helped focus on the individual and steer away from master narratives of ethnic oppression (171, 179). Last, the parties wanted to be sure that the emotions expressed were "genuine" and truthful (179) and participants felt a need to demonstrate their desire to move forward and establish renewed relationships through culturally appropriate means such as gifts and preparing food for the other (193). Both Peterson's and Burnet's comments show how the grassroots reality of reconciliation seems to offer an alternative to proposed official frameworks.

My contention is that literary narratives and other forms of imaginative representation present an additional pathway to accommodate conflicting experiences of trauma and to create awareness of the diversity of the personal experience of mass violence. Also, when those writing the narrative take into account the cultural reactions of ordinary people to the processes of forgiveness, reconciliation, and dealing with trauma as evoked by both Peterson and Burnet, they are able to provide a meaningful space for them in the narratives they create.

Literary Narratives, Rwanda, and "Interconnectedness-toward-Wholeness"

Having established some of the challenges and theorizing about trauma, truth, and reconciliation, I would now like to return to my initial remarks on the texts from the project *Rwanda: écrire par devoir de mémoire*. I do so to demonstrate how certain requirements identified in the foregoing as being conducive to reconciliation and healing were embedded in the project's narratives, as well as to examine how several concepts associated with "interconnectedness-toward-wholeness" were embodied in them.

The mere ability of a literary text to present a plurality of voices, including those of the marginalized and the silenced, is a step toward the creation of a shared narrative in dialogue with the community. If that narrative then also is able to problematize imposed collective identities and stereotypes, it establishes a safe space in which the trauma of the individual can be explored, irrespective of the group it officially belongs to. Furthermore, transforming the statistics of genocide into human beings with names and individual stories enables an author to invite the readers to recognize the humanity of the other. In addition, the authors from this commemorative project did not for the most part position themselves as writers or even as eyewitnesses, but rather as listeners, not speaking for the Rwandans but with them, thus creating what Alexandre Dauge-Roth (2009, 165) would call a "testimonial encounter" and Linda Alcoff (1991, 17) a "dialogic encounter."

Nicki Hitchcott (2009, 152–53) posits that the most "significant" aspect of this initiative was its unique composition of African writers who, though from a wide range of countries, shared the colonial experience and seemed to reflect the African identity both in its diversity and its commonality. During a discussion with Véronique Tadjo, prize-winning author and artist who had participated in this project, I asked her how the "African" composition of the group enhanced the existing body of representation of the genocide.[9] Her modest answer somewhat disappointed me: she was quick to assure me that Western writers were representing the genocide in a remarkable fashion and that "intrinsically," there was nothing that their project added to this. For her, at least in the answers she gave me at the time, it was simply a question of redressing the imbalance that existed because of the prominent Western media coverage of the event in contrast with the near-silence on the side of the African continent.

I felt, though, that a valuable link could be made between this literary project and Ubuntu ethics, both in the authors' desire to demonstrate their moral solidarity with their African brothers and sisters and because of the collective nature of their endeavor.[10] The project required these independent writers from countries as diverse as Djibouti, Burkina Faso, Senegal, Côte d'Ivoire, Chad, and Guinea to travel to Kigali as a group and participate in a two-month writer's residency.[11] The mandate was to publish their texts thereafter within a fixed period—not only in their capacity as individuals, but also as participants in a polyphonic project. This collective desire to show solidarity is reminiscent of the notions of a shared humanity and the value of community, in which Ubuntu is grounded and that Metz and Gaie define as the "combination of identifying with others and exhibiting solidarity with them" (2010, 276).

Apart from these general objectives of expressing solidarity and providing a collective response, I have identified certain features as giving an African frame to the texts from the project and its stated objectives. To my mind, these characteristics, such as allusions to the role of cultural values, the prominence of traditional wisdom in the form of sages and indigenous proverbs, and an insistence on the importance of burial customs and the relationship with the dead added a valuable perspective to the ones proposed by Western authors.

Many of the features that are present in the project coincide with characteristics often attributed to Ubuntu: the importance of cultural and traditional values; the concept of the "interconnectedness of human, animal, plant, inanimate environments and the cosmos" (Mphahlele 2003, 137); and the assertion that "a person is a person through other persons" or becomes more human(e) and complete through communal relationships; and Ubuntu's converse: that those who do not act in an appropriate manner toward others are like animals (Metz 2011, 537). In my analysis, I therefore focus on two main aspects of the project: first, its plurality and multivocality, which opens up spaces for the expression of silenced and marginalized voices, and, second, the elements that I identified earlier as providing an African frame to the texts.

Travels to Rwanda

Although examples are available in various texts from the project, I have chosen to refer mainly to Véronique Tadjo's travel account, *The Shadow of Imana: Travels in the Heart of Rwanda*.[12] This Ivoirian author appears to be intensely aware of the parallels between Rwanda and South Africa and places her narrative within the frame of reconciliation processes in South Africa. Even before arriving in Rwanda, she situates her first encounter with Rwanda in South Africa, where she has spent a few days at a conference (Tadjo 2002, 3–4). She describes her unsettling chance meeting with a Rwandan refugee in a parking lot in Durban, thus creating a distinct link between postapartheid South Africa and postgenocide Rwanda, and hopes wistfully that South Africa, a country that "forms part of our collective memory," might provide her with some answers to her own questions on reconciliation.

From the outset, Tadjo's text stages a chorus of voices: she is the first-person narrator, describing, questioning, and interacting with the inhabitants of the country as she travels "into its heart." But there is also the chapter in which her voice is subsumed by voices of the dead and of the soothsayer, and the people she meets speak directly on the pages of her text, assuming their own positionalities, styles, rhythms, and tones. Those who speak are seldom types who fit into monolithic categories; they are often at once perpetrator and victim, wounded human being rather than Hutu, Tutsi, or even foreigner. Russell West-Pavlov describes her text as a form of deliberate "border-blurring" in the face of genocide rhetoric, which employs "border-drawing" (2014, 118).

There is the child who does not yet have his own voice but who is born from rape and of whom his grandmother says "I don't want this one, he was born of the war. What are we to do with him?" (Tadjo 2002, 35). We hear from the group of women perpetrators waiting in prison, singing "songs of God," doing basketwork, praying aloud (100–101). We witness the suffering of Isaro, the widow of a man who committed suicide after being accused of being a perpetrator. Isaro will never know whether he was guilty; he has "taken the truth with him" (55). Then there is Froduard, the traumatized "young farmer turned murderer," who says "they gave us clubs and told us where to strike: it was them or us, and there was no greater fear than that, that they were the ones wanting to kill us if any of them survived" (102–3), and Anastase, the young Rwandan who raped his own sister. Thus, the people we meet in her text resist clearly defined stereotypes and the author often insists on remaining ambiguous about the ethnic identity of her characters.

Joséphine is introduced to us as a woman who did not want to tell Tadjo whether she was Hutu or Tutsi (Tadjo 2002, 105). West-Pavlov defines this ambiguity as "zones of indefinition" in which the author refuses to categorize, while at the same time not automatically exempting her characters from blame: "Refusing to reinscribe the very categories which have driven the genocide, and which continue to define the identities of perpetrators and survivors after the event . . . , the text perseveres with the young woman's story without categorizing her within the inevitably binary narratives of Hutu/Tutsi hostility. The episode does not release the character from intimations of culpability, or at the very least moral ambivalence, but stresses none the less the business of living on after the genocide" (West-Pavlov 2014, 120).

The narrative of Anastase and Anastasie is another pertinent example: when reading it for the first time, one assumes that Anastasie is a Tutsi. She is a victim of the genocide, she has been raped and she dies standing up against the militia. A closer reading, however, reveals that all is not that simple. It is her own brother who rapes her, and yes, she dies at the hands of the militia, but Tadjo never states explicitly that she is Tutsi, only that she belonged to a resistance group and that "all the Tutsis and those who had tried to defend them were massacred" in her neighborhood (Tadjo

2002, 67). Anastasie could in fact have been a moderate Hutu who helped to defend her Tutsi neighbors, and the question of her ethnicity remains open-ended.

Consolate's story constitutes another such case; she is described as having "a face of astonishing sweetness" and a smile that tastes of mango (Tadjo 2002, 27–28). We are not told whether she is Hutu or Tutsi, only that her father is dead and her mother and brother are in prison. Whether Hutu or Tutsi, she bears the marks of the trauma of genocide, someone who experiences rejection, exile, and betrayal in her own country, who "has mourned the future" and is caught up in the past, in her memory "frozen, fixed in time" (29).

The Kubwimana family, too, is not assigned an ethnicity; Tadjo describes them as an "ordinary family in a little provincial house, tucked away in the hills," a family with whom she exchanges addresses (23). We learn that they fled to Zaïre during the genocide, that the father was pro-Hutu before and that the sister's husband was accused of having participated in the genocide. We meet the son, Isaac, who has no direction in life, and who says bitterly, "The adults betrayed us. . . . They ruined our lives," and the small orphan girl adopted by the family, the "daughter of a friend" (21–23). Once again, we are not told whether the orphan girl is Hutu or Tutsi.

Tadjo describes her visit to a youth center where children "orphaned by the war, AIDS, or family dislocation" gather (86). The children that she meets at the center and who roam the rubbish dumps of Kigali are not labeled, either, in terms of ethnicity. What is more important is that they are a product of the genocide and represent the sad future of Africa; life holds little value for them, and they are ready to be given weapons and enrolled in armies. They are introduced to us as "children of the genocide," "the open wound of memory," and "the wound that might kill the country all over again," children who will grow up with "rage in their hearts" (87–88).

In various such micronarratives, the author complicates the creation of a common memory of the genocide: she seems to support the government's initiative to not distinguish between Hutu and Tutsi, but she takes it a step further and subverts the binaries of Hutu perpetrator and Tutsi victim often informing analyses of the genocide. Thus Tadjo contributes to the creation of a multivocal history of the genocide and subverts the monolithic image of the categories of humans into which society has placed itself. She also insists on showing us how victimhood, suffering, and traumatization are not confined to certain groups but are essentially a human experience.

Animals, Sages, and the "Wrath of the Dead"

Let us turn now to a number of examples of values that can be linked to an Ubuntu worldview that I want to consider in the light of Tadjo's text. The first one is the relationship between personhood and the treatment of the other. An aspect that emerges strongly from her text is the realization of the extent of man's inhumanity toward man and his ability to demote the other to the category of animal or subhuman. Tadjo's references to this ruthless cruelty toward the other remind us of Metz's (2011) statements that acquiring Ubuntu can be likened to "exhibit[ing] humanness" and that "Southern Africans would say of a person who does not relate communally that 'he is not a person.' Indeed, those without much ubuntu, roughly those who exhibit discordant or indifferent behaviour with regard to others, are often labelled 'animals'" (537).

It is not only the militants who give themselves over to brutality during the genocide; women, children, priests, and grandfathers participate too. Tadjo describes the cruelty of the women perpetrators, of whom she admits honestly that "we would have preferred them to be innocent" (2002, 102). And yet she acknowledges that it was these women who "helped men to rape, who sang to give them the courage to massacre, who betrayed, who pillaged, who decided to join in the act of cruelty. With machetes, they killed other women, mutilated children, finished off men" (101). By listing action after action, the author undermines the assumption that the women were all passive bystanders. She names the terrible price that they pay for their inhumanity: "Educated women, agitators, officials, accusers, organizers. These women killed their own destiny as women" (102).

The sense that the society has deteriorated into the realm of the inhumane is suggested by the many unflattering allusions and comparisons made to animals such as dogs, cockroaches, gorillas, and vampires. This extended metaphor demonstrates man's descent into inhumanity and cruelty and plays a dual role: it serves to demonstrate the decline of mankind, but equally to remind us that in genocidal logic, the life of an animal is often worth more than that of a human being.

Tadjo situates her remarks on this subject within the frame of Dian Fossey's work with gorillas, Rwanda's "principal tourist attraction," whereas the reader knows that ironically, after 1994, the genocide sites are competing for the primary position as "tourist attraction" (2002, 81). Of Fossey and the gorillas, she writes, "On the Rwandan side, the Volcano National Park has been given over to their [the gorillas'] use. Dian Fossey had made of it a kingdom. . . . Dian Fossey is dead, probably murdered by poachers. In the end, she loved animals more than the human race" (81–82). Tadjo shows how, ironically, the gorillas compete with the inhabitants of the country in terms of their value: "Yes, it is true that once upon a time, the villagers used to hunt the gorillas, but what did they know then of the terrifying creatures with their frighteningly human appearance? It took the establishment of the research station for them to understand that these creatures were Rwanda's most precious possession. More precious than themselves? The competition was on" (82). Eventually, the Rwandans come to realize that their lives appear to be less precious than those of the gorillas, and this logic is perversely confirmed by their own actions during the genocide.

In contrast, reducing a victim to the status of an animal or a slave, and thus interiorizing a dehumanizing image of that person, enables the perpetrator to kill more effectively: "To erase all humanity. To look no more into the face of others. Above all, to exchange no more glances. An animal, a heap of flesh. A skull cracking like a dry branch. . . . To drink enough alcohol to be released from all hesitation, and to wipe out all memory of daily life. To remain in ignorance of doubt so that the act is nothing more than a gesture of unbelievable power. To be master of the slave kneeling at one's feet. God made man" (Tadjo 2002, 117). This is the "breakdown in interconnectedness," the "undoing of the self," and the severing of the connection between the self and the other that Krog (2008), Brison (1999), and Herman (1992) have described.

The second concept, related to Ubuntu ethics, and which forms an integral part of Tadjo's text, is the notion of interconnectedness. This invisible link—both between humans and between the dead and the living, man and the universe—clearly shapes her narrative. Her strongest celebration of interconnectedness comes through her constant reminder that we are all part of a shared humanity.

In various ways, Tadjo (2002) demonstrates that the genocide did not happen only to the Rwandans, it happened to us all. She writes, "Yes, I went to Rwanda but Rwanda is also here in my country. The refugees are scattered all over the world, carrying within themselves the blood and fury of the abandoned dead" (37). The author bravely attempts to identify with and show solidarity to the Rwandans, inviting us to do the same: "In the dark night of absolute blindness, what would I have done if I had been caught up in the spiralling violence of the massacre? Would I have resisted betrayal?

Would I have been cowardly or brave, would I have killed or would I have let myself be killed? Rwanda is inside me, in you, in all of us. Rwanda is under our skin, in our blood, in our guts. In the very depths of our slumber, in our waking hearts" (37).

A further aspect of interconnectedness explored by Tadjo is the porous boundary between the dead and the living, an acknowledgment of the importance of indigenous culture and beliefs that may easily be overlooked by an author writing from a Western perspective. She explores this aspect of African ontology as it presents itself in the aftermath of genocide. An obvious link can be made here to the South African context and the desire of people to find and appropriately bury the remains of their loved ones; a quest that Peterson calls the "search for the disappeared" (2014, 221) and to which Mark Sanders (2007, 41–86) devotes much discussion in his text on the "ambiguities of witnessing."

It is commonly known that, after the genocide in Rwanda, burial customs were not observed properly, and many survivors were unable to find the bodies of their loved ones in order to bury them. Burial rites serve not only to appease the dead but also to lead the living through a process of grieving. Odile Cazenave (2004, 80) reminds us of the troubling questions provoked by the genocide sites in a culture steeped in animism: "What becomes of a society when its dead are not buried? . . . How to not see in a flying butterfly, an ululating owl, or a meowing cat the expression of a pained, wandering soul in search of rest?"

Tadjo admits in a recent article that the writers in the project "found it impossible to talk about postgenocide Rwanda without invoking the presence of the dead and their continuous impact on the memory of the living" (2013, 3). In her travel account, she addresses this aspect in a chapter written in the form of a tale in which the boundaries between the dead and the living are blurred and which she calls "The Wrath of the Dead" (2002, 39). She explains in an interview that this chapter was inspired by her own intimate knowledge of the burial rites prevalent in African cultures (Tadjo 2000b).

The tale, reminiscent of the oral tradition, and by her own admission "purely imaginative" (2013, 3), comes unexpectedly, inserted in the middle of an account that in many ways conforms to notions of the travel diary, with realistic descriptions of sites visited, survivors interviewed, and her own reactions to the events described. By simply interweaving these two forms of narrative, the author in fact subtly demonstrates how the cohabitation between the dead and the living is as real for the inhabitants as the places and people that surround them. She writes, "The town streets were filled with spirits moving around, whirling in the stifling air. They jostled the living, clambered on their backs, walked alongside them, danced around them, followed them through the crowded alleyways. . . . They were in every neighbourhood. You could feel them as they scurried past people" (Tadjo 2002, 41). The dead haunt the living, angry at being killed and fearful of being forgotten by those whose memory is "starting to fade" (41). Their presence is pervasive, tangible and inopportune, their rage "pierc[ing] the eardrums of the survivors" and "making the days and nights unbearable" (42). For them, as for the living, the desire to be heard is not tended to by the society. The author underlines the interconnectedness between the spiritual and the natural world by accompanying the wrath of the dead with related signs in nature: "Some of the dead were so enraged that they refused to go when the time came to quit the earth. There was one in particular whose head had been cut off and who was angry with everyone. His ally was a torrential downpour. . . . The rain fell furiously. An angry rain shrieking its refusal to open the gates to the other world. And it hammered the earth with great strokes in order to say: 'No!'" (42). A soothsayer is summoned to listen to the stories of the dead. He then asks the living to bury the bones of the dead according to custom, thus allowing them paradoxically not only to depart but also to return to the living and visit them "in peace" (45). Tadjo articulates the interdependence between the dead and the living in the words of the diviner who says, "We must ask them to yield up to us the secrets of life, which becomes triumphant once more, since only the living can bring the dead back to life. Without us, they no longer exist. Without them, we fall into emptiness" (45).

In this tale about the anger of the dead, the soothsayer plays a central role.[13] He is a traditional sage who represents traditional beliefs. He is respected by the community and operates in a well-defined role: that of mediation between the physical and the spiritual world. He is at once intermediary, negotiator, adviser, interpreter of the supernatural, and guardian of moral values. Tadjo admits in an interview to also having endowed him with the ability to "speak truths" (*diseur de vérités*) (Tadjo 2000b) about the society he lives in, and the capacity to denounce both its current and past ills because he is in direct contact with the spiritual world, and both the living and the dead listen to him. The role of intermediary attributed to him by the author enables him to offer advice on reconciliation and forgiveness.

He is also the one who accompanies the living in their work of mourning while intervening between the dead and the living.

The author herself refers to her writing as a form of "lifting the cloak of (in)visibility" (Tadjo 2013, 1). For her, the notion of invisibility is defined as "the belief that there is no separation between the spiritual and material worlds" and that there is therefore a "hidden world" that interpenetrates the living one (1–2). This belief is clearly illustrated in the words of the soothsayer: "The dead will be reborn in every fragment of life, however small, in every word, every action, however simple it may be. They will be reborn in the dust, in the dancing water, in the children who laugh and play as they clap their hands, in every seed hidden beneath the black earth" (Tadjo 2002, 46). It is this "hidden world" of the dead, permeating the lives of the living (Tadjo 2013, 2), with a huge impact on the postgenocide society that the author seeks to reveal.

Tadjo (2013) takes the notion of invisibility further by describing the genocide as "another form of invisibility" because the inhumanity and magnitude of genocide rendered the victims "anonymous" and thus "invisible" (4). This author clearly demonstrates that in the face of dehumanization and depersonalization, it is the duty of narrative to rehumanize: statistics and numbers become individuals, and she provides us with a striking example of this process during her visit to Nyamata church:

> The guide invites me to come and write in the register.
> I am number 7317.
> I write my surname and my first name.
> My address in Rwanda.
> My address abroad. (2002, 13)

In her narrative (Tadjo 2002), neither the victims nor the visitor who listens to their story can remain a number; all have to acknowledge their own humanity and that of the other. Thus, victims and perpetrators are endowed with names and faces through literature so that we could again see them as individual human beings.

Conclusion

The examples from Véronique Tadjo's genocide narrative demonstrate how elements of the Ubuntu premise of interconnectedness between humans and their environment(s) are embodied in her text. Her text leads us to "see the humanity of one another" (Staub 2006, 868), irrespective of our perceived roles as victims, perpetrators, or bystanders. Tadjo articulates dehumanization through demeaning comparisons with animals. That and her interweaving of multiple genres—whether realistic reportage, travelogue, or highly imaginative and metaphorical storytelling—helps readers uninitiated in such notions make sense of what Tadjo calls invisibility or the interpenetration of the spiritual and physical realms. Her text interrogates the tensions and dissonances between official interventions—which emphasize collective imperatives and interventions at the expense of individual and ethnic needs and experiences—and the more open-ended and ambiguous voices of individuals and marginalized groups.

The author invites readers who have not experienced the genocide to embark on the journey of listening with her[14] as a means of reconnection not only between perpetrator and victim but also between Rwandan and non-Rwandan—and ultimately between the individual and the other. The journey on which narrative takes us is then first to demonstrate our part in the breakdown of interpersonal bonds and the undermining of human dignity, solidarity, and humaneness and second to invite us to the possibility of moving toward wholeness through telling and listening. Literature and storytelling in general remind us again of their potential to provide a safe space in which to explore multiple and even contradictory voices, perspectives, and identities in situations where the political and physical landscape does not always allow us to do so. Narrative, at least the type that we find in *L'ombre d'Imana*, offers us a way toward healing the break in interconnectedness and restoring our collective humanity wounded by the depersonalization of mass violence.

Notes

1. This commission was chaired by Archbishop Desmond Tutu and was appointed in December 1995. Its main purpose was to promote reconciliation and forgiveness among perpetrators and victims of apartheid in South Africa primarily through public hearings.

2. *Ubuntu Colloquium: The Meaning and Value of Ubuntu*, held at the University of Pretoria, June 23–25, 2014.

3. The following texts were published as part of this commemorative endeavor :
   - *Murambi: le livre des ossements* (2000) by Boubacar Boris Diop from Senegal
   - *L'aîné des orphelins* (2000) by the Guinean writer Tierno Monénembo
   - *Murekatete* (2000) by Monique Ilboudo from Burkina-Faso
   - *La phalène des collines* (2002) by Koulsy Lamko from Chad

- *L'ombre d'Imana: Voyages jusqu'au bout du Rwanda* (2000) by Véronique Tadjo from Côte-d'Ivoire
- *Moisson de crânes: textes pour le Rwanda* (2000) by Abdourahman A. Waberi from Djibouti
- *Nyamirambo!* (2000), a poetry anthology by Nocky Djedanoum from Chad
- *Le génocide des Tutsi expliqué à un étranger* (2000), an essay by exiled Rwandan Jean-Marc Vianney Rurangwa
- *France-Rwanda: les coulisses du génocide; témoignage d'un rescapé* (2001), a testimony by genocide survivor Vénuste Kayimahe

4. Antjie Krog, award-winning South African poet, academic, and writer, defines her concept as follows: "Interconnectedness-towards-wholeness in this essay is more than just a theoretical knowledge that all things in the world are linked, it means both a mental and physical awareness that one can only 'become' who one is, or could be, through the fullness of that which is around one—both physical and metaphysical. Wholeness is thus not a passive state of nirvana, but a process of becoming in which everybody and everything is moving towards its fullest self, building itself; one can only reach that fullest self though, through and with others which include ancestors and universe" (2008, 355).

5. For more on the notion of listening to trauma and how it is demonstrated in this literary project read De Beer (2015).

6. Staub cites processes such as seminars, conferences, the *gacaca* proceedings, the release of prisoners, reconciliation projects at high school level, and others (2006, 882).

7. My own field work in Rwanda has taught me that the situation is extremely complex in postgenocide Rwanda and a range of interpretations exist with regards to the existing policies of reconciliation and unity. Burnet's findings on grassroots forms of reconciliation offer a valuable perspective.

8. In spite of the divisions between Hutu and Tutsi, it remains meaningful to speak of the shared Rwandan culture and tradition because the groups share elements such as language, customs, and religion that historically existed and still exist, notwithstanding the politicized divides.

9. Véronique Tadjo, in discussion with the author, July 2010.

10. I base this assertion on the following statement made by one of the initiators of the project, Nocky Djedanoum: "L'ambition principale de ce projet intitulé 'Rwanda: écrire par devoir de mémoire' est avant tout de témoigner de leur solidarité morale envers le peuple rwandais et de rompre la loi du silence [des intellectuels africains]" (Djedanoum 1999).

11. Not all of them were able to participate in the initial voyage and many of them returned for subsequent visits, either in a group or on their own.

12. Tadjo's original text, *L'ombre d'Imana: voyages jusqu'au bout du Rwanda* (2000) was translated by Véronique Wakerley in 2002. All citations are taken from Wakerley's translation.

I have proposed a similar analysis (in a previous article, De Beer 2015) of some of these aspects that Koulsy Lamko's (2002) novel embodies.

13. The figure of the sage is in fact present in many of the texts from the project and they either embody or subvert traditional belief systems. For more on this, read De Beer (2013, 254–58).

14. Here again, Tadjo's (2002a) writing demonstrates Mphahlele's (2003) description of the African tradition of telling and listening: "We are traditionally great talkers, find comfort

in talking to other people, and also want others to know that they can unburden themselves by talking to us" (138).

References

Alcoff, Linda. 1991. "The Problem of Speaking for Others." *Cultural Critique* 20 (Winter): 5–32.

Brison, Susan J. 1999. "Trauma Narratives and the Remaking of the Self." In *Acts of Memory: Cultural Recall in the Present*, edited by Mieke Bal, Jonathan V. Crewe, and Leo Spitzer, 39–54. Hanover, NH: University Press of New England.

Burnet, Jennie E. 2012. *Genocide Lives in Us: Women, Memory, and Silence in Rwanda.* Madison: University of Wisconsin Press.

Cazenave, Odile. 2004. "Writing the Rwandan Genocide: African Literature and the Duty of Memory." In *Reconstructing Societies in the Aftermath of War: Memory, Identity, and Reconciliation*, edited by Flavia Brizio-Skov, 70–84. Boca Raton, FL: Bordighera.

Dauge-Roth, Alexandre E. 2009. "Testimonial Encounter: Esther Mujawayo's Dialogic Art of Witnessing." *French Cultural Studies* 20:165–80.

———. 2010. *Writing and Filming the Genocide of the Tutsis in Rwanda: Dismembering and Remembering Traumatic History.* Plymouth, UK: Lexington.

De Beer, Anna-Marie M. 2013. *Le voyage de l'écrivain vers une voix, une histoire et un futur— une étude du projet littéraire, Rwanda: écrire par devoir de mémoire.* Unpublished thesis, University of Pretoria, Johannesburg.

———. 2015. "Ubuntu and the Journey of Listening to the Rwandan Genocide Story." *Verbum et Ecclesia* 36:1–9.

Djedanoum, Nocky. 1999. "Le Rwanda, terre de recueillement de mémoire." Accessed November 1, 2011. http://nocky.fr/ecrits-inedits/. Site discontinued: last modified 1999.

Gade, Christian B. 2012. "What Is Ubuntu? Different Interpretations among South Africans of African Descent." *South African Journal of Philosophy* 31:484–503.

Gaylard, Rob. 2004. "'Welcome to the World of Our Humanity': (African) Humanism, Ubuntu and Black South African Writing." *Journal of Literary Studies* 20:265–82.

Herman, Judith L. 1992. *Trauma and Recovery.* New York: Basic.

Hinton, Alexander L., and Kevin L. O'Neill. 2009. *Genocide: Truth, Memory, and Representation.* Durham, NC: Duke University Press.

Hitchcott, Nicki. 2009. "A Global African Commemoration—Rwanda: écrire par devoir de mémoire." *Forum for Modern Language Studies* 45:151–61.

Krog, Antjie. 2008. "'This Thing Called Reconciliation . . .': Forgiveness as Part of an Interconnectedness-towards-Wholeness." *South African Journal of Philosophy* 27:353–66.

Lamko, Koulsy. 2002. *La phalène des collines.* Paris: Serpent à plumes.

Metz, Thaddeus. 2011. "Ubuntu as a Moral Theory and Human Rights in South Africa." *African Human Rights Law Journal* 11:533–59.

Metz, Thaddeus, and Joseph B. Gaie. 2010. "The African Ethic of Ubuntu/Botho: Implications for Research on Morality." *Journal of Moral Education* 39 (3): 273–90.

Mphahlele, Es'kia. 2003. "Notes towards an Introduction to African Humanism: A Personal Enquiry—1992." In *Es'kia: Education, African Humanism and Culture, Social*

Consciousness, Literary Appreciation, edited by Es'kia Mphahlele, 131–41. Cape Town: Kwela.

Peterson, Bhekizizwe. 2014. "Dignity, Memory, and the Future under Siege: Reconciliation and Nation-Building in Post-apartheid South Africa." In *The New Violent Cartography: Geo-Analysis after the Aesthetic Turn*, edited by Michael J Shapiro and Samson O. Opondo, 214–33. London: Routledge.

Sanders, Mark. 2007. *Ambiguities of Witnessing: Law and Literature in the Time of a Truth Commission*. Stanford, CA: Stanford University Press.

Staub, Ervin. 2006. "Reconciliation after Genocide, Mass Killing, or Intractable Conflict: Understanding the Roots of Violence, Psychological Recovery, and Steps toward a General Theory." *Political Psychology* 27:867–94.

Tadjo, Véronique. 2000a. *L'ombre d'Imana: Voyages jusqu'au bout du Rwanda*. Arles, France: Actes Sud.

———. 2000b. *"Le pardon ne veut pas dire l'oubli."* Interview by Boniface Mongo-Mboussa. *Africultures*, October 31. http://www.africultures.com/php/index .php?nav=article&no=1611.

———. 2002. *The Shadow of Imana: Travels in the Heart of Rwanda*. Translated by Véronique Wakerley. Portsmouth, NH: Heinemann.

———. 2013. "Lifting the Cloak of (In)visibility: A Writer's Perspective." *Research in African Literatures* 44:1–7.

West-Pavlov, Russell. 2014. "'Regardez la vie reprendre': Futurity in Véronique Tadjo's L'ombre d'Imana/The Shadow of Imana." *Tydskrif vir Letterkunde* 51 (2): 114–30.

Wolfe, Stephanie. 2014. *The Politics of Reparations and Apologies*. New York: Springer.

ANNA-MARIE DE BEER is Lecturer in French and Francophone Studies at the University of Pretoria in South Africa.

10

UTU/UBUNTU AND COMMUNITY RESTORATION

Narratives of Survivors in Kenya's 2007 Postelection Violence

James Ogude and Unifier Dyer

THIS CHAPTER EXAMINES THE IDEA OF UBUNTU, a South African concept drawn from the Nguni languages but one that resonates with similar concepts in other parts of Africa. We found Ubuntu useful in understanding relational forms of personhood, seen by many as the defining principle in numerous African societies, and that is the principle that our personhood depends on our relationship with others: "A person is a person through other persons"—*Mutu ke mutu ka batho*, the Basotho say. In this chapter, Ubuntu is interchangeably used with its Bantu variant Utu from East Africa's major language, Swahili. It is captured through the axiom *Mutu ni utu*; translated, it reads "a human being is humanity"; or *Sifa ya mtu ni utu*, meaning "what essentially defines a human being is his/her humanity" (Kresse 2007, 139).[1]

This chapter, in part, seeks to deepen our understanding of the concept, which seems to speak squarely about the relationship between self and community; to ask whether values akin to Ubuntu, an indigenous knowledge-based value system, continues to manifest itself in the everyday practices and daily encounters of ordinary people. More important, we seek to ask whether the concept, which is rooted in a number of African societies and traditions, could be mobilized to reconstitute communities that have experienced forms of dislocation, violence, and trauma. In other words, whether it can be used in postconflict situations to appeal to our common humanity and to provide the grammar or a framework for speaking about forgiveness, redress, and reconciliation, since our humanity depends on our connectedness. Archbishop Desmond Tutu, in an astute and strategic move during the process of the South African Truth and Reconciliation Commission (TRC), used the Ubuntu concept and combined it with the Christian idea of *imago dei* theology (we are all made in the image of God and we are therefore the same) to appeal to the consciences of South African peoples across all barriers of color, race, class, and ethnicity. This critical moment in South Africa's history was marked by the difficulties of having to negotiate a peaceful transition from an oppressive regime to a new and desired democratic dispensation: the interregnum.

Following Tutu's use of Ubuntu in the context of the TRC, this chapter seeks to examine how traditional forms of redress could complement or even enrich Western forms of justice, especially in contexts of fragile democracy and postconflict periods. The argument is that in fragile democracies or postconflict periods, the institutions of justice and redress have either collapsed or have been compromised by the very corrupted custodians of these institutions. In such contexts, people tend to turn to para-literate zones of knowledge or simply the surviving value systems that continue to regulate their daily lives. They may range from religious institutions, modern and traditional, to indigenous systems of justice and redress still in vogue or simply lurking in the memory of community leaders.

Recent scholarship and practices have examined the value of traditional justice mechanisms in peacemaking and reconciliation after violent conflict. Indeed, attempts to evoke traditional justice instruments in peacemaking and administering justice must be seen as innovative when conventional judiciary systems are seen either as hostile or simply as unreliable. For example, how does one deal with persistent impunity often displayed by those who commit grave human rights abuses, especially when the powerful custodians of modern justice systems are involved? Concurrently, however, questions have been asked about the applicability of systematic prosecutions in contexts where regime change is an extremely delicate or complex operation. Local political and civil society leaders have pointed to the many political, social, economic, and cultural contingencies that may make it impossible for their societies to fulfill the duty to prosecute.

It is these doubts about the use of trials that have led to a search for alternative or complementary mechanisms to avoid the dangers of too much or too little criminal justice. The TRC, with its principle of amnesty for truth, was a turning point. It became clear that a combination of measures and instruments in search for justice and reconciliation was needed. As a result, a remarkable shift now points to multiple conceptions of justice and reconciliation: state and nonstate instruments; legal, semilegal, and nonjudicial techniques. As part of this important development, some postconflict societies have now turned their attention to their legacy of indigenous practices of dispute settlement and reconciliation. The argument is that traditional and informal justice systems may be adopted as an appropriate response to civil war and oppression.

In what follows, we try to provide an overview of the narratives about Kenya's 2007 postelection violence and to ask what forms of justice and redress would be appropriate in the Kenyan context. In order to do so and to avoid a predetermined outcome, we wade through personal narratives of both victims and perpetrators and political actors and community leaders in an attempt to surface their own understanding of the conflict and how the postconflict moment could be addressed. We pay attention to the language and the grammar they use to frame meanings, even when those very meanings remain elusive and contradictory and defy framing in ordinary language. It is out of this chaotic plurality of meaning that we attempt to go behind the filter of language to point to possibilities of redress, restoration, and reconciliation—a path that points to a profound, if sometimes shaky, belief in our humanity, way beyond a national and ethnic citizenship. But first, a brief background of Kenya's 2007 postelection violence. How did Kenya arrive at this ghastly experience in a country that was often seen as an island of peace in East Africa?

Background to 2007 Postelection Violence in Kenya

Kenya's 2007 postelection violence was not unique in the history of Kenya's elections since independence. In fact, its more recent electoral history is characterized by both spontaneous and politically orchestrated violence designed to undermine the popular vote and the democratic process. For more than three decades, Kenya was under single-party rule by the Kenyan African National Union (KANU). In 1991, Section 2A of the Kenyan Constitution was repealed, this was a law that since 1982 has made Kenya a one-party state. Kenya's 1992 elections, which saw multiparty registration, were meant to mark the end of single-party rule by nullifying Section 2A of the constitution, which prohibited plural politics. But this was not to be: Daniel Arap Moi would maintain single-party rule in Kenya for another decade. The 1992 elections were riddled with violence that was meant to disenfranchise and destabilize communities that did not support Moi and KANU. The violence took the form of land dispossession and killings of those deemed as foreign settlers, actions meant to enable the Kalenjin community (Moi's community) to occupy the land of victims who were uprooted from Rift Valley and also undermine the electoral process. In October 1991, state-manufactured ethnic tensions resulted in violence[2] when clashes broke out in the Rift Valley Province between Kalenjin on one side and Kikuyu, Luo, Kisii, and Kamba groups on other hand, which sealed the province's fate as the hotspot of election violence in subsequent elections. Violence preceded the elections themselves and the 1992 events are crucial in understanding violence that surrounded later elections.

The 1997 elections were characterized by similar politically motivated, state-sponsored violence. Violence in 1997 was targeted on coastal groups from upcountry, namely, Luhya, Luo, Kikuyu, and Kamba communities, displacing them and destroying their property. The violence was intended to disenfranchise communities from other regions that had settled in the coastal region as migrant workers and registered as voters in coastal region. But it was also intended to curry support and votes from Swahili-Arab and Mijikenda communities by evoking their long-standing land grievances. The elections saw the multiparty state stumble and stagger under Moi, who was reelected president.

With ethnic tensions already rising, the aftermath of the first multiparty democratic elections in 2002 laid down new foundations for ethnic conflicts. With the final removal of Section 2A from the constitution after the reinforced appeal of Section 2A in 1997, Moi was prohibited from running for another term. The replacement of Section 2A with Section 1A promised to introduce change from the one-party state to a multiparty state. Tensions in the 2002 elections were minimized by the rallying of diverse Kenyan communities, except Moi's Kalenjin community, behind the National Rainbow Coalition (NARC), an amalgam of two parties, the National Alliance Party of Kenya and the Liberal Democratic Party (LDP),[3] which intended to oust KANU, now led by Moi's anointed leader, Uhuru Kenyatta. Despite the decrease in election violence, more than two hundred deaths were reported. Symptoms of ethnic tension—which must be seen as essentially fabricated by political leaders however real the ethnic conflicts might be—would emerge in the years leading up to the 2007 elections, when firm lines were drawn between ethnic factions and underlying ethnic tensions that were ambiguous in 2002 surfaced with greater inflexibility.

After ballots were cast, NARC won, and Mwai Kibaki, the party leader, took office as president. After being sworn in, Kibaki failed to honor the Memorandum of Understanding (MoU) he had with Raila Odinga to share appointments of cabinet ministers and public appointments equally. To make amends for this breach of trust, it was agreed between the two leaders that Odinga would fill the newly created position of prime minister, although Kibaki only consented after the peace agreement brokered by the late Kofi Anan, the former secretary general of the United Nations, and only in the immediate aftermath of 2007 postelection violence. The betrayal of the MoU by Kibaki split NARC into NARC-Kenya and the LDP. The ethnically charged divide between Odinga and Kibaki became the fault line upon which the 2007 general elections were conducted. As it transpired, Kibaki's presidency was rife with signs of approaching danger and fissures.[4] Immediate demands over land grievances and constitutional reform that were not met ignited conflict, and historical grievances stoked the fire and its raging flames.

The election narrative relates elections that were held with a fair amount of cooperation and peace on December 27, 2007. The two major competing parties were Party of National Unity (PNU), also called the banana party, with Kibaki as leader, and the Orange Democratic Movement (ODM), also called the orange party, led by Odinga. Confusion occurred in the election tally when the election commission called Odinga ahead on the December 29 and a day later announced Kibaki as president. A rushed swearing-in ceremony followed under the watch of the chairman of the electoral commission of Kenya, Samuel Kivuitu. Within minutes of the announcement, violence broke out in towns and their surrounding areas. Most of the violence was concentrated in the largest province Rift Valley Province with the towns of Eldoret, Naivasha, and Nakuru most affected.[5] Large parts of Nyanza Province, located in the western region of the country, was also a hotbed, with the most violence reported in the provincial capital Kisumu. Western Province was equally affected by the splurge of violence. The Rift Valley Province in particular has been characterized by tensions around land taken from the Kalenjin community by the founding president, Jomo

Kenyatta. The outbreak in violence was swiftly followed by planned attacks on families and homes, with old grievances over land, power, and wealth reignited in a fresh wave of unprecedented ethnic attacks. Later they would be dismissed as merely spontaneous responses to election rigging (Branch 2011, 281). In this turbulent time of unrest, the refuge that victims and residents sought from the police and law enforcement was instead replaced by gross abuses. Prison guards and police were reported at such times to loot, rape, and refuse help to those from ethnic groups other than their own. It is not surprising that the most difficult abuse to report was rape, and many women remained silent. Later, when ODM protesters in major urban areas took to the streets in resistance against election results, the might of the police force was unreservedly unleashed on them.

Electoral history has shown an unmistakable trend in the use of politicized ethnicity to fuel violence by the political elite. State power and the resource control it grants became the central site of ethnic struggle, and loyalty was rewarded through unbridled exploitation of state resources. Under Moi, the Kelenjin ethnic group maintained hegemony; with Kibaki, it was the Kikuyus who maintained hegemony. Ethnicity had become the most visible rallying point and dangerously systematized endemic violence.

Land grabs and displacement has caused generations of unresolved grievances in Kenya, a gaping wound compounded by the continuation of land ownership by the former colonial population and the cooptation into the settler economy—since what was won was flag independence—by the rising African elite, whom the ruling Kenya African Union government gave land to settle on as far back as Jomo Kenyatta's presidency. Ethnicizing politics plays into the hands of what Garuba calls "naturalisation of identity through the body" (2002, 107). When identity is naturalized through the body, the body becomes both a site and tool of struggle for the riches of the state, which are indispensable but finite.

The landscape on which electoral dynamics play out is a highly centralized executive power and a precarious constitution, which combine to place the state far out of reach of ordinary Kenyans and accessible only through "big men" and "big sisters" or "big women" who dispense resources as patronage (Ogude 2009, 12). The state becomes a "site of eating" (Ogude 2009) and votes are cast in order to acquire a share of what Achebe calls the "national cake" (1988, 12). When Odinga and Kibaki finally agreed to a coalition government, which in the short term prevented the return of conflict, their agreement overlooked the Reform Agenda (Branch 2011, 279), neglecting the rights of Kenyans who had been displaced and had no place to call home—refugees in their own country.

The Kenyan scenario search for justice, healing, and reconciliation remains elusive, as in other African countries afflicted by conflict. The measures taken have been half-hearted, at best, and unstructured. Internally displaced people remain in camps with little hope on the horizon. The Kenyan National Commission on Human Rights, which was meant to be styled after the South African TRC, was veiled in secrecy and controversy from its very inception. Huge gaps in the process of restoration and reconciliation, compromised by internal doctoring of the final report for political purposes, left more questions unanswered than answered.[6]

Since the end of physical violence, because the psychological and social wounds remain, the focus has been on the main political players rather than on the ordinary victims and perpetrators. Manipulations to shift the focus away from the ordinary victims and perpetrators has spurred on tensions around ethnicity and deepened the political and national fractures. This was most evident when leaders of the two warring sides accused of masterminding the violence of 2007 elections came together to form an electoral pact in the 2012 elections.

Although the full agenda of this electoral pact may take years to unravel, what was not lost on many Kenyans was the fact that the pact principally served the personal interest and political expediency of the two political actors and displayed no particular attempt to bridge the ethnic tensions or show convincing evidence that the country was at last turning a new chapter. Indeed, attention continued to be diverted away from the victims to the powerful. The ethnic division among Kenyans over the International Criminal Court (ICC) case against President Kenyatta and his vice president William Ruto has revealed that Kenyans need a much more comprehensive justice process to achieve reconciliation and restoration of social cohesion.

To try to understand what must be done, we turned to personal narratives of perpetrators and victims recorded in Njogu (2009), written from extensive interviews with the victims and perpetrators, and *Kwani?* (Kahora 2008), a Kenyan literary annual that detailed views of victims, perpetrators, and witnesses or observers of the violence on what has to be done in reconstituting the postconflict Kenyan nation. The two-part fifth issue of *Kwani?* includes interviews with Kenyans affected or involved in

the violence around the elections. Its photographs document the fright-
ful period of conflict and offers historical narratives, personal experiences,
critical papers, poems, letters, and cartoon strips. The two parts of the 2008
edition, "Maps and Journeys" and "Revelations and Conversations," provide what the editor tells us is part of the narrative on "what we were before,
and what we became, during the epochal first 100 days of 2008" (Kahora
2008, 1).

The Value of Narratives in the Process of Mourning and Healing

Although narratives do not bring about direct healing, they are critical in
creating the framework within which healing can take place. Narratives
are important because they allow the nation, listeners, and readers to share
the burden of memory with the victims and perpetrators; they also allow
readers to bear witness to trauma and to create a community of listeners for
survivors. It is, narrative, as Ricœur tells us, that enables "a path to mourning" (Ricœur and Antohi 2005, 24). But narratives are also important to
the extent that they allow the players to have a voice; to speak, and in that
way to lead us into their inner feelings and conflicted attitudes toward what
justice and healing should entail.

An essential part of the process toward healing traumatic experiences
is the accessibility of a suitable audience, since as Martin Kopf (2010) tells
us victims constantly have to negotiate the dialectic of "conflict between the
desire to tell and the will to deny" (48). It is worth mentioning that many
of the critical avenues of redress on the postelection violence in Kenya have
been led by nongovernmental organizations (NGOs), often seeking to keep
memory of these gruesome events alive through documentary films, pho-
tography, stories, poems, and essays on and by the victims and perpetrators. NGOs often position themselves as neutral arbiters in contexts marked
by political partisanship and tension.

Narratives offer us a national archive of remembrance and keep dialogue on these issues alive in the minds of the present and future citizenry.[7]
On the value of narrative records Kimani Njogu opines (2009): narratives
"spell out the difference between official state-inscribed versions of events
and the people's history as it exists in popular memory. This memory is not
simply limited to the telling collected here, it exists in the landscape of new
donor-built homesteads and corrugated iron sheets freshly emblazoned

with the names of the benefactors; it is carried in the scars, limbs, thoughts and reactions of all who witnessed the violent events" (10).

In essence, memory is lived as an experience in the present that is informed by the past. The first archive sites are people and the spaces they inhabit. Etched in their new ways of living are the traumatic remembrances of what has forced people to grope for a language with which to frame their trauma. The "donor-built homesteads" and "scars" are what appear after the act of violence, and they remain as testimony of what violence forces people to become. It is how they move beyond the inevitable, the turmoil of bloodshed and hostility and the tools they appropriate for this task that we endeavor to investigate.

What do we glean from the narratives in the rightly titled *Healing the Wound* (Njogu 2009) and the personal narratives in Kahora (2008) of Kenya's postelection violence? What issues come to the surface about justice and forgiveness? In other words, Do these narratives point to possibilities of redress? and, In what idiom are they wrapped?

A significant aspect of memory making is narrative formation, and the grammar used depends on the story that is being told. Significantly, what the interviews from Njogu (2009) and Kahora (2008) reveal is the hard task of asking how experiences steeped in violent acts can be narrated, depicted, and archived. After asking how they can be, the point of departure we chose was a collective voice on what factors contributed to the rise and finally the spree of violent confrontations among communities in Kenya in the period before and after the 2007 presidential elections.

Ironically, the perpetrators and victims agree on a number of issues they believe triggered the postelection violence: political manipulation by political leaders using negative ethnicity and mobilizing ethnicity to get votes and lack of integrity by the Kenyan Electoral Commission foremost among them. Included also are a broad consensus on long-standing grievances over land leading to ethnic tensions, rivalry, and jealousy. Perpetrators and victims also both point to forces beyond human control, noticeably, the work of the devil. The devil here could be veiled grammar or a metaphor for a breakdown in the moral fiber of society that has led to otherwise seemingly inexplicable mistrust and suspicion among people who have hitherto lived peacefully. Violent atrocities point to a fundamental loss in values akin to Utu that uphold respect for life and living together harmoniously. It is not surprising that the elders who are supposed to be the custodians of moral values in the society are the ones accused of poisoning the youth, and the youth themselves point to lack of employment opportunities and poverty as the driving force behind their actions. When the welfare of the whole society is upset by poverty and lack of gainful employment, the moral fiber of the society is in turn affected and leads to the erosion of values such as Utu that maintain social cohesion.

Equally noteworthy is the occurrence of nepotism along ethnic lines, which creates the illusion in the minds of many that ethnic political power pays and it is only when one's ethnic group acquires that power that national resources can be accessed, social security provided to one's community, and economic mobility realized. Those with such privileges feel they have worked hard to attain the success they have and that other groups are either lazy, simply wanting to take what others have worked hard for or that they harbor jealousy toward those with greater material wealth. Framed this way, what forms of justice do the people desire? How do they think restoration can be achieved?

How Victims and Perpetrators Frame Their Understanding of Justice and Redress

Experiences of interiority documented in the narratives we study afford us alternative perspectives to dominant voices. It is through these texts that we begin to see a deeply personal and intimate relationship between people vis-à-vis the state. Embedded in the narratives of victims is an astute awareness that the balance of communal life has suffered destabilization and that this imbalance comes, in part, from ethnic factionalism and the erosion of values that affirm their humanity. This erosion is evident in many of the narratives that betray a language of violence and abuse, pointing to a loss of common social norms of humanness. For anybody familiar with Kenya's political landscape, the language of violence is largely drawn from the rhetoric of politicians, who have over the years perfected a grammar of exclusion, a language of them and us. Examples include the talk about "flushing out" foreigners and derogatory names such as "watu wa Bara" (the uncivilized from the hinterland) and "madoadoa" meaning "blemishes" or "stains" (Njogu 2009, 3, 86).[8]

Stemming from this kind of idiom is a general blame on *Wazee*, the elders (who are said to have trained young men to fight using traditional forms of combat learned during initiation), and on politicians (said to have "poisoned" the youth with their evocative words and material tokens;

Njogu 2009, 65).[9] It is significant that *Wazee*, who, in traditional contexts, should be the custodians and repository of positive societal values and therefore charged with providing the moral compass, are portrayed in the narratives as instigators of violence and negative ethnicity. One small-scale farmer from Ukunda regards the ethnic distinctions and ethnically tinged language as a government creation and is used as a political instrument manipulated by those unsatisfied with election results (Njogu 2009, 91).[10] It would seem that although the farmer is aware of the influence politicians wield and the role they play in igniting and even funding violence, political rhetoric still seeps into the language of ordinary citizens who are trying to assemble a narrative of national and personal trauma.

Juxtaposed against this farmer's sentiments are a considerable number of narratives that stress in the opening sentences of the interviews Njogu conducted, a high levels of integration of various ethnic groups into communities, and diverse ethnic groups who have lived peacefully together for generations. Many of the interviewees tell of how free movement was before the election violence imposed constraints and forced them to flee to parts of the country where their ethnic groups are dominant, creating the false perception that they are "returning" to their site of "origin" as a community. Previously, mobility among Kenyans was driven by a search for economic livelihood or employment opportunities. The constant assertion of themes of integration and forced return to ethnic enclaves points to the possibilities of national citizenship on the one hand and the actuality of disintegration and a return to purely ethnic identity on the other.

In spite of the tensions between the desire for national belonging and ethnic affiliation, a noticeable yearning for a form of integration or communal affinity that transcends ethnic and national attachments also emerges: an affirmation of a common humanity. In the majority of the narratives we have studied there remains a deep sense of belonging that supports the reintegration of victims and perpetrators into a community where they can enjoy the unity in diversity that they experienced before election violence erupted. Samuel Kinuthia in his narrative stresses that, when he returned home, no initiative was made to say "welcome back" (Kahora 2008, 42). He mentions, "We need to see the local chief, to tell him to ask our friends here to come and talk to us, so we can talk together" (42).[11] When presented with the question "Have your people forgiven the neighbours for what happened, or do they want revenge?" Samuel Kinuthia answers, "They have forgiven. They say, 'let them come, and we will talk'" (43). In spite of the deep fissure that violence has caused family and neighbors within the community, there is a concerted effort to renegotiate these relationship by facilitating dialogue, and most especially through the act of forgiveness, an indispensable tool that engenders agency in the forgiving and the forgiven. Appropriated in such a manner, forgiveness is a demonstration of restoration.

A sawmill operator from Londiani in the Rift Valley province offers an interesting observation on the conditions of forgiveness. His concept includes a system of gradation where the level of violence determines the punishment for the act. Violations of human rights require educational intervention and burning houses deserves no forgiveness. He does not, however, explain which human rights he means or what has to happen with those who are not forgiven. What is clear, though, is that there are conditions for forgiveness and there are also conditions under which it can be denied, highlighting the importance of forgiveness. Furthermore, articulated here is an understanding of the pertinent need to uphold human rights, through civic education, espoused and checked continuously and consistently. The path to reconciliation therefore necessitates a clarification of concepts such as forgiveness, punishment, and violation of human rights, and reconciliation also requires the establishment of dialogue between affected individuals, families, and communities.

The language of justice and reconciliation is layered, wrapped in ambiguity and the tentativeness of any work in progress and requires a constant desire to constitute the community afresh. This grammar of justice and reconciliation sometimes intones a religious register of forgiveness as a tool for redress and at other times gestures toward social systems like *kibageng* (Njogu 2009, 25),[12] which could inform structures of reintegration and reconciliation and which, according to the executive director of the Naivasha Disadvantaged Support Group, failed because victims of violence felt that "the people they suspect were leaders of the Naivasha violence are the ones they see in the peace committees so they feel that they are not making any headway" (Njogu 2009, 202). The Waki Commission hearings (convened to address what the Kenyan Commission on Human Rights overlooked) are the center of criticism in the comment. What remains central to these iterations on the restoration of shared values is the need for dialogue and communication across ethnic and party divisions in order to create an inclusive community.

In Kahora (2008), many of the sentiments presented point to a breakdown in communication between neighbors, which is replaced after the electoral violence by deep suspicion and unsettling silence. And yet isolated cases occur in which people who have returned to their communities to rebuild their lives have had their neighbors reach out for reconciliation by saying "we are sorry for that" (Kahora 2008, 45). Those most willing to extend these words of remorse are often the elders, even though the youth perpetrated the acts of violence. At this level, it is the elders who are once again forced to confront their dereliction of responsibility during the violence and become voices of reconciliation between the victims of violence (but also encompassing the community) and the perpetrators both at the individual and communal level.

Noteworthy is how, in fact, the language of the narrators also betrays that lingering desire for state citizenship and all the guarantees that are associated with it: security from poverty and education and the creation of employment opportunities. Narrators also express a desire for the rule of law and institutions of justice that can be trusted. Finally, the narratives also point to the need to give recognition to communal agency as opposed to people being subjected to changes and ideas coming from external actors. A good example is Operation Rudi Nyumbani, an initiative that a young man Johnson from Turbo tells us was meant to help people back into communities that was not recognized by community members, which left it largely ineffective (Njogu 2009, 275).

In spite of everything, a humanist discourse permeates Njogu's narratives. For example, the way narrators speak about those who have done wrong shows how they expect reconciliation to happen. Retaining relational ties such as neighbor(s) and friend(s) indicates the significance those relationships have for those who have found them corroded. The relational references do not change, even though the nature of the relationship has undergone tremendous strain. The felt importance of the relationships that existed between communities, pointing to their connectedness beyond ethnic and family affiliations, signals by that very fact not simply the desire to restore community, but also a lingering presence of the values that bind communities together; values that even a traumatic experience such as the postelection violence cannot easily erase. Refraining from labels such as "criminals" except in the case of politicians reflects a subtle and complex attempt to discriminate between perpetrators of violence and the politicians who masterminded the violence in the first instance. A common matrix of victimhood is therefore created between victims and perpetrators—the twin actors, both in need of healing.

This demonstration of relationality can be traced to specific normative prescriptions embedded in the fabric of communal thought and practice. The nature of the relationships, how they are formed and solidified, determines the role they play, and the significance afforded to them by the members involved. Ikuenobe (2006) tells us that relationships such as mother, father, uncle, aunt, sister, brother, friend, neighbor "prescribe communal norms, certain social responsibilities, and modes of behavior, which are learned in the context of the society and community in which the words have meaning" (70). These titles are loaded with responsibility to both the referred and the referrer. It is the weight, protection, and status of these relationships that makes abandoning them for harsher appellation impossible irrespective of the extent of pain and harm caused. The sharp awareness that violent acts were not isolated from the political violence of the state places repairing these relationships into sharp focus for those who value them more than the empty promises of political leaders.

People in Kenya feel a deep willingness and sense the necessity to preserve or restore broken and eroded relationships. Beyond this, reaching out and initiating communication takes a step toward repairing what has been damaged, looking at the wrong done and wrongdoer as a pertinent player in the journey toward restoration and healing. Reaching out restores a mutual recognition of humanity and embodies what we variously call Ubuntu.

One of the primary forms of imparting Ubuntu is through lifelong education, significantly through oral literature, the anchor of African expression and knowledge transfer. When the Londiani sawmill operator distinguishes forgiveness as a key prescription for determining how to carry on from a place of deep pain and then goes on to link this with education, he shows that the concept of forgiveness is not innate within people and needs to be taught and instilled. Although he wrongly delineates African modes of education as informal, Ikuenobe (2006) recognizes that "the idea of education involves the broad processes of learning, upbringing, socialization, initiation, acculturation, and teaching people the communal ways of life, tradition, beliefs, values, a broad range of prescribed conduct, and the general and moral principles that determine the acceptable actions and behavior" (73). Forgiveness as an identified value would be woven into the moral pretexts set by the community and disseminated as education. In conversation with a healer from Vhembe, South Africa, we asked what *vhuthu*, the Tshivenda equivalent of Ubuntu, is and we were offered a descriptive answer: "muthu arena vhuthu u na u vhavhalela" (a person with vhuthu is compassionate and benevolent; unwilling to cause any sort of harm)—and the attitude extends to people, the environment, animals, and all beings, animate and inanimate. In forgiveness, part of *vhuthu* would be an unwillingness to inflict harsh sentencing. Although the celebrated characteristic described to us by the healer was assumed to be uniquely part of the owner's personality, the sawmill operator and Samuel Kinuthia draw our attention to the exception of such an act and the necessity for initiative through education. This is all the more necessary in an environment where deep fissures have been caused by violence, as was the case in Kenya.

The Moral Concept Utu/Ubuntu and the Search for Justice and Restoration in Kenya

When faced with a rapid and destabilizing period of violence such as the one we have outlined in the case of Kenya after its elections, we must acknowledge that this is a national trauma. The moment itself was devastating, but its devastation also persist in its sobering effect on everyday life and national politics. People feel acutely that the state, its leaders, and its institutions cannot be trusted to implement justice fairly, nor can they be trusted with building bridges between victims and perpetrators.

From the narratives, we come to see that the greatest concerns in communities affected by election violence are the immediate communal issues. Communal issues, though, are often tied to the nation-state through direct community affiliations with members running for political office that have various degrees of access to the "big men in power," closing the gap between ordinary everyday experiences and the issues of the larger nation-state. It is as a result of such tethered relations that people become quite aware of the state and the power it wields in their lives and what they expect from it as citizens of a democratic state—albeit an unstable democracy.

Without close ties to the nation-state, it becomes a far removed entity and the citizenry relate to it more as a source of coercive power than as the custodian of their interests, as Mahmood Mamdani (1996) has argued. The state is therefore largely expected to bear the material burdens that victims have incurred, but no more. With the state predominantly left out (or willfully leaving *itself* out) of the processes of restoring balance and creating healing, what does the language of belonging, forgiveness, rehabilitation, rebuilding, reintegration, and reconciliation offer communities with their deep wounds and grievances?

It is for these reasons that Desmond Tutu, chair of the South African TRC, argues that "Western-style justice does not fit with traditional African jurisprudence. It is too personal." He writes that the African view of justice is aimed at "the healing of breaches, the redressing of imbalances, the restoration of broken relationships. This kind of justice seeks to rehabilitate both the victim and the perpetrator, who should be given the opportunity to be reintegrated into the community he or she has injured by his or her offence" (Tutu 1999, 51).

On paper, Tutu's African idea of justice may appear idealistic and altogether romantic, but in practice—especially in transitional and fragile democracies, such as was the case in the immediate aftermath of postapartheid dispensation, when real judicial and economic power was still in the hands of the minority whites, or in the context of Kenya, when the postelection violence left the country deeply divided and soon after had the perpetrators in control of the levers of power—a moral ethic such as Ubuntu, with its focus on restoration and dialogue, can prove central to healing. Court trials and conventional judicial process can easily turn into a farce in these scenarios.

Court trials may be impaired through lack of, or destruction of, evidence and absence of witnesses, as we saw recently in Uhuru Kenyatta's case at The Hague, which led to the ICC withdrawing the case against him. When lack of proof leads to the acquittal of evidently-guilty, let alone alleged, perpetrators, people's trust in the judiciary system or institutions of justice is damaged forever.

When time and time again the narratives point us to what enables people to reconnect and reintegrate into their communities, can we afford to overlook the deep introspection people do in the aftermath of such tragedies, especially if it reveals to us what they base concepts of everyday life on? What source do people draw from when they reflect on the damaged fabric of their society and nation as a whole, particularly in contexts full of political intrigues and power games? Many have argued that in such cases, trials instigated from below and rooted in indigenous justice mechanisms—and, indeed, indigenous forms of forgiveness—become relevant. In a locally driven hearing, one scholar writes, "The centre of gravity moves from the courtroom to the hearing, from the judge to the local civil society, from fixation on individual guilt to the search of societal patterns in atrocities, from legal retaliation to ritual reconciliation, from internationally driven retributive impulses to the full acknowledgement of the opportunities the local context offers" (Huyse and Salter 2008, 5).

It is in contexts characterized by political and democratic fragility that values such as Utu, the Swahili equivalent of Ubuntu, find resonance in forcing us to confront our humanness and our connectedness rather than our ethnic citizenship or national context. The social and philosophical concept Utu has its roots not only among the Swahili-speaking communities along the coastal region but also among the Bantu-speaking peoples of East Africa.

In understanding the way Utu is practiced in its foundational ethos, we need to move well beyond the axiom and grasp its relational principles, which underscore our connectedness as human beings. As a moral and ethical concept, it also points to the enduring possibilities of renewal; of communities reconstituting themselves, especially when they are forced to rediscover their Utu-ness.

As a socializing agent then, Utu, just like Ubuntu, is founded on the notion that "human beings are what they are through the presence [and, we could add, participation] of others" (Kresse 2007, 140). Appropriated as the foundation for personhood, it connotes a sense of shared identity with one another. Such identification is through a set of culturally defined rules of behavior. Utu is universal, is formal, is abstract, has a moral quality, and is mediated by individual action and social recognition.

Utu is characterized as a reward-earning system of which the markers are morality, respect, and acknowledgment of goodness. Furthermore, Utu itself is not a religious term despite how interchangeable its principles are with religious concepts. It is Utu's ability to incorporate hybrid notions that can assist us in understanding the shards of justice pieced from the narratives in Njogu (2009), and Kahora (2008). It is worth reflecting on such a question as, If people's daily lives are informed by notions of Utu/Ubuntu, is it surprising to find that after moments of trauma they wish to restore their sense of self through principles that echo Utu/Ubuntu?

Without attempting to impose a value system on a specific context, we wish to propose here that in the Kenyan scenario we could use Utu in this way to frame a discourse around postconflict processes of healing and restoration. People are quite aware of the culpability of the state in all such conflicts and how they too are implicated in the structure of violence, while equally conscious that they cohabit a single space either as victims or perpetrators of violence—hence the overriding need to reconcile and live together. After all, almost every narrative speaks of how people enjoyed the diversity of living among or accepting people from different ethnic groups. When people evoke the everyday grammar of forgiveness and restitution, reintegration and rebuilding new communities from the ruins of politically engineered violence, they are well on the path to how their trauma can be overcome. That path, this chapter argues, are pointedly linked to those relational values that both Ubuntu and Utu stand for. These are values that call for the recognition of the other's humanity.

A concept such as Utu could be effective because, as a knowledge system, it has an immense ability to withstand extended and continual periods of absolute change. We have witnessed how after periods of gross atrocities over long periods of time (apartheid) or short durations (multiple Kenyan postelection violence) the value of life is reinterrogated and the human lives affected placed at the center of the discussion. The initiatives that have been used with success tend to refer to humane values in confronting and dealing with situations of conflict, even when humane values are rooted in traditional and religious modes of redress. Most of the persons interviewed in Kenya in the aftermath of the election violence with great ease cite concepts akin to Utu/Ubuntu interchangeably with religious values. It is therefore possible to think of Utu as an ethos people can appropriate to enable a grammar of talking about healing (forgiveness, reconciliation, etc.) and also about retributive measures (political accountability, international tribunals). Although we cannot argue conclusively that Ubuntu/Utu as a moral and ethical principle will resolve postconflict tensions in Kenya, we can at least argue that it offers a framework for communication and dialogue that opens up possibilities for realizing healing and restoration in contexts of fragile democracy. We are in agreement with Luc Huyse that although tradition-based practices may not always acquire total legitimacy locally and internationally, they can "produce a dividend in terms of the much-needed post-conflict accountability, truth telling and reconciliation that is not negligible. Consequently, positive effects may be expected with regard to the more general transitional justice goals of healing and social repairs" (Huyse 2008, 192).

Notes

This chapter was first published in German in *Polylog* no. 34 (2015) and permission has been granted for the reproduction of the English version, with some modification, in this volume.

1. Hallen (2009) makes a similar point with reference to Gbadegesin's study of Yoruba values. According to Hallen, Gbadegesin concludes "that the moral values that distinguish 'traditional' Yoruba and, by implication, African culture delimits a form of humanism: cooperation, a healthy sense of community, generosity, and respect for others" (46). The concept of Ubuntu exists throughout the African continent and finds expression in the multitude of languages and cultures that color its geography. In southern Africa, it appears in the Nguni languages and other Bantu language subfamilies. In literature, Ubuntu is the most commonly used and comes from the Nguni languages. Some other variants include Vhuthu in Tshivenda, Botho is Sotho, Hunhu in Shona, and Umuntu in Kinyarwanda and Kirundi of Rwanda, to name but a few. Also see Ramose ([1999] 2002), and Kagame (1956).

2. One cannot ignore the statement made by Moi, who predicted that the 1992 elections would experience ethnic clashes because Kenya was not a cohesive nation.

3. NARC comprises Kikuyu, Luo, Luhya, Kamba, and various other communities. Ethnicity was less of a mobilizing tool in the 2002 elections than it had been previously or would become later.

4. Soon after the campaign against the November 2005 referendum (which aimed to dilute the centralized powers of the president, resolve land disputes, address the gender inequality in land ownership, and provide greater access to religious courts), Kibaki, having lost the referendum to the opposition, sacked all his cabinet and deputy ministers (something that had never occurred in Kenya's history) as an initiate to start afresh and replaced them with mainly Kikuyu members from his ethnic community. Kibaki's government targeted the media to weaken it—this was something that would emerge as a strategy in the midst of the postelection violence, when broadcasts reporting violence were banned. In tandem with these was a deliberate effort to grow and strengthen the administration police. Frustration was on the rise when levels of corruption had become apparent, especially with Anglo Leasing, the scandal in which the government was alleged to have awarded the British company Anglo Leasing Finance a printing license worth USD$30 million to change Kenyan passports, which turned out to be one among many phantom entities fraudulently used to extract higher taxes from Kenyans without delivering the promised services. Last, the electoral commission established in 2007 was unilaterally appointed by Kibaki, who blatantly overlooked the 1997 Inter-parties Parliamentary Group, which required that all political parties nominate their representatives to the electoral commission. What transpired next was even more problematic: the president's longtime lawyer, Kihara Mutu, became the vice chairman of the electoral commission.

5. Kenya is divided into eight administrative provinces: Central (predominantly Kikuyu), Nairobi (cosmopolitan capital city with diverse communities), Coastal (inhabited largely by the Mjikenda, Taita, and Swahili Arabs, among others), Rift Valley (predominantly Kalenjin community), Nyanza (predominantly Luo and Kisii, among others), Western (predominantly inhabited by the Luhyia community); Northeastern (predominantly inhabited by the Somali speaking communities); and Eastern (predominantly inhabited by the Kamba community, among others).

6. In the aftermath of the postelection violence, Kenya's president, Uhuru Kenyatta, and his vice president, William Ruto (both accused by the ICC of inciting violence), were moving around using state resources to give money to IDP's as an election ploy. The payouts were grossly uneven, with opposition strongholds receiving the least.

7. It is this will to remember that has shaped the metanarrative of redemption on the Jews' holocaust to date, so much so that when the student representative council president

of the University of Witwatersrand (South Africa), Mcebo Dlamini, praised Adolf Hitler on his Facebook page, the media, talk-show hosts, and listeners alike were united in their condemnation of his insensitive utterances. Many, not simply Jews, share the burden of the holocaust and the unforgettable memory of what it inflicted on our humanity. See "jewish-student-organisation-responds-to-dlaminis-hitler-comments," http://witsvuvuzela .com/2015/04/27/src-president-says-i-love-hitler/.

8. *Madoadoa* is used here to isolate immigrant communities as outsiders whose presence can only threaten the "purity" of the indigenous. Similarly, those violently referred to as "watu wa Bara" were attacked in Coastal Province and told to return inland and not vote in the province (Njogu 2009, 86).

9. Part of the training given to the youth is modeled on heroic narratives of conquest and pride of the "tribe" that are intended to bind the youth to a fabricated idea of ethnic nationalism or citizenship.

10. To further make this point, one businessman from Kericho town, in the highlands west of the Kenyan Rift Valley, describes distortions created by politics, even in long-standing grievances such as dispossession of land. Simply put, he says, "These [ethnic] clashes are not triggered by either land or tribes but by politics" (Njogu 2009, 123).

11. Such seemingly simple enunciations accepting community members who have been displaced from their homes back into the community is in fact at the heart of what a displaced person in Naivasha camp is distraught about when he exclaims, "I feel I am a refugee in my own country" (Kahora 2008, 144).

12. Annette Wairimu explains the interconnectedness that *kibagenge* works through as follows: the government "should urge the people to unite because even if the *'perceived enemy'* went away, no community can trade with itself. If all communities do not work closely together, they cannot engage in development. Only unity and working together can enable our children to learn (get educated). No single community can progress alone. For instance, in the church I belonged to a woman's group where we would give gifts to other people. These groups collapsed when people moved away from Kuresoi" (Njogu 2009, 25).

References

Achebe, Chinua. 1988. *A Man of the People*. London: Heinemann.

Branch, Daniel. 2011. *Kenya between Hope and Despair, 1963–2011*. New Haven, CT: Yale University Press.

Garuba, Harry. 2002. "Mapping the Land/Body/Subject: Colonial and Postcolonial Geographies on African Narrative." *Alternation* 9:87–116.

Hallen, Barry. 2009. *A Short History of African Philosophy*. 2nd ed. Bloomington: Indiana University Press.

Huyse, Luc. 2008. "Conclusions and Recommendations." In *Traditional Justice and Reconciliation after Violent Conflict: Learning from African Experiences*, edited by Luc Huyse and M. Salter, 181–97. Stockholm: International Institute for Democracy and Electoral Assistance.

Huyse, Luc, and M. Salter, eds. 2008. *Traditional Justice and Reconciliation after Violent Conflict: Learning from African Experiences*. Stockholm: International Institute for Democracy and Electoral Assistance.

Ikuenobe, Polycarp. 2006. *Philosophical Perspectives on Communalism and Morality in African Traditions*. Lanham, MD: Lexington.

Kagame, Alexia. 1956. *La philosophie bantu-rwandaise de l'être*. Brussels: Académie royale des sciences colonials.

Kahora, Billy, ed. 2008. *Kwani?* Vol. 5. Nairobi: Kwani Trust.

Kopf, Martin. 2010. "Trauma, Narrative and the Art of Witnessing." In *Slavery in Art and Literature: Approaches to Trauma, Memory and Visuality*, edited by Birgit Haehnel and Melanie Ulz. Berlin: Frank and Timme: 41–58

Kresse, Kai. 2007. *Philosophising in Mombasa: Knowledge, Islam and Intellectual Practice on the Swahili Coast*. Edinburgh: Edinburgh University Press.

Mamdani, Mahmood. 1996. *Citizens and Subjects: Contemporary Africa and the Legacy of Late Colonialism*. Princeton, NJ: Princeton University Press.

Naidoo, Riante. 2015. "SRC President Says 'I Love Hitler.'" *Vuvuzela*, April 27. http://witsvuvuzela.com/2015/04/27/src-president-says-i-love-hitler/.

Njogu, Kimani. 2009. *Healing the Wound: Personal Narratives about the 2007 Post-election Violence in Kenya*. Nairobi: Twaweza.

Ogude, James A. 2009. "The State as a Site of Eating: Literary Representation and the Dialectics of Ethnicity, Class and the Nation State in Kenya." *Africa Insight* 39:5–21.

Ramose, Magobe, B. (1999) 2002. *African Philosophy through Ubuntu*. Harare: Mond Books.

Ricœur, Paul, and Sorin, Antohi. 2005. "Memory, History, Forgiveness: A Dialogue between Paul Ricœur and Sorin Antohi." *Janus Head* 8:14–25.

Tutu, Desmond M. 1999. *No Future without Forgiveness*. London: Rider.

JAMES OGUDE is Senior Research Fellow and the Director at the Centre for the Advancement of Scholarship, University of Pretoria. Until his recent appointment, he was Professor of African Literature and Cultures in the School of Literature, Language and Media Studies at the University of the Witwatersrand, serving as the Head of African Literature and also Assistant Dean–Research in the Faculty of Humanities. He is author of *Ngugi's Novels and African History: Narrating the Nation* and he has coedited four books and one anthology of African stories, including most recently *Chinua Achebe's Legacy: Illuminations from Africa*.

UNIFIER DYER is Research Assistant with the Centre for the Advancement for Scholarship at the University of Pretoria and is an MA-PhD candidate at the University of Wisconsin–Madison.

INDEX

Abahlali base Mjondolo movement, 90–91
Achebe, Chinua, 211
Acosta, Alberto, 168
Africa, problems of, 34–35, 115–16, 118, 123, 155
African art, 11, 73, 76, 85, 91. *See also* artists
African culture and belief systems: animism, 199; bridewealth, 83, 84; conception of reality, 24; core principles, 25–27; dehumanizing aspects of, 123; divinities, 26; ecstasy in, 107; folklore and values, 79; importance of Ubuntu to ordinary people, 8; in literary narratives, 193–94; polygyny and lobola, 84; reconciliation and revenge in, 191; in solving current crises, 116; Ubuntu in context of, 23–25. *See also* Bantu culture; kinship systems
African humanism, 49, 143, 160, 224n1
African philosophical systems: *Bantu Philosophy*, 23–25; categories of, 153; challenges of, 80; diversity in, 98, 111n1; founding father of, 132; indigenous knowledge in, 2; need to systematize, 100; oral traditions in, 99, 109; Ubuntu as cornerstone of, 8, 29, 30–31. *See also* Kagame, Alexis; *muntu*; Odera Oruka, Henry; Ramose, Mogobe B.; Tempels, Placide; Ubuntu; vital force
African renaissance, 33, 74, 126, 151, 155–56
agency, 11, 13, 89, 166, 172n21
Anan, Kofi, 210
ancestral veneration, 8, 13, 101, 121, 122. *See also* elders as perpetrators; kinship systems
apartheid, South African: blacks as subpersons, 68; as breakdown in interconnectedness, 187; moral character of, 57; as obstacle to ideal state, 42–43; persistence of effects of, 7, 61; "separate but equal," 60; Ubuntu as concept in transition from, 151; victims and perpetrators, 139
Apel, Karl-Otto, 105
Appiah, Anthony, 11
Arendt, Hannah, 118
artists, 76, 78, 81–82

balance: between communality and individuality, 88, 136; cosmic, 157; in the good life, 157, 158; of good over evil, 134; and moral order, 85; in social contexts, 75; universe as balance of opposites, 50
Bantu, origin of term, 21–22
Bantu culture, 82–85, 87, 93n13, 100–102
Bantu languages: abstract forms in, 48–49; coinage of *Bantu*, 21–22; countries where spoken, 21; Kagame's metaphysics of spiritual existence in, 47; *muntu* to Umuntu, 48–49; noun classes in, 22, 24, 46, 50; *-ntu* suffix, 9, 13, 18n4, 22, 24–25, 108, 153–54; philosophical characteristics in, 153; Ubuntu as notion of, 103
Bantu Languages, The (Nurse and Philippson), 21
Bantu Philosophy (Tempels), 23–24
Battle, Michael, 2
Bergson, Henri, 50
Biney, Ama, 144
bin Robert, Shaaban: concept of human perfection, 49, 50–57; *Kusadikika*, 58, 59; Masolo's invocation of, 5; moral idealism of, 57–58; notion of "utu bora," 12; *Siku ya Watenzi Wote*, 58–59. See also *Utubora Mkulima*
black and African people, oppression of, 60, 76, 117, 166–67. *See also* apartheid, South African
Black Consciousness movement, 11–12, 74
black intellectuals, 9, 11, 77, 79, 91